"The achievement of *Cunning Folk* is to make premodern magic seem not only real, but also reasonable, interwoven into everyday life in ways that don't feel antiquated. Through lively and extremely well researched storytelling, Stanmore shows readers that for many people both medieval and modern, to believe in magic, to hope for magic, is part of being human." —David M. Perry, coauthor of *The Bright Ages*

"Before, during, and after the witch trials, purveyors of magic were in fact common, helpful community merchants. *Cunning Folk* brings us into this fascinating era with personal accounts that deepen and complicate the history of spellcasting, and offer inspiration for today's practitioners." —Michelle Tea, author of *Modern Tarot*

"A significant follow-up to Barbara Ehrenreich and Deirdre English's seminal *Witches, Midwives, and Nurses, Cunning Folk* offers a nuanced view into premodern spirituality, dispossessing us of the idea that all supernatural belief was relegated to 'devil's work.' . . . Connecting past to present, Stanmore proves that magic-seeking is deeply human; that medieval desires and impulses were not so different from today's." —Frances F. Denny, author of *Major Arcana*

"Packed with vivid historical anecdotes, this is an intriguing insight into the magical lives of past people and the history of our own superstitions today." —Marion Gibson, author of *Witchcraft*

"The best introduction to late medieval and early modern popular magic yet written. Comprehensive, humane, lively, and a great read." —Ronald Hutton, author of *The Witch*

"This is a brilliant book, written with wit and vigor, in which Tabitha Stanmore explores the premodern places where magic was real, offering not only practical solutions for ordinary problems but a way of feeling about the world, an emotional relationship between anxious humans, cosmic forces, and the mundane mysteries of their lives." —Malcolm Gaskill, author of *The Ruin of All Witches*

"Absolutely fascinating. *Cunning Folk* is a much needed book that draws attention to a little-known but important aspect of daily life. Like all good history books, it tells us about ourselves as well as the past. It will both inform and inspire readers." —Ian Mortimer, author of *Medieval Horizons*

"A fascinating and intricately researched book that opens a window into another world." —Tracy Borman, author of *Anne Boleyn & Elizabeth I*

"A window on the hopes, passions, and lives of Europe five centuries ago. We know the horror-film version of magic. Tabitha Stanmore—uncovering a whole treasure house of long-lost private lives—adds the rich, fresh, human version." —Michael Pye, author of *The Edge of the World*

"I adore *Cunning Folk*. A truly fascinating and human book." —Ruth Goodman, author of *How to Be a Tudor*

Cunning Folk

Cunning Folk

LIFE IN THE ERA OF PRACTICAL MAGIC

TABITHA STANMORE

BLOOMSBURY PUBLISHING

NEW YORK · LONDON · OXFORD · NEW DELHI · SYDNEY

BLOOMSBURY PUBLISHING
Bloomsbury Publishing Inc.
1385 Broadway, New York, NY 10018, USA

BLOOMSBURY, BLOOMSBURY PUBLISHING, and the Diana logo are trademarks
of Bloomsbury Publishing Plc

First published in 2024 in the United Kingdom by the Bodley Head, an
imprint of Vintage, part of the Penguin Random House group
First published in the United States by Bloomsbury Publishing, 2024

Bloomsbury Publishing Plc does not have any control over, or responsibility for,
any third-party websites referred to or in this book. All internet addresses given in this
book were correct at the time of going to press. The author and publisher regret
any inconvenience caused if addresses have changed or sites have ceased to exist,
but can accept no responsibility for any such changes.

ISBN: HB: 978-1-63973-053-7; eBook: 978-1-63973-054-4

Library of Congress Cataloging-in-Publication Data is available.

2 4 6 8 10 9 7 5 3 1

Typeset by Westchester Publishing Services
Printed and bound in the U.S.A.

To find out more about our authors and books visit www.bloomsbury.com and
sign up for our newsletters.

Bloomsbury books may be purchased for business or promotional use. For information
on bulk purchases please contact Macmillan Corporate and Premium Sales Department at
specialmarkets@macmillan.com.

To my family, and other magical creatures

Cunning, *n.*—wit, wisdom, intelligence.
From the Old English *cunnan*, 'to know'.

CONTENTS

Cunning Folk

INTRODUCTION

Ey, I warrant you, I thinke I can see as farre into a Mill-stone as another: you have heard of Mother Notingham, who for her time, was prettily well skill'd in casting of Waters: and after her, Mother Bombye; and then there is one Hatfield in Pepper-Alley, hee doth prettie well for a thing that's lost. There's another in Coleharbour, that's skill'd in the Planets. Mother Sturton in Goulden-lane, is for Forespeaking: Mother Phillips of the Banke-side, for the weaknesse of the backe: and then there's a very reverent Matron on Clarkenwell-Green, good at many things: Mistris Mary on the Banke-side, is for recting a Figure: and one (what doe you call her) in Westminster, that practiseth the Booke and the Key, and the Sive and the Sheares: and all doe well, according to their talent. For my selfe, let the world speake . . .

—Thomas Heywood, *The Wise Woman of Hogsdon*

IN THE AUTUMN OF 1637 MABEL GRAY LOST SOME SPOONS. After a morning spent tearing her house apart, she asked her neighbours for help in their recovery. Unfortunately no one had seen them, but Mabel's friends suggested that she should seek out a magician who might be able to help find the missing cutlery. Thus began a long journey across London, during which Mabel visited some of the seediest areas of the capital and met several wizards, in the hope of getting back what was hers.

She went first to a 'cunninge woman'—the kind of practitioner who specialised in simple spells—in Southwark. Travelling from her home in Westminster, Mabel would have had to catch a ferry across the Thames, probably disembarking at Stangate Stairs on the river's bank opposite Westminster Hall. Passing the warm red walls of Lambeth Palace on her right, she then walked about two miles east across fields filled with livestock to meet this magician. The journey was in vain, however: the court document that records Mabel's adventure tells us that the cunning woman was unable to help. Perhaps she didn't specialise in this sort of magic, for she recommended a man near Drury Lane who could supernaturally recover lost or stolen goods. The cunning woman gave Mabel an address. Mabel followed the directions, paying the ferryman a halfpenny to recross the river, before heading west. Lutners Lane, where this second magician lived, was not a notable or salubrious location. John Strype's 1720 edition of *A Survey of the Cities of London and Westminster* describes it as a 'very ordinary' place and 'but of small account either for buildings and inhabitants'. To an eighteenth-century reader this description would carry a sniff of derision. The buildings were probably in poor repair, and 'small account' suggests that the inhabitants were unlikely to be respectable.

Nevertheless, Mabel was determined. She knocked at the cunning man's door and explained her situation, begging for help in finding her spoons. The magician listened sympathetically, but unfortunately he couldn't help, either. He, in turn, suggested that she go and see a third wizard, a certain Mr Tunn, who knew how to recover lost goods like hers. He lived not far away, she was told, in Ram Alley just off Fleet Street. This news must have been a mixed blessing for Mabel. On the one hand, Mr Tunn was close by, and Mabel's feet must have been aching by this point; on the other, if Lutners Lane was 'ordinary', Ram Alley was considered debauched. Strype's *Survey* tells us that it was a street 'taken up by Publick houses' and a 'privileged Place for Debtors'—meaning that it was a safe place for debtors to lie low.[1] The alley's reputation might explain why Mabel paid the cunning man three shillings to go with her to see Mr Tunn: she may not have felt safe going alone. Fortunately the wizard agreed, and they set off to find the third—and, hopefully, final—magician.

At last Mabel found a practitioner who claimed he could help. She agreed to pay Mr Tunn five shillings in cash and a further three in wine to tell her where the spoons were and, if they had been stolen, by whom. The answer was vague, but delivered with confidence: Tunn assured her that 'the thiefe was in the howse that had the spoones . . . and the spoones should come agayne they should not know howe and be laid in the same place from whence they were taken'.

Why did Mabel spend a day travelling across London and at least eleven shillings (a week's pay for a skilled tradesman) to find these cunning folk? It is obvious that her spoons were incredibly valuable to her: in a time before mass production, even simple household utensils were time-consuming to make and worth keeping for decades. If they were made of metal—especially silver—they might have been her most valuable items, perhaps even her sole heritable property. Recovering them, therefore, was worth her time and money. But in a world where there was no formal police force or insurance, who could help when such valuable items were lost? For Mabel and many others like her, the first port of call was often a magician. We don't know whether Mabel recovered her spoons—I hope she did—but either way, she clearly thought her investment in magic was worthwhile.

The kinds of help a magician might offer varied widely. Sometimes their service was straightforward—like divining where a thief was hiding—while at other times it could be more complex, even morally ambiguous. This was especially true for magicians who dealt with affairs of the heart.

Mary Woods lived in Stratton Strawless, a parish eight miles north of Norwich. The epithet 'strawless' suggests that the land around the village was not arable; indeed, it might have been densely wooded. It's tempting to imagine that Mary was a cunning woman dwelling in the depths of the forest, in a home difficult to find and shrouded in mist. Despite her out-of-the-way location, though, Mary doesn't fit this stereotype. She was married to a man named John, travelled a lot and was well connected. Unlike the cunning folk visited by Mabel Gray, Mary seems to have been of relatively high standing or at least carried a degree of social credit, if her acquaintances are anything to judge by. We know from her court testimonies, when she was interrogated four times between 1612 and 1613 on the orders of Robert Cecil, Secretary of State to King James I, that she visited Norwich several times to divine the future and administer love spells. She even went as far as London on at least one occasion. Given the state of seventeenth-century roads, the 120-mile journey each way would have been a significant and costly undertaking. What is more impressive, though, is the social status of her clients and what she was asked to do for them.

We first meet Mary in the early days of summer 1612. She had recently been bidden by one Mrs Suckling to do some fortune-telling—specifically, to find out how long the woman's husband, Dr Suckling, would live. This in itself might not have been an ominous request: the death of the head of a household could lead to financial ruin as well as potential heartbreak, and being forewarned meant being forearmed. Mary happily assured Mrs Suckling that her husband was bound to live a long time. If she expected this to bring comfort to her client, it had the opposite effect. Apparently distressed at the news, Mrs Suckling offered Mary Woods a 'large reward' to poison the doctor. According to Mary's court testimony, she refused the money and the request, but we may wonder whether we can believe her. For by February of the next year she had gained clients significantly more illustrious than a doctor's wife: namely, Frances Howard, Countess of Essex. Clearly Mary had started to make a name for herself.

Frances asked Mary for a strikingly similar service to that requested by Mrs Suckling: that she procure a poison to kill her husband, from whom the countess dearly wanted to be free. Frances' marriage had been a political arrangement, intended to raise the fortunes of the Howard family by uniting with the lineage of an old enemy. She was just fifteen years old when she wedded Robert Devereux, the third Earl of Essex (himself only in his early teens) in 1606, and the couple spent very little time together thereafter. Devereux might have been an object of scorn for Frances: he was the first-born son of Elizabeth I's disgraced favourite, who had been executed for treason only five years before. Perhaps the political cloud hanging over Robert's head, combined with his apparently surly temper, was not something Frances was prepared to tolerate for the rest of her life. Her request to Mary Woods was specific: Frances wanted a poison that would take several days to take effect, in order to allay suspicion.[2]

This time, Mary's plea of innocence in the court was harder to defend. Although once again she claimed not to have accepted the job, it turned out that she had received money and a diamond ring from the countess. Such substantial gifts would not have been given for a trivial request, and it later emerged that Mary was promised a further £1,000—an extraordinary sum, worth about £260,000 in today's money—upon receipt of the poison. Given the evidence against her, Mary eventually confessed to the arrangement, but swore that she had repented and fled London rather than carry out the poisoning. Perhaps this is true: Robert Devereux would live for another thirty-three years. In any case, by the end of 1613 Frances had successfully annulled the marriage by claiming that Robert was impotent (in his own defence, Devereux responded that he was only impotent around Frances). She married her lover, Robert Carr, less than two months later. It is clear enough, therefore, that Frances really did want to escape the union. Yet by 1615 she was embroiled in a second murder charge, this time for killing her new husband's friend and confidant, Thomas Overbury, who had tried to stand in the way of their marriage. Frances was found guilty of multiple attempts to kill Overbury and of eventually succeeding through the use of a poisoned enema. She confessed to the crime and she and Carr were imprisoned in the Tower of London until 1622, narrowly escaping execution.

While Frances Howard was by far her most celebrated client, the court accused Mary of conspiring to kill the husbands of at least three women over a two-year period. She was also charged with practising palmistry, possessing a 'familiar spirit' and healing people harmed through witchcraft. Perhaps Mary's reputation as someone who could end bad marriages was born of her own supposed attempt to poison (and, failing that, divorce) her husband John, with whom she had been miserable for years. The specifics of

Mary and John's relationship do not survive, so we don't know what caused her murderous dislike of her spouse. Maybe, as with Frances and Robert, the couple had married out of obligation rather than affection, and over time indifference had evolved into loathing. Equally John might have been cruel, and Mary trapped. Or perhaps John was simply not as ambitious as Mary, and she did not want to be held back in pursuing her dubious talents.

Still, it seems that no poisoning attempts were ever conclusively proved against Mary and she drops out of the court records after the annulment of Frances and Robert's marriage. We can only speculate about what happened to her. Most scholars assume that she was nothing more than a charlatan, who blackmailed her clients by threatening to make up stories about them having murderous intentions. Perhaps that's true; perhaps, after undergoing investigation for the attempted assassination of an aristocrat when her bluff went too far, she got scared and changed her approach. But such an interpretation rings hollow, particularly given Frances' later hand in Thomas Overbury's death. Moreover, other future-tellers of the period were asked similar questions about how long spouses might live, and attempting murder through magic was not uncommon.

Magic, then, clearly had a dark side: a magician could harm as much as help. Enduring an unhappy and perhaps abusive marriage, some women were keen to know how long it might last; but clearly there were others for whom this wasn't enough, and who were willing to take matters into their own hands. It is impossible to know precisely how many spouses turned to magic to end a relationship, or indeed how many used it to start one. What appears in the historical record inevitably provides only a small insight, but even from the limited number of cases we have, it seems that Mary Woods' clients were not uncommon in their requests, and that Mary herself was just one of many people who offered such services. She might well have carried on telling fortunes and offering solutions to unhappy lives—it was certainly lucrative enough. After her brush with Frances, though, she might have avoided associating too closely with the great and the good.

Mary and her clients may have been driven by greed, ambition or simply a desire to live a better life than the one mapped out for them. There were also those who may have turned to magic to seek professional advantage. According to the late medieval *Chronicle of Westminster*, in 1366 a master carpenter was found to have sold his soul to the Devil in order to excel in his craft. The *Chronicle* is hazy on details about the man's life—particulars like his name, where he was from and his age are omitted—but we can gauge something about him from ancillary information. The fact that he is mentioned in a chronicle of Westminster suggests that he was settled just outside the City of London; and the fact that he is described as a 'master' carpenter implies he was a full member of the Carpenters' Company. Carpentry was a skilled and prestigious profession: it required specialist tools, an exceptional knowledge of different kinds of woods and patterns of tree growth and, by the fifteenth century, at least seven years of training. Most buildings were made from timber in the medieval period, and even stone houses and churches relied on wood to create their magnificent hammer-beamed roofs. Carpenters were therefore constantly in demand, and those with experience and talent were highly prized. That our carpenter had earned the title of 'master' suggests that he was at the top of his profession, having completed his years of apprenticeship and having gained a reputation of being very capable. By the time his story came to light, he had apparently excelled over other carpenters for fifteen years: he must have had several apprentices working for him by then, and likely contributed to the urban fabric of much of medieval Westminster.

Unfortunately, this success was not to last. After a decade and a half of achievement, the carpenter unexpectedly announced that he was about to die. This must have come as a surprise to those around him: he cannot have been more than forty-five years of age at the time, and the fact that he was still working in his profession suggests that he must have been in relatively good health. What he did next, though, was even more surprising. Having told his friends and associates—some of whom might have been fellow members of the Carpenters' Company—of his imminent demise, the carpenter gave instructions that he should be left entirely alone, as there was a very serious risk that he would do harm to others. His friends complied with his wishes, locking him in a room for the night in the hope that he might sleep peacefully and perhaps the fear that had overtaken him would pass. It didn't. Shortly after putting him to bed, his companions were roused by his agonised cries. In the words of the *Chronicle*, 'they entered the room and found him extracting his own bowels from his belly'. His friends rushed forward, trying to stop his clawing and to patch him up, while someone ran to fetch a priest. The explanation for his grisly actions would have surfaced when the carpenter gave his final confession. According to his testimony, he had served the Devil for fifteen years, trading his soul for the chance to be the best at his craft. We don't know exactly how he had struck this deal with the Devil and whether it involved the help of a magician: the *Chronicle* is more anxious to tell readers that he died shortly after receiving the Last Rites, thus ending his life in the Catholic faith.

This story, with its pact between an overly ambitious person and a demon ready to take advantage of human weakness, may sound familiar. It provides the basic premise for Christopher Marlowe's *Doctor Faustus*, as well as countless folk tales from across Europe. The moral of the story for fourteenth-century listeners was to put faith in God rather than in demons, and that ambition can come at a painful, perilous cost. For modern readers, though, it also confirms the contemporary belief that supernatural powers were everywhere: people knew themselves to be living alongside a magical realm that could be manipulated for material gain. Many supernatural activities were formally condemned by the Church; and other than it being a noteworthy event in itself, the story of the carpenter in the *Chronicle of Westminster* was intended to dissuade others from forging similar pacts. Indeed, the fact that it leaves out particulars about who the carpenter was means that the tale might be told more widely and thus serve as a warning.

◆

We will see throughout this book that magic was the fallback option when things went wrong—or even when life wasn't going as well as one might like. For the most part, this wasn't wishful thinking or the preserve of gullible people being misled by tricksters (though that certainly happened too).

To the pre-modern mind, magic was a rational part of the supernatural universe in which they lived. God and the Devil, angels and demons were all real and could affect people's lives: it made perfect sense that men and women—rich and poor, high-born and low-born—would try to harness the powers around them. Whether using magic was strictly moral (or acceptably Christian) was another matter, but both the Church and the worldly authorities could turn a blind eye when the spells were harmless. They were more likely to take action when magic was used in nefarious ways or to sinister ends, but even then there was a good chance that, if both magician and client were discreet, their activity would go unnoticed.[3]

Although they are mentioned throughout, this book is not about witches. Our focus on witches and the sensationalism of witch trials make us forget that there was a whole host of magical practitioners in the late medieval and early modern periods.* That concentration has blurred the picture, to the point where we tend to view pre-modern life as dominated by superstition, misogyny and paranoia. But it is important to remember that not every person who practised magic was considered a witch. Some theologians were categorical in defining a witch as anyone who worked through the aid of demons, which in their eyes applied to any person with supernatural abilities other than the Christian saints. In practice, however, people tended to put magical practitioners into two distinct categories: those who used magic out of spite to harm others, and those who used it as a tool to positively affect the world around them. The former were counted as witches—powerful people who could raise storms, inflict disease and cause anguish in revenge for even the slightest insult. The latter were generally viewed positively by their neighbours, or perhaps as morally neutral: they used their powers as directed by their clients, who shared in the guilt if their

---

*   A brief note on the time period covered in this book. Both 'medieval' and 'early modern' are broad terms: every historian will probably give a different start and end point to both periods, according to what—and, crucially, where—they focus on. This isn't the place to pursue such a discussion, but when I refer to the late medieval and early modern periods I mean roughly the fourteenth to late seventeenth centuries.

requests were sinister. They provided a service to their neighbours; historians therefore describe their activity as 'service magic'.

These two groups of people—those accused of witchcraft and the service magicians (or 'cunning folk')—rarely overlapped in people's imagination or, indeed, in the courtrooms of the time. In England only a handful of wise women and men were tried as witches: for every one that was, there would have been hundreds who continued their practices unhindered. The shocking exceptions to this rule include Ursula Kemp, a cunning woman hanged for witchcraft in Essex in 1582. Ursula's end was a tragic one: she had a long-standing reputation as a healer who even specialised in lifting the curses placed on people by malevolent witches. Despite her services, she ended up being executed as a witch herself after her neighbour, Grace Thurlowe, went lame.[4] Heartbreaking as her story is, Ursula was one of very few cunning folk in England to end up this way. In fact, as fear of malevolent, demon-derived magic increased at the height of the witch trials that spread through Europe and North America in the sixteenth and seventeenth centuries, so did service magicians' business: magical protection, 'unwitching' (removing curses) and helping to identify witches were some cunning folk's bread and butter.

If the vast majority of magicians weren't witches, we would be equally wrong to view them all as quacks. Some undoubtedly were; but in a world where reputation counted for everything, they would have been out of business if people found that the services they offered did not—somehow— work. What's more, as we saw earlier, people believed that magic was part of the universe in which they lived. Catholic priests too dealt with the numinous on a daily basis: they exorcised demons, blessed fields for good harvests and performed small miracles through the Eucharist—literally turning bread and wine into the body and blood of Christ—every day. The idea that a priest is somehow the same as a magician might sound absurd, but both fundamentally work with supernatural forces.

Between the extremes of the divine servant and the witch sit the service practitioners. They could move around the spectrum: some cunning folk were also priests, and some, occasionally, were executed as witches. Many would live relatively quiet lives and perform magic for their neighbours. What they had in common was an ability to manipulate the world in a way that most mortals could not—and a willingness to sell that skill.

This book, then, is about those people who practised 'useful' magic and the people who bought it. It is about their hopes and desires, their fears and their vulnerabilities. It is about the kinds of problems that people faced every day in medieval and early modern Europe, and the solutions they found. It is about life, belief and how magic was intimately woven into the mundane. We will look at the different applications for magic, ranging from the seemingly trivial, like divining the right day to start a journey, to the deadly serious, such as finding a missing person or saving a life. Along the way we will meet some devious wizards and desperate clients, as well as kind-hearted practitioners who offered their powers to anyone who needed them. We'll see that magic wasn't confined to naïve country folk with peculiar beliefs, but was also commissioned—and feared—by the most powerful and best educated in society. And far from magic being suppressed by the Church, priests were regularly found selling spells over their altars.

By the end of our journey we will have learned how to go about recovering lost goods, discovering buried treasure, finding love, getting revenge and healing the sick. We will come to understand why dark magic might feel like the only solution at times, and how to cancel out a curse once it has been cast. And if we were suddenly to find ourselves transported back to the sixteenth century, we will know where to go to find a magician with the necessary skills and how to tell the real ones from the charlatans. Most of all, though, we will have a chance to glimpse the world through medieval eyes: a place where it's possible to meet the Devil on the road, control the future through the stars and employ a fairy to help find gold.

CHAPTER 1

HOW TO FIND THIEVES AND LOST GOODS

THE WARDENS OF ST MARY'S CHURCH IN THATCHAM, Berkshire had a problem. It was their responsibility to maintain the fabric of the building—including its impressive tower, complete with four bells—manage the accounts and take care of the church's sacred possessions. Unfortunately, in 1583 they failed in their duty. The Communion cloth, which covered the altar while parishioners took the Eucharist, had gone missing, along with two other decorative textiles. The altar cloth especially played an important part in religious practice at the time. Despite the movement towards more austere church interiors following the Reformation, Queen Elizabeth I still required that the altar be covered during Communion, out of respect for the Last Supper held by Christ for his disciples. Losing it, therefore, was a disaster. It could have consequences for the spiritual health of the parish, not to mention the reputations of the unlucky wardens.

At a loss for what to do, and with no leads to follow after an initial search, the churchwardens sent one of their own to Burfield, a Berkshire hamlet about ten miles to the east. It was known that a 'cunnyng woman' lived there, and the delegate of St Mary's Church was tasked 'for to make enquire' of her about where the cloths might be. We know this because the wardens diligently recorded the man's travel expenses—and presumably the wise woman's fee—in their account book: the trip cost a total of sixteen pence, about £250 in today's money.

That churchwardens would ask a magician for help may appear surprising. They were, after all, respected members of their community with responsibilities towards maintaining orthodox religious practices. That they would put their faith in a woman's magic may seem outlandish to us, but it is a testament both to how seriously the wardens took their duties and to how well respected cunning folk could be: we enter a world where reputation is everything.

A missing altar cloth was a major concern, but as we saw earlier in the story of Mabel Gray, losing even small items could have a significant impact on a person's life. Today we might appreciate items if they are particularly expensive or useful, or if they carry sentimental value, but otherwise we are comfortable with the fact that things will get broken, wear out or simply be thrown away. But back when everything was handmade—thus requiring skills and a significant outlay of time to produce—even the lowliest items were carefully looked after and sorely missed if they were lost. We can get a glimpse of the appreciation people had for their possessions through some of the inventories that survive from the period. The astonishing level of detail in some of these documents gives us an idea of the worth placed on items, ranging from sizeable possessions like beds and jewellery, all the way down to food and rags.

Thomas Grafforte, a French immigrant who lived and worked as a merchant tailor in St Giles Cripplegate, London, is a good example. Upon his death in 1661, an inventory was taken of his goods. The recorders were thorough, moving from the garret at the very top of his house through each of the rooms, then down to his workshop where he kept his tools. They finished with an appraisal of his clothing. Thomas seems to have been quite wealthy: he lived in a house with at least six rooms, his workshop included four weavers' looms and his goods were valued at £30 7s 4d. Each of his possessions, regardless of their monetary worth, was carefully itemised, even the '2 old greene ruggs' and 'one blankett'. The sum of his clothes consisted of '3 old Suites of Cloath 1 Stuffe cloake 1 cloath cloake [and] 2 old hattes'.[1] Thus even for someone as well established and successful a craftsman as Thomas Grafforte—and a tailor no less—his clothes and other possessions were limited.

At the other end of the spectrum, those living in poverty could own almost nothing. In some cities, civic authorities would routinely record the possessions of everyone on their death, so as to avoid disputes between heirs and neighbours. A heartbreaking inventory from 1544 in the Bavarian city of Nuremberg records that an elderly man had 'absolutely nothing . . . except for his daily clothes, specifically a tattered blouse and pair of pants, and the same type of thing from his late wife . . . There is therefore no need to take an inventory other than this.'[2]

The fact that even wealthy households felt it worthwhile to keep and reuse rags, and that some people only owned one suit of clothes, tells us quite how important belongings were to their owners. This is the context we must bear in mind when exploring the frequency with which people consulted magicians about recovering lost items. It explains why John Somer, a labourer from Morpeth in the north-east of England, put his faith in a 'wyff of Newcastell' to recover his stolen shirt in the 1570s. He paid fourpence for the privilege—about half a day's wages—but that was cheaper than trying to replace it. The shirt may have made all the difference between John being warm or cold, looking respectable or distinctly shabby. It's perfectly possible that the shirt was his only spare item of clothing.[3] Luckily, the magic seems to have worked: the shirt reappeared—miraculously—after a few days.

There was also the question of reputation to consider. With the vast majority of people living in the countryside, clusters of families were grouped together in small communities composed of a few smallholdings. In most villages everyone would know everybody else, and neighbours were the first port of call for support when something went wrong. Being 'of good report' or honest reputation, therefore, was vital to a prosperous life. If, on the other hand, you were known to be lazy, a drunk or a thief, you would be shunned. When a household fell on hard times, it was largely down to the goodwill of the local church and neighbours to see the family through. This might come in the form of donations of food and fuel, clothes and medicines, or of labour (such as helping with repairs or tilling fields). If that goodwill was lost, the consequences could be severe, and your survival and that of your family might be at stake.

As figures within the public eye, churchwardens had a long way to fall if they failed in their duties. They were elected from their community and were judged to be people who stood out for their trustworthiness, competence and reliability. Losing valuable public property could ruin this carefully built reputation. It could heavily impact on a man's status in a community—wardens were almost exclusively male—reducing his stake in collective decision-making processes and forever change his standing in the eyes of his neighbours. It is not surprising, then, that the churchwardens at Thatcham would go to any lengths to get their altar cloth back. How would the village react if they knew these men had managed to misplace it, or if they learned that there was a thief in their community?* The fact that cunning folk were a go-to for lost or stolen goods tells us something about their reputation too. A magician's authority and power would have been based on the successful help they had provided in their communities in the past. Nobody would hire a known charlatan.

◆

In 1390 Lady Constance Despencer, Countess of Gloucester and granddaughter of King Edward III, had a valuable item stolen from her: a scarlet mantle with a fur trim of 'cleansed miniver' (miniver being the white fur taken from the winter pelt of red squirrels). Constance approached a cunning man named John Berkyng about her loss. We do not know how

---

* As we only have the churchwardens' account book to go by for this case, unfortunately we don't know whether they got the altar cloth back. Given the success of other magical missions to recover lost goods, though, there is a chance that they did.

she knew Berkyng, though perhaps someone in her household recommended him. Either way, he assured Constance that he 'well understood incantations and the art of magic' and could easily identify the thief.[4] So impressed was Constance by his claims that she recommended Berkyng to her father, Edmund de Langley, the Duke of York. Edmund eagerly enquired as to the fate of two silver dishes that had recently gone missing from his home on the Strand, at that time a neighbourhood located just outside London. Berkyng rallied to the task, naming three individuals as the culprits: John Geyte and Robert Mysdene, he claimed, had taken Constance's cloak; and William Shedewater, a serjeant in Edmund's own service, was responsible for the missing silver. The three men were duly seized, severely beaten and imprisoned for their supposed crimes. They were also ordered to swear that they 'would never [again] come within ten leagues of the hostels of our Lord the King, the Duke of York . . . or the Duke of Gloucester [i.e. of Lady Constance]'. It meant that they would have to leave their homes and never return to the City of London or its environs. This was an incredibly severe punishment, given that none of the stolen goods had been found on the defendants: all the evidence rested on the word of the cunning man and the influence of his noble clients.

Fortunately, all three men were absolved of the thefts and were let go before their exile was effected. Each 'made plaint' that they had been 'falsely and maliciously' named by John Berkyng and that all the accusations were little more than slander. Berkyng then found himself before the mayor and commonalty of London to justify his actions: something that he was unable to do satisfactorily. Eventually he admitted that he had committed a falsehood in naming Geyte, Mysdene and Shedewater as thieves, and the court punished him accordingly. Because, the judgement read, through his 'art magic, and falsities . . . murders might easily ensue, and good and lawful men be undeservedly aggrieved and defamed in their name and reputation', John was put in the pillory in the centre of London for an hour, imprisoned for two weeks and then was himself exiled from the city.

Justice was done in the end for the three accused, but they would still have endured a good deal of trauma. The initial arrest and assault that the men underwent was probably enacted by the guards of Constance's and Edmund's households before they were turned over to the London authorities. It was only after the men appealed that the truth came out. Many people who were overawed by their social superiors (or simply did not wish to receive another beating) might not have spoken up and would have been exiled for a crime they didn't commit.

While the episode reveals the power of a magician's word, it also shows some of the risks magicians were taking when selling their services. Cunning folk did not wield any official authority and were liable to prosecution, both under Church law for their superstitious actions 'against Holy Writ' and under secular law for causing disturbances to the peace. We don't know whether John Berkyng deliberately lied about who had stolen Constance's and Edmund's goods: he might well have reached his conclusions via his magic art and been sincere in his accusations. The fact that he was employed by the nobility suggests that he had a strong reputation as a goods-finder and might have been performing such services for years. In which case, John might be one of the many cunning folk who trod a fine line between being a respected member of his community who offered valuable services and a troublemaker liable to prosecution by clients and disapproving bystanders. Perhaps we should also remember that although John Berkyng comes across as the villain in this particular story, in many respects he was as vulnerable as those he accused—unlike his noble clients, for whom there appear to have been no repercussions.

Lower down the social hierarchy where people did not have the power to simply order someone's arrest, clients acting on a cunning person's word had to confront supposed thieves themselves. And instead of seeking legal resolution, they had to rely on reputation and social pressure to ensure a good outcome. Galvanised by a magician's advice, in 1509 Alice White felt empowered to publicly accuse Richard Facques of stealing money out of her bag. Initially Alice tried to settle the matter quietly, by speaking to the wife of Richard's business partner about her suspicions. After waiting about three months for Richard to come clean and return the money, though, she decided to go and find him herself. Marching into the house of Julian and Anna Notary, where Richard was conducting business, she loudly declared, 'I pray you God, may Facques let me have my money . . . the which I lost and that was taken from me.'[5] She felt confident about accusing him thus in front of his neighbours and business associates because she had consulted a cunning man. The soothsayer had told her that a man with a blemish on his face had taken the money; and as Richard Facques was the only person with such a mark in the vicinity when the goods were stolen, she surmised it must have been him.

It is notable that Alice originally tried to settle the matter through a mutual friend. But she nevertheless had enough faith in the magician to escalate matters when this quieter route failed, putting herself and Richard in the public spotlight and potentially incurring the opprobrium of her community in the process. We know that after she accused him, Richard sued Alice for defamation. Whether or not she was required to pay damages we do not know, but the magician's advice would have had a serious and potentially catastrophic impact on her life: if convicted, Alice's standing in her neighbourhood would have been severely damaged. Cunning folk may not have had any legal authority, but the result of their work could often be as punitive as any legal outcome.

The examples above paint magical practitioners in a poor light. They come across as frauds who wielded too much power and caused destruction and pain to others. But this is not an entirely fair picture. Although there were certainly some frauds who took advantage of people's trust—just as there are plenty of charlatans today—it seems likely that the vast majority genuinely believed in their own abilities. It is an irony of history that most of the records that survive relate to when service magic went wrong, rather than when things went well. For every complaint or wrong suggestion recorded about a cunning person, there are almost certainly dozens of instances where magicians genuinely helped people. Happy customers are rarely of interest to a court of law, though, so these successes were seldom recorded and preserved for posterity. What we do know is that the church-wardens of Thatcham, the Duke of York, the Duchess of Gloucester and Alice White would all have trusted magicians for a reason. They must have known of others who had been helped in the past and recommended the practitioners they consulted.

In spite of the general rule outlined above, we do sometimes find evidence in the court records that cunning folk had, indeed, satisfied clients. There is the case of John Chestre, who was indicted for failing to identify a thief in 1375. On the face of it, Chestre looks to be as much of a charlatan as Berkyng. Chestre's client, John Porter, had paid a large sum to find who had stolen his goods. The surviving record does not tell us what it was that Porter had lost, but it must have been valuable, given that he handed over nine shillings and tuppence for its recovery. It is no surprise that Porter was bitterly disappointed, therefore, that Chestre came up with nothing. Feeling thoroughly cheated, Porter brought a case of common plea against the magician in London.

Chestre was summoned to defend himself on a chilly day in late January. The Court of Husting dealt with a range of common plea cases, presided over by the mayor and aldermen at the Guildhall. A brief look at the other people appearing before the court that day gives us an insight into the varied matters the aldermen dealt with, and the wider connections that London enjoyed. As the Husting was the only court that would admit 'foreigners'— anyone who was not a citizen of the city—Chestre was surrounded by a range of characters as he waited to be seen. First before the mayor was John, Bishop of Macedonia (possibly a diplomatic delegate who held a titular bishopric, or a bishop in exile), who publicly paid off his debt of 23½ marks to the spice-and-pepper importer, Stephen atte Wode. Presumably to get his business squared away in one day, Stephen atte Wode remained in court to establish a trading arrangement surrounding the importation of four tons of tin from Cornwall. That being dealt with, John Patyn was summoned and fined forty shillings for attempting to flout the rules of his guild. Patyn was a fletcher—someone who made arrows and the feathers, or fletches, for them—but had sent an apprentice out of London to make longbows on his behalf. Fletchers were separate from bowyers, or bow-makers: by making bows, Patyn had effectively stolen work from others. The fine was probably so high because the bowyers and fletchers had only become separate trades in 1371, and a fierce rivalry had sprung up between them. Patyn had been reluctant to relinquish his skill as a bowyer to specialise solely in fletching, so it is unsurprising that he was found to be flouting the ordinance of separation four years later.

After Patyn was dismissed, the aldermen finally turned to the magician John Chestre. He was accused of 'trespass' by his client, because despite making a covenant with Porter to 'invoke and inform him of the person or persons who had stolen certain goods of his at Clerkenwell', Chestre had given him no useful information. We will never know whether the aldermen were more interested in this incident than in those that came before: the record treats it as fairly routine business. This is not surprising—many of the magicians mentioned throughout this book were not prosecuted for their supernatural activities per se, but rather for the potential disruption they caused within their communities through false accusations (as in John Berkyng's case), superstitious practices or fraud.

Chestre was determined to show himself in the best possible light, however. Although the magician admitted that he had failed in his purpose, he defended himself against the claim that his services were useless. Chestre described how he had 'turned a loaf with knives'—a practice to which we will return below—to try to identify Porter's thief, and though it had not worked on this occasion, he had been very successful for other clients. He cited an instance when, using the same technique, he had recovered a mazer—a kind of drinking bowl—for a man at the 'bell othe hoppe' (presumably a tavern called the Bell on the Hoop). More impressively, Chestre claimed that on another occasion he had returned £15 in cash to a man living near Garlickhythe, a landing place for boats on the Thames, known for its garlic market. That Chestre was so specific about the locations in which he practised is telling: the court could check that he was a reliable magician. While providing the evidence that he had not intentionally cheated Porter was critical for clearing himself of the charge of trespass, it was equally crucial for his reputation. It is obvious that Chestre performed his services frequently. We have another record from early January of the same year that shows him formally committed 'to inform John Balsham, skinner, before Easter as to the whereabouts of certain goods and chattels which had been taken from his house about the Feast of St Hilary last past'. His skills were in demand, therefore, and Chestre could not afford to lose clients because of a single failure.

Ultimately, his pleas succeeded: the court seems to have been convinced that Chestre had not meant to defraud Porter, but the magician was told to return the money. He was to remain in prison until Porter was repaid, but he received no specific punishment for trespass. The following Monday, 29 January, both parties appeared in court declaring they had reached an agreement and Chestre was released. One final matter remained to be dealt with, however. Chestre's magic was deemed to be a deception to the public, and he was ordered by the Husting not to do it again. This ruling sounds severe, but in practice it probably didn't make a great impact on Chestre's activities. Unlike Berkyng, his magic had not caused any lasting damage, so he was not exiled; nor was he fined, like John Patyn, the rogue fletcher. Essentially Chestre was given a warning and, given that he clearly earned a living from his magic, it is doubtful that the warning was heeded. He does not appear in the court records again, so it is possible that he gave up spell-casting—or maybe he simply chose less litigious clients in the future.

◆

The level of anguish with which some people appealed to cunning folk for help must have been heightened when it was a living thing that had gone missing. Although it was far more common to use magic to recover inanimate objects, it could still be called upon when people or animals disappeared. Of course every case of finding people was unique: while objects can only really go missing for one of two reasons—they have been either mislaid or taken—people might have accidents, get abducted or get lost. In some cases, they might run away and not wish to be found. This is probably true of one Mistress Redman, who disappeared from her home in Sutton-in-the-Isle, a small but prosperous village just outside Ely in Cambridgeshire, in the late 1610s. It is likely that she left of her own accord, because her husband John was indicted for employing magicians not only to identify her whereabouts, but also to bring her back. It is not clear how the cunning folk were expected to do the latter part, though perhaps it involved some sort of sympathy magic using magnets and 'poppets' (little dolls made to represent husband and wife) to draw Redman back to her family. That John employed magicians to help him achieve this suggests that it cannot have been an easy task, which in turn may imply that their marriage was not a happy one. For a wife to abscond was comparatively rare: for financial, social and safety reasons, women tended to be closely tied to their kin and communities. For Redman to have fled to a location distant enough for her husband not to know how to follow her, there must have been a strong motivation. We will return to the ups and downs of romantic relationships in the next chapter.

Other instances of using magic to find missing people bely similarly unhappy circumstances or are simply tragic. John Garnett, from Ormskirk in Lancashire, consulted an unnamed cunning man in the early 1630s after his friend went missing. After performing his conjurations, the magician told Garnett that his friend had been murdered and his body thrown into a marl pit. Marl is a type of natural fertiliser that became common in agriculture from the sixteenth century. It was especially popular in the north-west of England, where small quarries or pits were dug all over the landscape. Essentially, Garnett's cunning man was telling him that his friend was dead and buried in one of dozens of patches of unconsecrated ground, likely never to be recovered. Whether this was true or not, as far as we know, Garnett's friend was never seen again.

Although outside our time period, a final case of person-finding outlines the method one might use for this service. In 1760 Timothy Crowther, the cunning man and town clerk of Skipton in Yorkshire, was approached by two concerned friends about a man who had been missing for twenty days.

Timothy was about sixty-five and was well known for his skill in astrology and goods-finding, so when he said he needed a boy of about twelve to help him with the spell, his request was met. Jonas Rushford was brought, and Timothy gave him a mirror, put him to bed and covered him with a blanket so that Jonas lay in the dark. Timothy then asked Jonas whom he would like to see, and the boy replied—bless him—'my mother'. As soon as he said this, suddenly Jonas' mother appeared in the looking glass 'with a lock of wool in her hand, standing just in the place, and the clothes she was in, as she told Jonas afterwards'. The test-run having succeeded, Timothy told Jonas to keep looking into the glass and this time try to see his neighbour—the man who was missing. In Jonas' own words, as related by the person who recorded the story:*

> I looked and saw him riding towards Idle, but he was very drunk; and he stopped at the alehouse and drank two pints more, and pulled out a guinea to change. Two men stood by, a big man and a little man, and then they went on before him and got two hedgestakes, and when he came up on Windhill common, at the top of the hill, they pulled him off his horse and killed him, and threw him into a coal-pit.

Jonas led the concerned friends to the spot he had seen in the mirror, and sure enough the missing man was found in the pit with 'his handkerchief . . . tied about his mouth and fastened behind his neck'.[6] Though a sad end, at least this man was found, unlike the Lancashire friend of John Garnett.

Locating missing persons through magic appears less regularly in the records than finding stolen goods. This may be partly due to the latter occurring more regularly than the former, but it is surprising nevertheless. As we saw earlier, magic is often turned to in difficult times when other

---

*   The incident was, incidentally, recorded by John Wesley, the founder of Methodism.

options are either limited or seem hopeless: a loved one disappearing is surely one such situation. That so few instances survive could be an indication that many cunning folk were wary of offering such services. Getting the answer wrong—either declaring that someone was alive and well and would soon return, when they were in fact gone for ever, or declaring someone dead just before they come walking back through the door—would be embarrassing at best, a cause for reprisals at worst. Even so, there must have been at least some people who were prepared to shoulder this burden of risk. It might also be that clients and cunning folk were reticent about mentioning this particular service. As we will see in a moment, when it came to finding lost goods there was some practical benefit to claiming publicly that one had visited a magician. When trying to locate a missing person, telling everyone that a magician had been consulted did not necessarily add much to the search—unless their information proved useful.

◆

What emerges from all these stories is that cunning folk were clearly believed by their clients to deliver the goods, both literally and figuratively. The question remains, though, why they were so trusted, and how they could be so confident about their powers. People in the past were not stupid—at least, no more so than we are today. Recourse to magic cannot, therefore, be explained away simply by claiming that its users were gullible or superstitious. That said, it is not my place to say whether the magic practised by cunning folk was real: I don't know, I wasn't there. What we can say is that there was a variety of spells to draw on, and that they got results often enough to maintain belief in their efficacy.

Methods for recovering lost goods varied from the very simple to the excessively complex. John Chestre, whom we met above, had an approach that was at the more basic end of service magic. 'Turning the loaf with knives' was fiddly, but could only be used to answer binary, yes-or-no questions. It involved taking a loaf of bread—probably one that was a couple of days old, so that it was slightly stale but could still hold its shape—and inserting four knives at right angles so that they made the shape of a cross. We know from another case in the 1380s that the next step was to insert a peg into the loaf. The contraption would then be imbued with supernatural power through the incantation of certain words, before the magician asked the questions. The peg would be held so that the bread could turn like a spinning top—one way for yes, the other for no. The bread was not eloquent enough to give actual names of suspected thieves or the locations of lost items, so the client would need to offer some options. With a list of potential culprits supplied, the magician would simply observe which way the loaf spun as their names were called. If the client suspected one person in partic- ular, they might 'encourage' the loaf to turn in such a way that confirmed that suspicion. Whether a magician would doctor the results in this way might be determined by their client's needs. A customer who merely sought external confirmation of their suspicions might welcome such an interven- tion, while others who were at a loss might want the wizard to make full use of their magical skills. When Lady Constance and Sir Edmund employed John Berkyng, they may already have had suspects in mind and simply wanted validation: they were clearly willing enough to accept Berkyng's pronouncements. Another factor was the magician's own conscience and professional pride; assuming they genuinely believed in their abilities, they might refuse to pronounce anyone's guilt unless it was confirmed by the spell. This could explain why Chestre failed to identify a thief for John Porter—Chestre obviously thought highly of his skill, so maybe the loaf just refused to turn towards 'yes' for any of the names he was given.

'Turning the loaf' was not the only binary form of thief identification. In fact it was not even the most popular—references to the method are sparse in the historical records. Working on the same basic principles, the 'sieve and shears' and the 'book and key' methods were much more common. It makes sense that the sieve-and-shears technique was more widespread, as it was both less fiddly and used ubiquitous, hard-wearing items. Most help- fully, the deposition record of William Hasylwoode, a sixteenth-century cleric, explains how the items were to be used. Apparently, William 'dyd take a seve, and a payre of sheeres, and hanged the seve by the poynte of the sheeres, and sayed thees wordes—by Peter and Paule, he hath yt, namyng the partye whom he in that behalf suspected'. Like the loaf stuck through with knives, the suspended sieve would turn according to whether the named person was guilty or innocent.

The point of using a sieve in everyday life to sift the bad from the good may explain why this standard household item acquired magical significance. The invocation of Sts Peter and Paul also has a logic behind it: one cunning woman, Ann Bellett of Worcestershire, even claimed that these Apostles had invented the method. Although there is no mention of such a feat in the Bible, apocryphal texts from the second century onwards attribute a range of miraculous actions to Peter, including a dramatic contest between him and the renowned magician Simon Magus. The Acts of Peter relate that the saint was able to bring a dead man back to life, while Simon only pretended to resurrect a corpse; and through prayer Peter also successfully stopped Simon from flying up to heaven. Medieval people would have been familiar with Peter's superior intercessory power, which may explain why he was invoked in spells.

Within Catholic Europe, particularly before the Protestant Reformation, saints were seen as the intercessors between humanity and God and were believed to wield extraordinary powers. Requesting their assistance was part of orthodox Christian practice at the time, so it should come as no surprise that their power would also be harnessed for activities like identifying thieves. Alongside Peter and Paul, practitioners using the sieve and shears might also appeal directly to the Trinity, reciting, 'In the name of the Father, the Son, and the Holy Ghost' before asking each question. If simply recovering the goods was deemed more important than identifying the thief, then the story of St Helen (c. 250–330 CE) and her discovery of the True Cross might be invoked. Helen, mother of the Roman emperor Constantine, had converted to Christianity in her later life and became incredibly devout. She dedicated herself to eradicating any traces of polytheism from Jerusalem, replacing all temples dedicated to the Roman gods with churches. The story goes that Helen ordered a temple to be torn down and the land beneath to be excavated. In the process three crosses were uncovered, one of which was proved, through subsequent miracles, to be the cross upon which Jesus had died. Helen's discovery was remembered throughout medieval Europe, and she was regularly invoked to help find lost items—especially those suspected of being buried underground. A practice in fourteenth-century Flanders apparently involved the magician lying flat on the ground with their arms outstretched—thus making the shape of a cross—and performing the action four times in the cardinal directions of the compass. While so doing, the magician would call on the ground to give up the location of the lost goods, just as the earth had swallowed, and then returned, the true cross to Helen.

The ecclesiastical courts generally disapproved of such methods. In Catholic Europe, such activities were seen as blasphemy as they misused divine power; in Protestant regions, appealing to saints teetered dangerously close to Catholic superstition. Nevertheless, the practitioners probably did not see themselves as behaving badly. William Hasylwoode, whom we met earlier, was a clergyman who no doubt believed that calling on the Lord and the Christian saints was perfectly acceptable. The same attitude perhaps explains the popularity of the book-and-key method. This involved taking a psalter (a book of psalms) or a Bible, placing a key inside and holding the book between one's hands. Upon asking yes-or-no questions, the book was either expected to turn or the key to fall out when the answer was in the affirmative. As sacred texts, the Bible and the psalter bore power. The spoken words accompanying the ritual drew on the same well of energy. Most often a section of Psalm 50 was recited: *Si videbis furem, correbas cum eo, et cum adulterem portionem tuam ponebas*—'When thou sawest a thief, then thou consentedst with him, and hast been partaker with adulterers'. That the passage condemns thieves is likely the reason it was chosen as an incantation for goods-finding: in a sense, it calls for divine retribution.

Other practitioners opted for the simpler incantation *Deus deorum* (God of gods), invoking the ultimate power in the universe that could see all and tell all. That the Latin version of these words was used in England even after the break with Rome in the 1530s tells us something about the potency that

Latin was thought to hold: alongside Hebrew, Arabic and Greek, the language was deemed innately powerful. By and large, the book-and-key method was only available to clerics, who would have easy access to a Bible or a psalter and were also the most likely members of the community to have a good working knowledge of Latin. As we will see throughout this book, training in orthodox religious practices could easily be repurposed for less conventional uses—and sometimes ones that were far more disturbing than recovering missing goods. That priests were willing to use sacred objects and words for such purposes, though, must have sent a message to their parishioners that there was nothing wrong with practising magic in principle. Priests came into contact with numinous forces every day through church services, prayer and Communion: as the spiritual experts in their communities, they would have set an example of where to draw the line between acceptable and unacceptable involvement with the supernatural.

The central place that priests held in their communities put them in a prime position for selling magic and may even have helped to ensure that it worked. Priests' responsibilities towards their flock meant they needed an intimate understanding of community relations and of people's private lives. In Catholic areas they would gain a great deal of knowledge while taking confession; but in all regions of Europe they might be appealed to as arbitrators in community disputes and, of course, administer the Christian rites at births, marriages and deaths. In addition, they were likely to have superior learning to most other villagers: even if they had received only the most rudimentary clerical training, they would at least have basic literacy skills and a smattering of Latin. Their spiritual authority, knowledge and, crucially, their right to involve themselves in their parishioners' affairs positioned them ideally for a career in moonlighting as cunning folk.

It's not surprising, therefore, that clergymen were consulted in efforts to find missing items. In 1473 William Dardus, vicar of Patrixbourne outside Canterbury, seems to have caused quite a stir in this small village when he reportedly boasted about his supernatural powers. The episode started when Mrs Byng's linen went missing, possibly stolen from outside her home after washing day. She consulted Dardus about it, who told her to leave it with him. Shortly afterwards he went around the parish telling his flock that he could summon the souls of the dead and ask them questions. Having sown the seeds in everyone's minds about his powers, a few weeks later Dardus made a show of taking some of the Eucharist home with him. The purported purpose was to conjure a spirit to discover who had stolen Mrs Byng's linen. Having made it very clear what his plans were, Dardus then told 'Byng's wife to close all the windows [of their house] except one'. While Dardus conjured and Mr and Mrs Byng waited quietly at home, the linen conveniently reappeared through the open window.

Dardus seems to have employed a clever strategy. He was playing on the widespread belief that, because they had the spiritual authority to perform exorcisms and bend demons to their will, priests also had the power to summon and communicate with spirits. His public claims made clear to the culprit that he would use these powers if the stolen goods were not returned, thus giving the thief a chance to do so himself. Dardus then ramped up the pressure by actually performing the conjuration. Fearing discovery, and having been given a way to return the linen anonymously, it seems that the thief quietly did so.[7] We don't know whether Dardus actually had the power to summon spirits, but it does not really matter. His claim that he would be able to do it, and his position at the centre of the community, giving him a captive audience that he could berate through sermons about the consequences of stealing, were sufficient. Having observed his parishioners' activities for weeks, perhaps he also had his suspicions about who the thief might be and would have named the wrongdoer if the linen hadn't reappeared. Dardus was treated sympathetically by the Church authorities investigating his case, probably because he was attempting to do good by the magic that he supposedly performed.*

Leaning on the fears and guilty conscience of the thief might have been the underlying strategy of other goods-finding spells. Several iterations of

---

* He may still have been something of a cad, though: when questioned for his unseemly priestly behaviour, Dardus denied all wrongdoing other than allowing Mrs Byng to 'handle his private parts'.

'trial by ordeal' were employed in medieval and early modern Europe, most of which worked on the basis that the guilty party would expose themselves through unusual behaviour. The trick was to build up anxiety in the suspect. As with Dardus' strategy, time was probably set aside to spread the word that an item had been stolen and that a cunning person was on the case. This would make the thief nervous: aside from the guilt potentially weighing on their conscience, the pervasive belief in magic's efficacy was bound to fray their resolve. All of the suspects would then be invited to a meeting place, which might be the victim's or the cunning person's home, or perhaps even the local church. Attendance would not be compulsory—cunning folk held no legal authority—but refusing to appear would be tantamount to admitting one's guilt. Once all were gathered, the ritual would begin. The actual method and materials varied by region and, presumably, the magical practitioner's own knowledge. Some would involve blessing and eating foods, others touching a blessed item and waiting for it to prove one's innocence or guilt.

The ordeal of eating was widespread in Britain, and is illustrated in the case of Jane Bulkeley of Caernarfon in North Wales. Jane had identified ten suspects for a local theft, whom she summoned together, along with the injured party. She took a piece of cheese (presumably quite a large one, given the next stage of the process), cut it into ten chunks and then wrote a charm on each. Unfortunately the records of the case don't elaborate on how she did this: in my limited experience of cheese-carving, anything more complex than a short word or two would have resulted in the morsel crumbling away. Perhaps she simply etched a cross into each piece and spoke a charm over it. Either way, to those in the room the charm would have imbued the cheese with supernatural power. Then, one by one, the ten suspects ate their piece. In some versions of the spell, each suspect would be expected to recite words along the lines of 'Lord, if I be the thief, may this morsel choke me.' If one person was strongly suspected of the crime, maybe they would be placed later in the queue to make them feel increasingly nervous. While every innocent party waited to eat their morsel, feeling insulted perhaps that they were undergoing this humiliating ritual, the guilty person's mouth would be getting drier and drier. With every suspect who swallowed their cheese easily and had their innocence declared, the thief would know that they were all the more likely to be exposed. When their turn came, they would inevitably struggle to swallow the hard, dry cheese (which it almost certainly was: soft cheese would be impossible to carve and there would be no point wasting good, fresh food on potential felons). As they choked on the holy morsel, their guilt would be proclaimed.

Simple psychology therefore played an important part in these rituals. In other versions, the cheese would be replaced with bread (probably also quite a stale loaf) or the act of eating would be replaced by touch. One—albeit rarer—method put all the suspects in a dark room with a dirty, sooty cooking pot. They would be told to touch the pot, and through God's intervention all those who were innocent would come away with miraculously clean hands. It seems the expectation here was that all those who were confident of their own innocence would touch the pot and leave with dirty hands. The one person whose hands were clean would be the guilty party, as they had not dared to touch the pot in the first place.

Other trials relied more heavily on direct divine intervention. A preferred method on the Italian peninsula, in particular, was to draw a picture of an eye on a wall and drive a nail through its centre, right into the pupil. The suspects would then be asked to walk past the eye, which in turn was expected to start weeping when the culprit appeared in front of it. In this case, although the thief might in theory expose themselves by acting nervously or refusing to go near the eye altogether, the part of the spell that was meant to expose the culprit was truly miraculous: walls do not normally cry. This is worth remembering because, as we will see throughout this book, although there are often psychological—and, to us, slightly cynical—explanations for how a spell might work, we should refrain from treating magic as nothing more than tricks and mind-games.

A combination of detective work, educated guesses and a varying degree of psychic power probably went into most goods-finding services, and the level of respect that a cunning person enjoyed would also have influenced the likelihood that stolen items would be returned. Often the stakes for cunning folk to be accurate could be high, especially if their client was demanding or the goods lost were valuable. Goods-finding was, however, the thin end of the wedge compared to many other issues on which cunning folk were consulted. We will now encounter how magic might be used in more personal matters.

CHAPTER 2

HOW TO FIND LOVE

For certes, I am al Venerien
In feelynge, and myn herte is Marcien.
Venus me yaf my lust, my likerousnesse,
And Mars yaf me my sturdy hardynesse;
Myn ascendent was Taur, and Mars therinne.
Allas, allas! That evere love was synne!
I folwed ay myn inclinacioun
By vertu of my constellacioun;
That made me I koude noght withdrawe
My chambre of Venus from a good felawe.

—GEOFFREY CHAUCER, *THE WIFE OF BATH'S PROLOGUE*

THE CHRISTIAN IDEAL OF MARRIED LIFE, IN WHICH A heterosexual couple pledged their troth to one another, stayed faithful and had numerous children, was as difficult to live up to in the past as it is now. Every step had its hurdles: finding an eligible partner and having the financial stability to support a family wasn't the least of them. Being fertile, surviving childbirth and actually liking your spouse were among the many factors that could not be guaranteed, despite the intense pressure to meet such expectations. The insistence that one should be chaste up until marriage also proved to be an impossible ask for many. With romantic relationships filled with potential dangers and pitfalls, one solution to the myriad problems was the use of spells. From seduction to marriage, conception to widowhood, there were charms and rituals to aid every stage of a person's love life.

In many ways, pre-modern Christian life was riddled with impossible double standards. There was the ideal, underpinned by religious doctrine, of what sex and relationships should entail. Then there was reality, which, as Chaucer's Wife of Bath reminds us, was tormented by human emotions and urges. By and large, the Church was responsible for both promoting the ideal and untangling the mess when reality got in the way. Ecclesiastical courts dealt with moral misdemeanours such as adultery and premarital relations, and it is partly thanks to their records that we know so much about what medieval and early modern people got up to in their private lives. They also tell us about the use of magic when things got tricky.

Love magic is a broad category, encompassing spells to bring couples together and to break them up, potions to conceive, and methods to improve marriages. The importance of heterosexual, married relationships to pre-modern people cannot be overstated: the family unit was seen as a fundamental building block of society, so how and when sex and marriage took place was of wider social concern and was not limited just to the immediate parties involved. By looking at love magic, therefore—what it was used for and by whom—we are not only gaining an insight into people's romantic lives, fascinating though that may be; we are also getting to look at society in microcosm.

Private matters became public very quickly. When a man and woman married—same-sex relationships, though recognised as occurring, were illegal—it really meant the union of two families. Both sides made material and moral commitments: the woman's family via a dowry, the man's through certain guarantees that the woman would be taken care of and any resulting children provided for. In much of north-western Europe the newly-weds would traditionally leave their parents' households and set up on their own; in southern and eastern Europe the bride would usually join her husband in his parents' house, splitting off into a separate household only after several children were born. In both systems the family was paramount: it supported the new couple and expected contributions in return. The pair would provide for their parents in old age; share the load of running a household by helping with farming, domestic chores and trade; and raise children who, in time, would do the same. This semi-self-sufficient unit also had a clear hierarchy that was thought to reflect the divine order of things: the (male) head of the household ruled and directed the rest of the family, supported by the wife/mother, both of whom should be obeyed by their children. Civilisation was imagined to function on a similar hierarchic principle: a country was, ideally, ruled by a supreme (male) head, supported by priests, a military class, merchants and labourers.[1] Stable family units contributed to a healthy community, and vice versa.

To be outside the system was dangerous, both for an individual and for society at large. There was a strong belief, informed by religion and some branches of medicine, that women could not be trusted to make important decisions.[2] Although in practice this could not be avoided, a woman without a father, husband or other male relative to guide her was nevertheless treated as something of a liability. Likewise young unmarried men were seen as problematic: pent-up sexual frustration was recognised as leading to rash decision-making, violent outbursts and all-round riotous behaviour. Sex outside marriage, meanwhile, could lead to fatherless children who would be a burden on the parish and a mark of shame on the mother. A stable marriage was, therefore, seen as the ideal—both for the individuals and for the wider well-being of society.

Of course this was easier said than done. In north-western Europe, men and women tended to get married surprisingly late, in their mid- to late twenties. While more couples in southern and eastern Europe would marry in their teens, most men here would wait until their thirties and then marry a much younger bride. These patterns of marrying late inevitably led some people to seek out premarital sex, and there were charms to help make that happen when one's own charms were lacking.

◆

The fish had been delicious. Expertly cooked, it had been seasoned with savory and sea holly, and something else that the man couldn't quite put his finger on. What he did know was that he felt happy and warm; very warm actually—his blood felt like it was simmering. He looked up at the woman beside him, who was watching anxiously to see that he'd enjoyed his meal. How had he not noticed her beauty before? Well, he was noticing it now, and he'd never wanted anyone more in his life.

I've made up this story, but food, herbs and certain secret rituals played a key role in seduction magic. Although there are very few court records that describe how people were using spells, priests' manuals—guides for how to care spiritually for their flock—cookbooks and popular literature, like plays and ballads, tell us about the kinds of charms that were in circulation. The use of fish and bread is rather graphically described in a thirteenth-century priests' manual written by William de Montibus, who demanded that a woman do penance if she had 'given either a fish which has died in her vagina, or bread which was made on her buttocks with blood, or menstrual blood to her husband to eat or drink so that his love will be more inflamed'.[3] The method is first mentioned in an eleventh-century book of canon law, warning churchmen of the sorts of immoral acts that women might be getting up to. Strange though it may sound to us today, the method would have made good sense to medieval people: here was an attempt to create a sympathetic link between the man and the woman through his consuming her blood and other bodily fluids. Blood in particular was a potent substance in Christian culture: after all, it was Christ's blood that had washed away humanity's sin. In medical terms, blood was also the humour—or physical element—that filled a person's body with heat and vigour. What's more, blood gave life: according to the Greek physician Galen, it was the base substance from which both sperm and breast milk were formed. By using her menstrual blood to charm a man, therefore, a woman was using a powerful, intimate material that was inherently linked to sex, passion and life.[4]

Bread also had a strong significance. It was a crucial foodstuff in people's diets, again given supernatural power through its use in Holy Communion. The manual process of kneading bread was also ritually important as it transferred some of the woman's essence into the dough, especially if she did it with her behind, before baking it for her intended lover. The name often given to these loaves—'buttocks' or 'cockle' bread—further emphasises their sexual nature: 'cockle' is an old slang word for the labia minora.[5] The practice of inserting a fish into one's vagina perhaps doesn't require further explanation.*

Thankfully, these were not the only attraction spells that someone could turn to. There were plenty of love philtres that might be used instead, whether made at home or bought from cunning folk. In 1582 Goodwife Swane of Kent was boasting that she had a recipe for a drink so powerful that 'if she [did] give it to any young man that she liketh well of, he shall be in love with her'. In London at around the same time, the sorcerer John Prestall was gaining a reputation for selling similar drinks to lovesick young men and women. He was so respected for his skill, he claimed, that 'he would never be hanged [for his sorcery] . . . for 500 gentlemen would have lain in the way to his execution' rather than allow his death.

What made these drinks so powerful? While their contents varied according to who was making them, they would likely have contained ingredients associated with heat, reflecting the belief that warmer bodies were more inclined to lust. Pepper, cinnamon and savory were all thought to carry heating properties and were a staple for aphrodisiacs from the sixteenth century onwards. Wild pansy—also known as 'love-in-idleness' and well known for its lust-inducing juice—makes an appearance in Shakespeare's *A Midsummer Night's Dream* as the plant that causes Titania

---

* Or perhaps it does: the first question I'm asked whenever I mention this practice is 'What kind of fish?' William de Montibus doesn't specify, but my guess is that it would be determined by regional availability and the practical, logistical aspects of the operation.

to fall in love with the first creature she sees. Mixing these ingredients in wine, beer or honey, adding some bodily fluids of the woo-er (blood, spit, perhaps even semen) and giving it to one's intended was probably one of the most common, and direct, means of magical seduction.

Other ingested love spells could be more complex. The *Picatrix*, a Latin book of magic that circulated throughout Europe from the mid-fifteenth century, describes an elaborate ritual for seducing a woman:

> Take 2 oz. each of dried hare's blood and wolf's brain; three grains' worth of melted cattle fat; two grains each of amber and nutmeg; three grains of camphor; and 2 oz. of the blood of the person doing the ritual (that is, the person on whose behalf it is done). Place this blood in an iron container over the fire until heated. Once heated, toss the other medicines on top. Mix everything. Remove them from the fire, and mix with wine or honey, a dish of meat or fowl, or with whatever dish you please. While doing the above, keep your mind firmly on the woman who is the target of this ritual. Afterward, take a small amount of incense and an equal amount of galbanum gum, and throw them into the fire. While the smoke is rising, say:
>
> '*ye deyluz, menydez, catrudiz, mebduliz, huenehenilez! I move the spirit and desire of this woman N. by the power of those spirits and this mixture. I move her spirit and desire with a feeling of anxiety as much in her waking and sleeping as in her walking, standing, and sitting. May she have no rest until she obeys those spirits that we will name: hueheyulez, heyediz, cayimuz, hendeliz!*'
>
> Once you have done the above, give to eat the entire mixture to whomever you desire until nothing is left. While this medicine sits in the stomach of the consumer, she will be unable to rest—rather, she will be moved by a powerful emotion. Obeying it, she will go to the place you desire.

The fact that the *Picatrix* was circulated in Latin, as well as other internal evidence, suggests that the intended reader was male, but fish dinners and 'buttocks' bread indicate that the desire to find sexual partners was not restricted to just one gender. The *Picatrix* and other texts also show us that seduction spells were not just for casual sex, but were sought in order to entice someone into marriage. For example, John of Kent's confession manual, written around 1215, instructed priests to ask parishioners whether they had used sorcery 'before marriage in order to have someone as your wife or know who you will have [as your bride]'. The *Picatrix* also contains a spell to create 'a perfect, durable love between the two [people]'. Seduction, therefore, could be the initial stage of a marriage proposal. We need to remember that weddings at the time did not have to be strictly formal affairs: a verbal contract and consummation of the union could be enough, providing there were witnesses to affirm that the couple had agreed to the match. If one wanted to secure another person as one's spouse, therefore, feeding them a potion that inspired irrational lust might do the trick.

Sleeping with someone did not always guarantee a wedding, though. What if rational concerns around personality or finances got in the way? Even more than today, a major consideration for marriage in the medieval and early modern periods was a person's financial prospects: a man who had the means to set up his own household and provide for several children was probably at the top of many brides' lists. For the man's part, a woman who could bring a substantial dowry to the household—whether in cash, furniture, land or livestock—was especially attractive. Physical beauty and a good temperament were also important, although one's true nature might not be revealed until after the marriage had taken place.

Given such concerns about financial security, it is perhaps unsurprising that a lot of marriage magic was used to try to woo someone above one's own social station. Although not a hard-and-fast rule, it seems that this kind of magic was used more by women than men, which is understandable, given the constraints women faced in founding their own businesses or embarking on a professional career.*

---

* Women might also have sought out marriage spells due to premarital pregnancy. Patricia Crawford estimates that, in the period 1550–1800, between 16 and 35 per cent of women's first births

In 1492 Margaret Geffrey seems to have been at the end of her tether. She was a widow living in the parish of St Bartholomew the Less, just outside the walls of London and right on the edge of Smith Field. From these details alone we can guess that she was vulnerable. Despite—or perhaps because of—the thriving weekly livestock market there, Smith Field was an unruly place. There was drinking, fighting and gambling, and it had one of the few streets where sex workers were permitted to go about their business (the street in question was affectionately called Cock Lane). To top it all, it also served as a site of public punishment, where Londoners would come to witness the brutal executions of condemned thieves, heretics and traitors. Perhaps Margaret lived here because her late husband worked at the market, or maybe she and her family moved to the area after his death because the rent was cheap.

Being a widow could be a blessing for some, as English law dictated that a woman's dowry should be returned on her husband's death, and in some cases she might also have the right to dispose of his property. This gave widows a level of financial freedom to which 'maids' and wives were not entitled. But widowhood could also ruin a family: outstanding debts had to be paid on the husband's death, which could leave the widow with nothing. Add to this the need to support children, and many bereaved women found themselves in dire straits. The best option was to remarry, but potential husbands could be difficult to come by, with children in tow: in addition to being more mouths to feed, the late husband's property would normally be reserved for his children and would not be at the disposal of a new partner.

Margaret appears to have been the less fortunate type of widow. Alone and responsible for both her mother and her children, she needed to find a new husband fast. One day a neighbour named Richard Laukiston

---

were conceived before marriage. Given the intense social stigma around bearing illegitimate children, pregnant unmarried women might have turned to magic to ensure their lovers followed through on their promises. Patricia Crawford, *Parents of Poor Children in England 1580–1800* (Oxford: Oxford University Press, 2010), p. 91. Again the court documents that record such cases give us only a small snapshot of people's lives, and we rarely discover the outcome of the predicaments they faced. Even so, what emerges from these records is often heartbreaking.

approached Margaret. 'Thou arte a poore widow,' he told her, 'and it wer[e] almes to helpe the[e] to a mariage.' The use of the familiar 'thou' rather than the formal 'you' suggests that Laukiston and Margaret were on good terms, which might be why she was willing to trust him. He told her of a cunning man who 'can cause a woman to have any man that she hath favour to', and he was certain that, if Margaret wanted, this cunning man could find her a husband worth a thousand pounds. For context, the average skilled tradesman in the 1490s might expect to earn about tenpence a day, so this was a fantastic amount of money. Of course such services came at a price. Richard offered to be the go-between for Margaret with this unnamed magician, and asked how much she would be able to pay. All Margaret had were two mazers, or drinking bowls, worth a little over £3 16s. She handed them over with trepidation as, in her own words, 'if thei wer sold and I faile of my purpose, I, my moder, and my children wer undoon'.

While these drinking bowls were her only valuable belongings, Margaret had reason to hope that the gamble would pay off. She trusted her neighbours, and she might even have heard of others who had found new husbands this way. Court records reveal that this sort of magic was being employed across the country. In 1446, for example, Marion de Belton and Isabella Brome were brought before the ecclesiastical courts in Durham for claiming to be able to procure desirable husbands for local women through magic. More than this, it was widely rumoured that the late queen consort, Elizabeth Woodville, had married Edward IV through similar means.

Elizabeth, like Margaret Geffrey, was a widow when she married the king in 1464. She had two surviving sons from her first marriage and, though of noble stock, she had few connections that made her a desirable match, from a political perspective. Moreover, she was about twenty-seven years old: aristocratic couples tended to marry younger than the wider population, and there were concerns that Elizabeth had only a few years left to safely bear children. Why then did the newly crowned monarch, whose hold on the throne was precarious at best, choose Elizabeth as his bride? Sorcery seemed like a plausible explanation to many, both at the royal court and across the country.

Perhaps Margaret, our widow in 1490s London, was heartened by these rumours about the royal couple and convinced herself that such spells could be relied upon. In her case, unfortunately, they could not: the reason we know about her is that nothing came of her agreement with Laukiston. No rich husband appeared after handing over her mazers and, as she feared, she was close to being 'undone' as a result. Ever resourceful, though, she took Laukiston to court for fraud. Surprisingly, given that she was a woman representing herself, Margaret won: Laukiston was made to return the drinking bowls or their equivalent value in cash. Her success had a downside, however: she had to perform public penance for trying to employ a cunning man. This was a humiliating ritual that was likely to have entailed walking barefoot to her parish church bearing a lit taper-candle and announcing before the congregation what she had done, begging forgiveness. No doubt Margaret felt this humiliation was worth it in order to get her money back and to warn others of Richard's deceitful nature. We can only hope that she found a husband or some other means of supporting herself and her family, for after this episode Margaret drops from the record, fading back into the mists of time.

Once again, the surviving records mostly provide insights when spells went wrong. While Margaret's case is an example of how people dealt with cases of fraud, others tell us about how violent magic could be. Some of the love spells used by men were especially disturbing. Although some would resort to potions like those described above, others chose to be more overtly coercive. One example is that of William Divers, a Canterbury man looking for love in the 1590s.

Divers was ready and eager to marry. He even knew whom he wanted as his bride: Elizabeth, daughter of Agnes Williams of the parish of St Paul's, Canterbury. Given that Agnes was in charge of the marriage negotiations, we can assume that Elizabeth had no father, uncle or adult brothers to answer to. Perhaps this made Elizabeth an easy target, and possibly also an attractive one, if she was the sole child able to inherit her parents' property. Either way, Divers seems to have been far more enthusiastic about the union than the Williamses were. He asked an acquaintance to act as an interme-diary between him and the mother and daughter. Third parties were common in marriage negotiations: such delicate topics as dowries, jointures (how much a wife would gain in the event she was widowed) and portions (the amount of an inheritable estate given in marriage) had to be broached, and often these discussions would be conducted by representatives of the potential couple. The importance of one's word, which served as a real legal bond, also meant that witnesses were highly significant in any transaction, so it is not surprising that Divers chose two respectable men to represent him to Agnes and Elizabeth: William Walsall, clerk at St Paul's, and Mr Ralph Grove, a gentleman of the same parish.

At first the wooing seemed to be going well: Walsall and Grove appeared to be honest men who did credit to Divers' petition. Agnes accepted tokens of affection on Elizabeth's behalf, and it looked like an engagement might soon be announced. But Elizabeth prevaricated, and no arrangement was agreed. Perhaps it was Divers who got frustrated, or maybe Walsall got bored: either way, the wooing turned to threats. Walsall later denied it in court, but the Williamses claimed that he got far too pushy. When Agnes would not consent to her daughter's marriage, Walsall took a new tack, telling her that 'if you . . . will not geve your consent that William Divers shall have your daughter Elizabeth I will . . . so deale with you that your mynd will never quiet in the day tyme and in the night you shal be trubled and vexed with straunge sightes and noises which you shall se[e] and heare'.

He did not say how exactly this would happen, but it seems that Divers was threatening to conjure a demon to torment Agnes. As a literate man—Walsall was a clerk—he would have had access to forms of ritual magic not available to most of the population, including magic books such as the *Picatrix*. These texts provided spells, often involving advanced rituals in Latin, Arabic and Hebrew, as well as careful plotting of celestial alignments, to summon spirits to do the spell-caster's will. We can only speculate whether Walsall really had the ability to conjure demons, but he could easily have relied on his reputation as a learned man to at least pretend he could control devils.*

This sort of threatening, coercive tactic seems to have been used almost solely by men, and sometimes they were successful. Agnes Williams reported Walsall for his excessive actions, and he was forced to back off. Edetha Best was not so lucky. In 1585 John Meere, a law student at Temple, London, was trying to seduce her. Meere threatened that if Best did not sleep with him, he would torment her with the sight of the Devil until it drove her mad. Despite Edetha being a married woman, and Meere being warned to stay away by her manservant, she consented to an affair out of fear. Whether she really experienced such an apparition—today we understand psychosomatic trauma—doesn't really matter: the threats would have been real enough to her. We don't know how many women were coerced into marriage through similar means, but demonic love spells were certainly a strategy that some men used to woo prospective partners. We can safely assume such marriages were unlikely to be happy ones, but as we will see later, there were spells to deal with that, too.

◆

By and large, magic that aided conceptions was treated quite leniently by the authorities—perhaps because the ultimate end was a socially positive one. Children were a fundamental part of romantic relationships in the period. While pregnancy was the almost inevitable consequence of

---

* On top of the theory contained within magic books, Catholic tradition supported the notion that demonic love spells worked. St Cyprian, an early Christian convert from Carthage, North Africa, is a good example. In the third century CE Cyprian was employed by the pagan father of St Justina to force her into marriage. The (as-yet-unconverted) Cyprian conjured demons and sent them to cloud Justina's mind with lustful thoughts, expecting that she would give in to the impulse and throw off her Christian vow of chastity. Only Justina's exemplary piety was enough to beat the demons back, and with Cyprian's attempt thwarted, he converted to Christianity. Despite the failure of this magic attempt, the reason that both Justina and Cyprian were canonised is because this kind of demonic intervention was assumed to work on most people.

sex—contraceptive methods were fairly unreliable—children were both the hope and the expectation in marriage. They also played an important part in the household. When young, they would watch livestock, help with food preparation and mind younger siblings. When grown, they would be expected to support their parents in old age. Children were also crucial for forming alliances between families through marriage. For those lucky enough to have heritable property or titles, children were the means to continue a dynasty. Quite aside from wanting them for their own sake, therefore, children were an important feature of a successful life.

What happened, then, when a couple remained childless? It was widely recognised that men could be infertile, but the social pressure and attendant shame of being unable to conceive were probably felt more keenly by women. Infertility was valid grounds for a marriage annulment in canon law, which added even more pressure—especially to noblewomen, whose ability to provide an heir was one of the greatest measures of their worth. Eleanor Cobham, second wife to Humphrey, Duke of Gloucester, seems to have felt this especially strongly.

Eleanor's marriage to Humphrey had been something of a surprise. He was the son of Henry IV, brother to Henry V—the hero of Agincourt—and uncle to Henry VI. Besides his noble lineage, Humphrey was a powerful and intelligent man in his own right. He acted as Lord Protector of England while his royal nephew was in his minority, and led armies in France for his brother during the Hundred Years War. Eleanor's stock, meanwhile, was less impressive. She was the daughter of Sir Reginald Cobham of Sterborough, a relatively minor knight and not a member of the peerage. In terms of land and connections, Humphrey could certainly have done better.

But the couple fell in love. Eleanor was intelligent, beautiful and engaging—far more so, apparently, than Humphrey's first wife, Jacqueline of Hainault. That marriage had been one of convenience: Jacqueline had recently annulled her marriage to John IV, Duke of Brabant, and was seeking a new protector. Humphrey had an eye on Jacqueline's hereditary lands in

Hainault. Claiming these lands as his own proved more difficult than he anticipated, however, and he found comfort in Eleanor's arms when his diplomatic missions failed. Their affair eventually convinced Humphrey to annul his marriage to Jacqueline, and the pair were free to wed in 1428.

Eleanor would have been in her late twenties at this point, so she may already have been anxious about bearing Humphrey a child. While they waited for Eleanor to fall pregnant, though, the couple built a life together, indulging their interests in the arts and natural philosophy by patronising some of the most eminent scholars, musicians and poets of their time. Their manor at Greenwich was cultivated into an impressive garden, named La Pleasaunce. By 1440, though, this idyllic life was looking less rosy. The couple still had no children: no heirs to inherit the beautiful manor or, indeed, Humphrey's titles. Humphrey did have two illegitimate children (their mothers aren't known to us), but although he recognised them as his own, their 'natural' status meant they could not enjoy any heritable rights. In the early 1440s Humphrey was also heir presumptive to the throne, as Henry VI was not yet married. At the age of forty, with her years for giving birth relatively safely having now passed, Eleanor must have been feeling the pressure. Desperate times called for desperate measures— measures that almost cost Eleanor her life.

Enter Margery Jourdemayne, a cunning woman who specialised in rela-tionships. She had been arrested for sorcery in Windsor in 1430 and spent two years in prison there until her husband paid a bond of £20 and she herself swore not to practise magic again. Margery clearly did not intend to keep that promise. It seems that, on returning to her home in Westminster, she immediately got back to work, discreetly selling spells and love potions to courtiers.[6] Eleanor might have known Margery from around then: a contemporary chronicler recorded that Eleanor had commissioned her 'sorcerie and wicchecraft' for a long time.[7] This might simply be malicious rumour espoused by a disapproving clerical writer, but Eleanor was known to patronise scholars interested in the occult arts. With her interest in 'natural' magic such as geomancy and astrology, it is perhaps not surprising that she would also have a cunning woman in her service.

The women had certainly met by the early 1440s, because in 1441 they were both arrested for conspiracy to magically murder Henry VI. Eleanor's motive for doing such a thing was obvious, at least to the investigators: if Henry died childless, her husband was first in line for the throne and she would therefore become queen. As evidence for this plan, the prosecution presented figures of wax and lead made by the magician Roger Bolingbroke, which Margery Jourdemayne probably also had a hand in creating. Eleanor vehemently denied the accusation, admitting only that she had employed Roger for a horoscope and Margery 'forto have borne a child by hir lord, the duke of Gloucestre'. These images could have been fertility charms, but they could just as easily serve a lethal purpose. Wax dolls and ciphers could be slowly melted, pricked with pins or buried, with the intention of causing harm to the person they were meant to represent. Everyone's lives were at stake in this investigation: if they had been producing love charms, Eleanor and her service magicians were breaking ecclesiastical law, but to a harmless end. However, if the images were proved to be of King Henry, as the prosecutors alleged, then they were committing the most appalling treachery. And the punishment for treason was death.

Margery was nobody's fool: when she and Eleanor were accused of heresy, witchcraft and treason, she was quick to condemn her employer and throw the blame away from herself. For Eleanor's part, she attempted to protect both herself and her retainers by steadfastly insisting that they were only attempting conception magic. The argument was a partial success in so far as Eleanor's life was spared, but Margery and Roger were not so lucky. Margery was burned alive at Smithfield for heresy—an odd charge, given the circumstances. It's likely that, as practising magic was not a capital offence and there was not enough evidence to find her guilty of treason, the prosecution opted for heresy as a means of making a spectacle of her death and thus deterring any other regicide plots. Roger, against whom there was much stronger evidence for a treason charge, was dressed in a conjuror's robe and made to confess his actions before being hanged, drawn and quartered. Eleanor used her noble status to protect herself, and was thus handed down the lesser sentence of public penance and a life sentence under house arrest. Her marriage to Humphrey was annulled and she spent the rest of her days under a cloud of infamy.

Let us consider Eleanor Cobham the woman, rather than the scheming Duchess of Gloucester she was reviled as by her contemporaries. Despite her wealth and status, her powers were limited by her fertility. Eleanor may well have been ambitious and may have dreamed of becoming queen. But beneath that aim there probably lay a very real fear that she couldn't have children. Given the money and contacts she had, why would she not employ cunning women and ritual magicians to help her?

Women of lower social standing may not have had the same resources or such high stakes attached to their reproductivity, but they would have felt similar pressures. They too resorted to conception magic at times, employing various methods. Communion bread was believed to carry numinous powers, and medieval priests' manuals warned that women might hide the bread under their tongues when they took the Eucharist, then use it in fertility spells at home.[8] We don't know how exactly the bread was used, though healing charms sometimes involved writing prayers on Communion wafers and eating them. Wearing a little pouch around the neck containing powders was another method offered by Mary Woods to her clients in the early seventeenth century. The most unusual measure we know of was boasted by Edith Hooker of New Alresford, near Winchester. By the early 1530s Edith had made a name for herself as someone who could help women conceive '*sine virili semine*'—that is, without a man's sperm. The method tried on at least one woman was to use 'medicine [that] was made from the spawn of a trotter', namely, from pig semen.

How conception *via porcus* was an improvement on human sperm is not explained in the court documents that record the case, but it indicates that the women seeking Edith's help thought that the fertility problems lay in their partners. Male impotence was believed to have natural explanations—hence Shakespeare's remark in *Macbeth* that alcohol 'provokes and unprovokes'—as well as sometimes being caused by witchcraft. If the latter was the cause, there were a host of remedies. The twelfth-century lawyer

Roffredus of Benevento lamented the different lengths to which a couple might go to restore a man's virility:

> The bewitched man should not run to enchanters or diviners, so that they can use their medicines or incantations. And I have heard that many women do this. They make their bewitched husband hold his trousers on his head for a whole day and night; or they take a piece of cheese and perforate it with a bore and they give the husband what they collect from the perforation to eat; or each of them may take their belts and tie them and put them in the open air overnight; or they make the poor man stand naked all night under a stole when the weather is fair, or similar things.[9]

An alternative to these methods was to identify the witch who had caused the impotence and try to make the curse rebound, through some form of reflective or 'unwitching' spell. The enactor of impotence magic was often suspected to be a jilted lover or someone acting on her behalf—it could be the last resort of an abandoned sweetheart. If a man had broken a promise of engagement and could not be convinced to return, impotence magic could be both a means of revenge, ensuring that the man was privately and publicly humiliated, and a last-ditch attempt to win him back. As impotence could be grounds for annulment, 'unprovoking' spells could end a marriage before it really began. Some spells were quite sophisticated and ensured that the target was only impotent with his new wife; for example, a common charm involved tying knots into string before throwing it under the newly-weds' feet while they danced at their wedding celebration. As the groom passed over the knots, his genitals would be 'tied', and presumably the association would be bound up with the new bride. If the marriage failed as a result, the original lover might be able to reclaim her partner, who would not be impotent with her.

Questions of fertility and fidelity were all bound up with the pursuit of stability and happiness. As is true through the ages, happiness can't be taken for granted. Even with a prosperous spouse, children and a family home, kindness and affection could still be lacking. Sometimes an unhappy wife or husband would take extreme measures to try to remedy their situation.

◆

Alice Suttill looked up at the door for what felt like the hundredth time that day. The bells of Canterbury Cathedral had struck the hour long ago, and yet Alice was still waiting expectantly for her visitor. He had promised that he would come and see her today—and he would bring her something to make her life happy, or at least a little easier to bear.

She was waiting for Thomas Fansome—medical practitioner, service magician and, eventually, confidant. They had met several months earlier in 1590, originally to treat an ailment of Alice's. He had stayed long after the medicine had been administered, caught up in conversation, and returned several times thereafter at Alice's request. She revealed to Thomas that her physical health wasn't her main concern: she was deeply unhappy. Married to a man who didn't love her and wouldn't even come near her except with brutal intentions, she felt her life was becoming intolerable. She didn't know what to do. Formal separation was technically possible in Protestant England, but it was an expensive and elaborate process that was unavailable to most people. A more common way out of an unhappy marriage was simply to abscond; yet it was a route taken more often by men than by women, who generally lacked the financial and other means to just disappear. Convention also held women (and men) back from ending bad relationships—even a simple separation, not to speak of adultery, could turn someone from a respectable person into a social pariah.

Alice didn't think leaving her husband was an option, therefore, but she was still unhappy enough to seek help. After he was arrested for his 'sorcerye', Fansome claimed that he had helped Suttill 'because until he had done he could not be in quiet', so insistent was she for his services. Pestered or not, he was certainly rewarded handsomely for his trouble: apparently over the course of their acquaintance he received payments in food, clothes and money, as well as a ring. Eventually Fansome gave in to her requests and provided Suttill with a piece of paper, scribbled with 'dyvers prayers', to carry around her neck. One of Alice's maidservants swore that she never took it off, but wore it night and day. The little charm was meant to make Alice's husband, William, love her.[10]

Written charms appear to have been quite a common method of casting affection magic. In the 1670s Peter Banks was plying a brisk trade selling magical contracts that would bind a husband's goodwill and make him kind to his wife. Yet like other contracts and leases, Banks' charms would expire after a set amount of time, and the wife would have to pay to 'renew' the spell. One of his clients, Jane Crossby, apparently bought a year-long contract in exchange for ten shillings and two new shirts, and found it to be very effective. However, when she refused to renew the spell at the end of the year— maybe she thought her husband had changed for good—her spouse immediately went back to his old ways.[11]

Contracts and written spells like these were expensive. They relied on men who had the literacy skills to write out the prayers, and perhaps also possessed astrological learning to enhance their power by tying them to the right planetary alignments. Many unhappy wives would not have been able to afford them, or to find people with the skills to issue them. Such learned practitioners were easier to find in large towns and cities; indeed, Thomas Fansome and Peter Banks operated in the substantial settlements of Canterbury and Newcastle respectively. For clients in rural areas in particular, more homely methods were available. Joan Squyer hit on a cheaper method in the 1470s, which involved washing her husband's shirts in holy water. She was advising her neighbours to follow her example, as her husband had become 'humble and obedient to her will' ever since—much easier to live with than his usual self.[12]

Although Joan was pleased with her solution, to the ecclesiastical authorities she was doing a double wrong. She likely took the water from the font of her parish church, and she would not have been the only parishioner to do so: because holy water was widely recognised as possessing extraordinary powers, medieval fonts were often locked to stop people taking it to irrigate their crops or to heal ailments. Even more unacceptable, though, was Joan's attempt to assert her will over her husband. It marked a dangerous endeavour to usurp the divinely ordained hierarchy of husband above wife, man above woman, which formed the foundation of an ordered society.

The fear that women were trying to control their husbands might explain why so many cases of marital love magic devolved into trials for attempted murder. Indeed, this was how Alice Suttill's situation came to light. Although both she and Fansome claimed the 'dyvers prayers' around her neck were to make William kind and loving, the pair were still initially accused of trying to kill Alice's husband. We don't know whether the charge was true: it could well be that Alice first tried to make her relationship better, but when that failed, she resorted to death magic. Or perhaps William, knowing what a poor husband he was, suspected that malevolent witchcraft was being directed towards him when he saw that Alice was dabbling in magic.

Like Suttill, in 1559 Frances Throgmorton was accused of attempting to kill her husband, this time by feeding him poison. If we are to believe Frances and her parents, George Throgmorton was quite a brute. The marriage was probably arranged, given that Frances was the daughter of Baron Chandos, and George was the younger son of the ancient Throgmorton lineage, a gentry family with landholdings in Wiltshire and Gloucestershire. Despite the appropriateness of the match, Frances soon discovered that George was a violent man who felt himself above correction or the law. We know very little about the ins and outs of their marriage, but when George accused Frances of mariticide, Frances' mother, Elizabeth, decided to intervene. She petitioned William Cecil, then Secretary of State, to give her daughter a fair hearing and impartial judges, whom she claimed would easily clear Frances' name. She also said that George, far from being incapacitated with poison and fearing for his life, was bullying the witnesses and enacting violence upon them. In her own defence, Frances cited the same excuse as Alice Suttill: that she had indeed employed enchanters, but only so that George might be kinder and more loving towards her.[13]

If a husband was also unhappy in his marriage and wished to be rid of his bride, accusations like this might have been strategic. Attempted murder by whatever means could lead to execution, and the method of execution for killing one's husband was especially grisly. It counted as a form of 'petty treason'—disrupting the social hierarchy through killing one's superior—and was punishable by death by burning. The same sentence was given to servants or apprentices who killed their masters, and to children who killed their parents. Accusing one's wife of attempted murder was therefore extremely serious, and was almost as extreme a way of ending a marriage as murder itself.

Beyond the possible malevolence of such an accusation, though, perhaps William Suttill and George Throgmorton really were afraid for their lives. Research on magic use in medieval Russia has revealed that fear of social inferiors prompted many of the sorcery accusations that arose.[14] The rigid hierarchy and brutal treatment of people lower in the pecking order was recognised as breeding resentment, and while servants might try to buy magic that would keep them in their masters' good books, the masters themselves could easily interpret such actions as malicious. A powder sprinkled in food, or a charm made up of unknown symbols, is impossible to identify definitively as harmful or kind: all an accuser has to go on is their own fear (and guilt). Meanwhile, all the user of the spell has to defend themself is their own protestations, and the hope that the magician they bought the spell from will support their testimony.

◆

Relationships in the medieval and early modern periods were fraught with pitfalls and tensions. From seduction to marriage, childbirth to widowhood, there were duties to fulfil and desires to grapple with, while partners would have sought at least some form of joy. Frances and George Throgmorton's marriage reveals how pressure from families and wider society could drive couples to extreme choices. Clearly neither partner felt that the relationship was going well, but with such high expectations maybe the death of one or the other party really did feel like the only option. For others, though, there were less harmful alternatives: Joan Squyer and her magical laundry shows that there was a middle road between putting up with a bad situation and attempting murder. We will never know how many women tried to alter their husband's behaviour through spells, but it is safe to assume that the surviving cases are only the tip of the iceberg.

For the destitute widow or the unmarried woman, on the other hand, the marriage state was something that could be keenly sought. Margaret Geffrey exposes a dream that was no doubt shared by many: that remarriage to someone both kind and prosperous was possible—with a little magical help. A Norfolk servant named Joan Hall went down a similar route in the 1550s by paying a go-between to consult a ritual magician on her behalf to get her a 'rich marriage'. As with Margaret, the magic failed, but clearly the hope of a fortuitous union permeated all levels of society.

Whatever the particular outcome, the variety of spells that were available, and the range of service magicians who could perform them, demonstrate how fervent the demand was. Magic in all its forms is ultimately the expression of a desire to have power in a situation that may feel outside one's control. In the visceral, painful, passionate realm of love and sex, it isn't difficult to understand why it was something to which so many would turn. We still use magical thinking in our relationships today: although 'buttocks' bread might (hopefully) be a thing of the past, the internet abounds with modern witches offering to cast spells to help their customers find soulmates. 'Couples horoscopes' can be commissioned to verify whether or not we have found 'the one', and even on dating websites it is common to state your star sign. How seriously we take these predictions is variable: some wholeheartedly believe in them, others think it a bit of fun. But in a part of life as unpredictable as love, it is no surprise that some cunning folk remain in business.

CHAPTER 3

HOW TO WIN AT TRIAL

IT WAS A COLD DAY IN EARLY FEBRUARY 1355 WHEN C. DE D., champion of William Montagu, second Earl of Salisbury, stepped into the arena. We don't know his full name, but we know that he was a hardened warrior and, as was customary, had been training for this battle for weeks. Even so, he must have been nervous. Trials by combat were dangerous affairs. Although he personally was not the injured party seeking justice, he was expected to fight for his lord as if he were, with all the fury and resolve of the aggrieved. He was risking life and limb and knew that his opponent, Robert Shawel, was doing the same. Why was it, then, that Robert seemed to look so relaxed as he faced him? Did he know something that C. de D. did not? It wasn't a good sign.

Lord Salisbury had employed a trained fighter to resolve a dispute between himself and Robert Wyville, the Bishop of Salisbury. Both parties claimed to have ancient rights over Sherborne Castle, a wealthy estate built by a previous Bishop of Salisbury more than 200 years earlier. The law courts had been unable to solve the issue and neither side was willing to give up their claim. The only remaining solution was to resort to divine arbitration. Trials by battle were an established means of putting questions of justice to the Almighty, and worked on the same principles as the ordeals for finding thieves that we encountered previously. God favoured the innocent and was expected to intervene to protect them: the party with the more righteous cause would therefore triumph in a pitched battle and the guilty party would be revealed. Judicial combat was a feature throughout medieval Europe and could be invoked by people of any social rank to resolve a whole range of disputes. A so-called Fight Book written by the Swabian martial expert Hans Talhoffer in the mid-fifteenth century enumerates the many disagreements that formal combat could settle. The long list includes 'murder, treason, heresy, acts of betrayal towards one's lord, betrayal of one's given word when captured, fraud and the abuse of a woman'.[1] The disagreement between the two magnates of Salisbury could conceivably fall under fraud, because presumably one party was lying about their rights over the castle. But what this case really shows is that there was an even broader range of uses for judicial combat than Talhoffer's list implies.

When initiating the process, complainant and defendant could choose whether to fight the battle themselves or have a champion stand in their place. In theory almost any appellant could fight, including women or 'foreigners' (anyone not from the local area), but in practice many people preferred to appoint a champion, if they were able to do so. It made sense that Bishop Robert asked a champion to fight for him: under the decrees of the Fourth Lateran Council, held in 1215, clerics were banned from engaging in duels. This was part of a wider prohibition on the clergy committing any form of bloodshed (including surgery). It is less clear why the Earl of Salisbury did not choose to fight: Montagu was twenty-six or twenty-seven years old at the time and was apparently a very capable soldier. Perhaps he saw it as beneath his dignity to fight a mercenary in single combat. Whatever his reasons, both Robert and William would have paid their men handsomely. The record from a different case in 1277 details that one champion was paid £46 for his services—about £40,000 in today's money, or the equivalent of twelve years' pay for a skilled craftsman.[2] No wonder: these battles often led to serious, permanent injury, and in some cases even death.

In theory, at least, there were rules to ensure that any judicial fight was fair. If they needed practice, each side could train for up to six weeks beforehand. In their efforts to restrict the use of judicial combat, local authorities outlawed biting, scratching and eye-gouging; indeed, customary laws dictated that hair and nails should be cut so that the temptation to scratch or pull each other's hair was reduced.[3] Each person was also given a greased, close-fitting leather suit to wear, which was meant to protect them and make grappling less likely. Sharp weapons were allowed only if agreed in advance: if just one combatant knew how to use a sword—if, for example, the fight was between a knight and a labourer—then swords would not be permitted.

Despite all these precautions, in reality these battles were brutal. We know from contemporary accounts that the fights could quickly devolve into undignified ruthlessness. A fifteenth-century chronicle describes a trial by combat in Winchester:

> [the defendant] smote at the peler [appellant] that hys wepyn breke; and thenne the peler smote a stroke to the defendent, but the offycers were redy that he shulde smyte no more, and they toke a-way hys wepyn [weapon] fro[m] hym. And thenn they fought to gederys [together] with hyr [their] fystys long tyme and restyd [t]hem, ande fought agayne, and thenn restyd agayne; and thenn they wente togedyr by the neckys. And then they bothe with hyr tethe, that the lethyr of clothyng and flesche was alle to rente in many placys of hyr bodys. And thenn the fals peler caste that meke innocent downe to the grownde and bote [bit] hym by the membrys [genitals], that the sely innocent cryde owt. And by happe more thenne strengythe that innocent recoveryd up on hys kneys and toke that fals peler by the nose with hys tethe and put hys thombe in hys yee [eye], that the peler cryde owte and prayde hym of marcy, for he was fals unto God.[4]

Although there is some semblance of honour early on in this combat—the armed party was not allowed to fight an opponent who was weaponless—acts like biting, scratching and gouging were clearly not off-limits. In a fight around the same time in Valenciennes, in modern-day France, one participant had both eyes gouged and his stomach crushed by his opponent's knees as he was strangled.[5]

Even if the fight in Winchester was dirty, the outcome was deemed to be conclusive by those present. Indeed, the appellant—who in this case was one of the combatants—agreed that he had been judged by God and admitted his crimes. Given that trial by combat did not rely solely on prowess with a particular weapon, many fights could easily go either way: hence it was seen as a reliable way of understanding God's will. Even so, there was always a nagging concern that a fighter might cheat to gain an edge. So let us return to the Salisbury trial and see why Robert Shawel was looking so confident as he squared up to his opponent.

On the face of it, both champions were evenly matched and equally equipped. Both were given the same white-leather, thigh-length bodysuits to wear, as well as red surcoats bearing the arms of their employers. In terms of weapons, each man was allowed a full-length shield and a baton, but that was all. Both had taken Communion beforehand and commended themselves to God, in case they died in battle. When they arrived in front of the judges, dressed and ready to begin, they were also expected to take an oath, calling on the Lord's grace to aid them if their side was just. The tension must have been palpable. But then, shortly before it was to begin, the duel was delayed. Both parties were ordered to go into another room and remove their armour, so that it could be checked for any tampering. But neither warrior complied. It may have been a point of pride or perhaps they feared that this was a trick; either way, they refused to leave until the judges themselves rose and 'with difficulty made them go'.[6] Shawel had an additional reason to avoid taking off his coat: sewn all over the inside were prayers and charms that would ensure he won the battle.

The discovery of these spells must have been an embarrassing moment for both Shawel and his employer, Bishop Robert of Salisbury. Presumably Robert had recommended the use of charms; maybe they had even been supplied by the bishop himself, or made by a cleric within his diocese. The move suggested, though, that this man of God did not have enough faith in his own cause—or, worse, in the Lord's ability to adjudicate. Or maybe, in his desperation to win, he believed that he was advancing the case of God. The late medieval period was marked by intense competition between the

Church and secular lords over land, legal jurisdictions and other powers, such as the right to appoint bishops and to sanction monarchs. Bishop Robert Wyville was clearly dedicated to advancing the privileges of the diocese of Salisbury and made the challenge over Sherborne Castle his cause célèbre. Perhaps, therefore, by giving his champion an occult edge Robert thought he was doing God's work, ensuring that things were not left to chance. After this revelation, however, Robert Shawel was made to promise 'that ye shull [not] have . . . stone of vertue, nor hearb of virtue; nor charm, nor experement, nor none other enchauntment by you, nor for you, whereby ye trust the better to overcome C. de D. your Adversarie'.[7]

Bishop Robert was not the only one to try to win trials by combat through magic. Indeed, the practice of utilising spells was so common that most fighters were obliged to swear a similar oath before they entered the arena. Subverting trials in this way had been recognised as a problem as early as 1020. The eleventh-century *Decretum*, a book of canon law written by Burchard, bishop of the city of Worms in the Holy Roman Empire, set a penance for any magician who tried to pervert the course of a trial through enchanted food, drink or objects. This text set a precedent for religious law across Western Christendom, and we see similar prohibitions in local legislation. The Arundel Penitential, first written in eleventh- or twelfth-century England, specified a full three years' penance for anyone who used *maleficium*—harmful magic—to sway a trial by combat.[8] Similar concerns are reflected in the ecclesiastical law of sixteenth-century Muscovy (the tsardom of Russia), where the Stoglav Synod of 1551 condemned the use of magic in judicial combat. Russian spell books of the time give us an idea of the sort of thing the Church council had in mind. One recommends that the warrior wrap the tongue of a black snake in green-and-black cloth, then place the bundle in their left boot. For extra potency, 'also put three garlic cloves in that same boot, and under your right armpit tie a hand towel and take [it] with you when you go to court or to the field of the duel'.[9]

What exactly Shawel's charms and prayers consisted of is not specified. They might have invoked angels or demons to come to his aid or taken the form of protective talismans. A wide range of talismans intended to protect the bearer from harm circulated in medieval Europe. One, recorded in a fifteenth-century manuscript now housed in the Bodleian Library, Oxford, consists of a list of the names of God. If the bearer wrote out these names on a slip of parchment, carried it on their person at all times and looked at the parchment every day, it was believed they would be immune to death by fire, water or the sword and impossible to beat in battle. Such a talisman would obviously be useful during most trials by ordeal, not only those of combat. 'Swimming' tests—where the accused was dunked in water to see if they sank (innocent) or floated (guilty)—and trials by hot iron or coals—in which the defendant had to carry a piece of heated iron nine paces—would present no challenge to the wearer.[10]

Along similar lines, a popular tradition sprang up in the twelfth and thirteenth centuries that if a person witnessed the consecration of the Eucharist during Mass, they would be safe from harm for the rest of the day. This protective benefit would apply to anyone who attended Mass, and not just those about to undergo a trial by ordeal, but it is worth remembering that every defendant was expected to attend Mass before their ordeal began. Those who paid attention during the Eucharist were therefore not only showing their devotion, but potentially also giving themselves some super-natural help in the lead-up to their trial. Exploiting a holy ceremony in this way would be treated as superstition by the Church, but even so it seems highly likely to me that anyone nervous about an impending duel would take precautions, if only for their peace of mind.

In the end, Bishop Robert won control of Sherborne Castle without recourse to magic or trial by combat. The matter was settled through a compromise in court, whereby Earl William relinquished his claim in exchange for 2,500 marks or £1,666—roughly £1 million today.[11] Bishop Robert was not punished for equipping his champion with spells: the only recorded repercussion was the oath that Shawel was made to swear. In truth, single combat was an increasingly uncommon means to settle 'right of writ' disputes by the fourteenth century, so it may always have been hoped that an agreement would be reached before the fighting took place. The delay caused by Robert's underhand tactics might even have encouraged both sides to find a peaceful resolution. Regardless, the incident—and the magic involved—should not be disregarded. Bishop Robert clearly took great pride in his victory: it even features in the list of achievements inscribed on his grave. The brass that still decorates his tomb in Salisbury Cathedral depicts the bishop praying in the window of a castle, with a champion ready to do battle standing in the doorway below. The Latin inscription translates as follows:

> Here lies Robert Wyvill . . . among his other innumerable benefits, he recovered, like an intrepid champion, the Castle of Sherborne to the said Church, which for 200 years and more had been withheld therefrom by military violence.[12]

Despite the poetic licence Robert takes in likening himself to the champion he employed, the inclusion of an armed fighter alongside this inscription shows that he took the challenge to the Church's authority seriously and was proud of his achievements. It also exposes the dirty tactics that the great and the good were prepared to adopt in order to win. Robert would have known perfectly well that using spells in a duel was both against the rules of fair combat and forbidden by the religion he represented. That he did it anyway reminds us that the judicial system was vulnerable to corruption. We will see more evidence of this below, in the cases of Aleyn, Prior of Bodmin, and Thomas Lake.

Spells were not only used in legal cases settled by ordeal. Magic texts and recipe books from throughout the medieval period list various amulets and talismans that could aid an appellant or defendant during a trial. These varied in complexity and accessibility. One recipe stipulates that the heliotrope plant should be picked when the constellation of Virgo is in the sky and wrapped in laurel leaves with the tooth of a wolf. It was contended that if the bundle was carried on one's person, no one would be able to speak ill of them. Another spell consisted of reciting three Paternosters (the Lord's Prayer) and three Ave Marias, to stop enemies speaking evil; and if they did so, the charm-wearer would be able to overcome them. A much simpler custom was to carry a sprig of mistletoe to protect the individual from losing a case in court.[13]

Each of these methods seems based on the premise that an opponent could have their thoughts or opinions influenced, and that the user could therefore gain an advantage. Unfortunately we don't know how exactly this was expected to happen. Perhaps such measures were intended to make a person more likeable, so that no one would want to litigate against them (even if they were guilty). Maybe the charms would make them appear more intimidating, so that their enemies would no longer wish to cross them. Indeed, the inclusion of bay laurel in the first recipe might have been in recognition of the plant's properties in classical literature, indicating that the charm was supposed to offer wisdom and eloquence to its carrier.

Most recipes did not get into these sorts of specifics, however. A written charm found on Fedka Popov, a prisoner in a Moscow gaol in 1649, for example, merely states what the spell's outcome would be. The charm was inscribed with the words 'Whoever carries this letter on his person, in trial the guilty will be found innocent and the innocent guilty', to which was later added, 'Whoever dies with this letter on his person will escape eternal torment.'[14] The second spell would have been inspired by the fear that the first part might fail. If Fedka was found guilty, the failsafe built into the charm would save, if not his life, then at least his soul. We know that Fedka could not read, so he may have been relying on the magic of the item itself rather than on the words per se. This tells us something significant about these spells, and about magic as a whole: it was the belief in their efficacy that ultimately fuelled their power.

Yet there were more direct—and sinister—methods for winning at trial, adopted by those who were either completely unscrupulous or truly desperate. One such case again reveals the unethical behaviour of some churchmen in their struggle against their secular rivals. This episode takes us into the year 1440 and to the heart of Cornwall.

◆

Aleyn was a powerful man. He was the head of the Augustinian priory in Bodmin, known as St Mary the Virgin and St Petroc. It was a monastic institution with origins so ancient that it was already well established by the time of the Norman Conquest in 1066. Indeed, the name Bodmin is thought to originate from the Cornish *Bod-meneghy*, meaning the 'home or abode of monks'. By the mid-fifteenth century, when Aleyn was its prior, Bodmin could boast of being one of the largest settlements in Cornwall, and among the wealthiest. The priory was a major landholder in the area and, as such, had both spiritual and secular control over many of the people who lived there. Abbots and priors (as well as their female counterparts in nunneries) tended to be well-educated, exceptionally capable individuals, skilled at negotiating donations of land and buildings from secular lords afraid for their immortal souls, who hoped that their generosity would be rewarded in the next life.[15] They also knew the value of the land they were given and could put it to work. Monasteries frequently acted as secular landlords and harvested rents and taxes from their tenants. These charges took the form of 10 per cent of their produce, known as the 'tithe'. The vast tithe-barns that still dot the landscape of northern Europe are testament to how much income such land management brought in. This wealth and influence did not mean that religious institutions were immune to criticism, however. Even before the arrival of the Reformation in the first half of the sixteenth century, there were widespread grumblings across Europe about the excessive power wielded by abbeys and monasteries. Reproaches were also levelled at individual clerics who abused their authority, and Prior Aleyn appears to have been one of them.

What exactly precipitated the dispute we are about to witness is unclear, but we know from a petition in the Court of Chancery that Aleyn had an 'oyer and terminer' issued against him, in or before 1440. This was essentially a direction for judges of the Assize courts to investigate a criminal offence. As a clergyman, Aleyn was largely exempt from secular law, so we can assume that whatever crime he had committed was in his capacity as a secular land-lord. He was sued by a squire named Richard Flamanak, who engaged the gentleman Henry Hoigges 'of Bodmyn of the counte of Cornewayll' as his attorney. Aleyn, meanwhile, does not seem to have sought legal advice. Instead he called upon the priest John Harry, who in the court documents is described as the 's[er]v[a]nt of the said priour'. While he was not well versed in jurisprudence, John had other valuable skills. What he could offer his master was 'malys & evele wylle' and knowledge of the 'sotill [subtle] craftys of enchauntement wycchecrafte & sorcerye'. Surprisingly, perhaps, neither Aleyn nor John was coy about the fact that they intended to destroy Henry Hoigges, and ruin Richard's lawsuit in the process. And it seems that John's spells were working: apparently he had caused Henry to 'brake is legge, and foul was hert; thurz [though] the weche he was in despair of hys lyff'. But such physical pain was only the beginning. John made it clear that if the lawyer continued with the suit, then the outcome would be fatal, as he would turn his magical efforts towards making Henry's 'nekke . . . breke'.[16]

Henry believed that his life was in danger and that John needed to be restrained. The way he framed his petition to the Chancery Court, though, is interesting. Evidently a true lawyer at heart, Henry put great emphasis on the fact that John was attempting to pervert the course of justice, and stressed that if he was allowed to get away with it, then both John and Aleyn would be subverting the rule of law. His petition begs the Lord Chancellor 'to considere the gret myschef harme & damage [John Harry] do un to yo[ur] said suppliant; & also the gret myschef th[at] may falle to hym here aft[er], & to all other th[at] buth suturs & atto[r]neys in availe to our sove[r]yn lord the Kyng, & to ther client in all maters as reson & consience askyt and requyryth'.[17] Although he complained of the ill-treatment and threats he had experienced, as one might expect, it is fascinating that Henry seemed genuinely concerned that spell-casting could risk the outcome of other suits in the future: that it would put in jeopardy the very foundations of law and order. Petitions like this, as well as Church injunctions against such behaviour, show us how seriously magic was taken as a potential force in the justice system. But Henry would have been very afraid too: his body and mind had taken a battering from John's spells, and he must have had little doubt that if no one stopped John, he might end up murdered.

As with many Chancery Court records, a copy of the petition survives, but not the action taken, so we don't know how the Chancellor responded. Bodmin Priory continued to thrive until it was dissolved in 1539 as part of the Henrician Reformation, but whether Aleyn continued as its prior or was removed as a result of his apparent corruption remains a mystery. It is possible that, like Bishop Robert Wyville, Aleyn was only lightly censured and was otherwise allowed to continue in his duties. What we can be confident of, however, is that Aleyn and John Harry were neither the first nor the last to use magic in order to triumph in a lawsuit. Concern over the employment of sorcery in trials continued well into the early modern period, reaching its height in the seventeenth century. It seems that no one was immune from corruption and magical meddling in lawsuits—not even the king himself.

◆

What were the consequences of trying to muddle the mind of a monarch? A man named Peacock found out the hard way in 1619. Details about Peacock's life are sparse: much of what we know comes from a letter from the Lord Chancellor, Francis Bacon, to James I, and reports the rumours flying around the royal court. What we can glean is that Peacock was 'a very busy brained fellow' who worked as a schoolmaster and minister of the Church before he attracted the attention of Sir Thomas Lake, who was junior Secretary of State for domestic affairs and, until recently, had been a trusted favourite of the king.[18] It seems that Peacock and Lake's relationship began when the latter was in the midst of a crisis. But in order to fully understand the importance of Peacock's services, we need to delve into the complex and dangerous realm of aristocratic family politics.

Thomas Lake had risen to his position as state official and royal favourite from relatively humble origins. He was born in the bustling port town of Southampton in 1567 to a minor customs official and attended the local grammar school. Like the infamous Thomas Cromwell a generation before, he climbed the ladder first of Tudor, and later Stuart, society by being a capable and efficient administrator. When James VI of Scotland succeeded Elizabeth I as ruler of England in 1603 (thus becoming James I of England), Thomas was among the welcome party dispatched north to acquaint James with his new kingdom. He quickly managed to ingratiate himself with his new king and was awarded a position in government. Thomas had married upwards in 1591, aligning himself to the formidable Mary Rider, the daughter of an alderman and later Mayor of London, and the couple had at least three children. For the next two decades the Lakes seemed to be firmly on the up, culminating in the extremely advantageous marriage of their daughter Anne to William Cecil, the sixteenth Baron Ros. William was the great-grandson of Elizabeth I's favourite, William Cecil, Lord Burghley. The Cecils maintained their position under the Stuart regime: Burghley's son Robert served as Secretary of State, Lord Privy Seal and Lord High Treasurer of England at various points under James I. By uniting themselves with the Cecils, the Lakes were marrying into one of the principal families in the country.

Unfortunately, what looked good on paper was far less successful in practice. Within a year it was clear that the newly-weds, Anne and William, absolutely loathed each other. From what came out in the investigation in 1619, infidelity might have been involved. What's more, the supposed affair was inappropriate in the extreme: Anne alleged that her husband had been committing adultery with his step-grandmother Frances, the Duchess of Exeter. The accusation was not as outlandish as it sounds: Frances was the second wife of William's grandfather, Thomas Cecil, and was thirty-eight years her husband's junior. She seems to have been an intelligent woman who certainly took an active interest in her step-grandson's affairs, whether or not the rumours of romantic involvement were true. Even so, to the early modern mind, family ties through marriage were as powerful as those forged through blood, so the idea that William might have slept with his grandfather's wife was viewed as appalling and incestuous.

Whatever the original cause of the rift between Anne and William, the Lake family was not prepared to accept that its experiment had been a total failure. Anne moved back into her family home sometime in 1617, and she and her parents tried to find ways to turn the unhappy marriage to their advantage. William had mortgaged a property, the wealthy manor of Walthamstow in Essex (now in north London), to his father-in-law to help fund a diplomatic mission to Spain in 1616, and the Lakes pressured him to sign it over to Anne, possibly in exchange for a divorce. It is possible that Anne and her mother, Mary, also threatened to publicly proclaim that William was impotent if he did not relinquish the manor. Lord Ros was prepared to accept the loss of his land in order for all of this to go away— until Frances and his grandfather got wind of the situation. Frances now did everything she could to stop the scheme, putting herself into the Lakes' crosshairs in the process. It was at this point that the inappropriate relationship between her and William was alleged.

The whole situation was referred to King James in 1618. Frances and Thomas Cecil claimed blackmail and corruption; the Lakes cried adultery, incest and the attempted murder of Anne (supposedly planned by William and Frances, after Anne discovered their affair). William was unable to testify in his own defence, having fled to Italy earlier that year to escape the relationship, where he died shortly afterwards. It quickly became clear that Anne and Mary's evidence for the affair was shaky at best, and at worst fraudulent. The letter that Anne produced, purportedly written by Frances confessing to her affair, was found to be a fabrication, as was the testimony of Anne's servant, Sarah Swarton. Sarah claimed during the Star Chamber investigation that she had witnessed Frances confessing all at William and Anne's house in Wimbledon, but when the king himself travelled to the house to investigate, the curtain she was supposed to have hidden behind was found to be too short to conceal her. The Lake family's position declined rapidly thereafter.[19]

The Lakes must have felt backed into a corner at this juncture, their case doomed. Both the aristocracy and the people of London lapped up the scandal. The fall of an influential family, a fascination with salacious detail and a genuine concern about moral corruption at the heart of the Stuart government made the affair the talk of the town. Ballads were sung in the streets, most of them shockingly lewd and misogynistic, branding Mary Lake and Anne Ros as villains.[20] With their reputations slipping and the investigation going against them, the Lake family became increasingly desperate. Sir Thomas offered £15,000 to George Villiers, the Duke of

Buckingham and a firm favourite of James I, to intercede with the king on his behalf. This was an extraordinary amount of money, the equivalent of about £2 million today, but despite this inducement, Villiers initially refused to get involved. There was a tactical element to this—the fewer favourites around the king, the higher the rewards for the select few—but Villiers probably also sensed that it was a lost cause and not worth his time. Eventually George was prevailed upon by his mother to have a word in the king's ear, but the attempt was half-hearted. The amount of money Thomas was prepared to spend, and the endeavour's failure, show just how dire the Lakes' situation had become. Now, with this context in mind, let's return to our man Peacock.

Unusually for the seventeenth-century rumour mill, there was little public commentary about the use of magic in this case. The surviving ballads do not mention Peacock at all, and a 1650s play that makes several references to the scandal is similarly silent. Even so, we cannot doubt Peacock's existence or the very real threat he was thought to pose to King James' government. A letter from Sir Francis Bacon to the king tells us how seriously Peacock was taken. Francis Bacon, who is now remembered primarily as a philosopher, was in 1619 the Lord High Chancellor of England. He was a meticulous and competent jurist, and before assuming this powerful role he had served as Attorney General for two years. He now took charge of Peacock's investigation, alongside the celebrated barrister Sir Edward Coke. Bacon was generally known as a measured man who shied away from extreme forms of interrogation, such as the application of torture. This makes it all the more surprising that he recommended torturing Peacock.

The letter, dated 10 February 1619, is coy about what exactly Peacock was thought to have done, but the alarm Bacon felt is palpable. It states that Coke and Bacon:

> proceed in Peacock's examinations . . . yet certainly we are not at
> the bottom; and he that would not use the utmost of his line to

sound such a business as this, should not have due regard neither to your Majesty's honour nor safety . . . if it may not be done otherwise, it is fit Peacock be put to torture. He deserveth it as well as Peacham did.[21]

Edmund Peacham was a Puritan minister who in 1614 was discovered to have written a scathing sermon condemning James I and predicting the king's death and an ensuing rebellion. The sermon was treated as indicative of a treasonous plot, and torture was used to discover the conspiracy's extent. Eventually it was concluded that Peacham was acting alone, but he was found guilty of personally advocating the death of the king. The fact that Bacon took Peacock's alleged offences as seriously shows how dangerous they were thought to be.

Peacock was feared to have practised 'to infatuate the King's judgement by sorcery . . . in the business of Sir Thomas Lake and the Lady of Exeter'. It seems that if bribery would not do the job for Thomas Lake, magic would—or, at least, that was the idea. As James had taken a personal interest in the case, manipulating the king's mind so that he was positively disposed towards the Lakes was hoped perhaps to mean acquittal and rehabilitation for the family. Unfortunately it did not work, and Peacock bore the brunt of the failure. He was tortured using the 'strappado' method. This was a brutally painful exercise, involving tying the subject's hands behind their back before hanging them up by the wrists, then having heavy weights (often a wooden beam) suspended from their feet. The torture usually resulted in dislocated shoulders and torn ligaments: no wonder Peacock was 'very impatient of the torture and swooned once or twice'. Through the pain, Peacock acknowledged that he had tried to sway James' judgement in the Lakes' favour, but insisted that he did not plan to harm or kill the monarch. This information may have been what Bacon was ultimately trying to discover. For there was a precedent. Malevolent witches had famously tried to kill James in 1590, by raising a storm to sink the ship he was sailing in. It was reported that James actually saw the witches in the storm, bobbing evilly around his ship in a sieve.[22] Having survived at least one magical assassination attempt, we can perhaps see why the king would want to investigate rumours of any others.

As Peacock was 'only' trying to ensure his client won in the upcoming trial, he was not prosecuted for treason in the end. However, he was imprisoned in the Tower of London, where he may have died: we lose track of him after the investigation was concluded. Even if he was released, the torture he went through would have disabled him for life. Sir Thomas Lake, Mary Lake and Anne Ros were also incarcerated in the Tower, fined and ordered to beg forgiveness from the king and from Frances Throgmorton. Anne did so more or less straight away and was pardoned; Thomas followed suit soon afterwards. Mary, however, refused to submit for about a year and was not released until she had done so. The family did eventually recover from the scandal, and Thomas was even reconciled with King James within a couple of years. We cannot be sure that he did not dabble in magic once more to regain his stature at court. As we shall see in Chapter Eight, sorcery would also be employed to (re-)climb the social ladder.

It seems that aristocratic attempts to gain the upper hand were not exclusive to England. In Russia, one Prince Volkonskoi was found to have directions for a useful spell in 1649/50 'to influence a suit in the Great Treasury Court'.[23] The script read:

> By the mercy of God, lover of mankind, look at me, slave of God, Prince Ivan Volkonskoi, with angelic and paternal and maternal heart, [so] that Kostentin Teterevin . . . will not be able to bring suit against me. And as you go out of the courtyard, pick up the first linden bark that drops from a tree and crush it in your hands. Then, when you come to the court, throw that bark under him, and as when that bark is crushed, it has neither mind nor memory, so when that Kostentin comes to the court, he will have neither mind nor memory.

As with the Lake case, the cunning man who wrote out the spell bore the brunt of the resultant investigation, while the noble who employed him escaped largely unscathed. Voinko Iakunin, a chancellery clerk, was tortured for information about how he had come across the spell and the intention behind it. Interestingly, Voinko had apparently learned the spell in his youth from a Cossack named Fedor Aleksandrov. It is possible that all three of these individuals—the clerk, the Cossack and the prince—had used the spell at least once in their lives, showing how far up and down the hierarchy such magic could reach.

◆

The disruptive power of magic—and the weak point in judicial systems—comes through clearly in the episodes we have encountered in this chapter. But I think we can spare some sympathy for the characters we have met, and understand their motivations for using spells and charms. A warrior who was facing vicious single combat would seek to win and would hope to avoid the debilitating injuries such trials often produced. A family facing public ridicule and a complete reversal of their fortune would want to tip the scales of justice in their favour by any means possible. Yet this thoroughly human impulse also made judicial magic dangerous. Unlike finding stolen goods, which essentially restored the natural order of things by returning items to their rightful owners, cheating at trial deliberately upset that balance. Perhaps this underhandedness was why Peacock's spell-casting was treated so harshly. It is certainly the argument that Henry Hoigges used to prosecute John Harry in the 1440s: that such techniques unsettled the cosmic order and, importantly, the rule of law.

The Lake case also shows the heightened concern over magic—particularly disruptive magic—in the seventeenth century. It is worth noting that even the deliberately harmful spells performed by John against Hoigges were not afforded the same attention or policing as those attempted by Peacock. This is partly a sign of the concern over meddling with royal government versus local affairs, but also demonstrates how anxiety over magic-use fluctuated over time. As we will see in the next chapter, attitudes and punishments varied wildly across time and geographical region. Although not a hard-and-fast rule, even performing magic to do harm could be overlooked before the mid-sixteenth century. From the 1560s onwards, though, this relatively relaxed attitude morphed into something much more hostile.

CHAPTER 4

HOW TO GET REVENGE

ELIZABETH ROBYNSON'S STOMACH GNAWED AT HER, BUT she didn't mind. In fact she embraced the feeling. The pangs of hunger that flashed across her empty belly were proof that her fast was working, and she was glad of it. Her life had been difficult of late: she had lost her husband, John, towards the end of 1515, and the following November she was summoned to stand before the local ecclesiastical court. Someone from her community in the Bowland area of Lancashire had reported her for 'unlawful possession of a parcel of tithable property and also of a tithable calf'. Presumably she had not declared this property after John had died, either because she did not want to pay the fine due upon the death of the head of a household or because she could not afford to. To her chagrin, she was ordered to repay the associated tithes, which would have brought her considerable financial hardship. Three years on, when she next appears in the consistory court records, things do not seem to have improved much. Elizabeth had not remarried, and at this point she was not getting on with her neighbours, either. Her relationship with a man named Edmund Parker had gone particularly sour. In fact things had got so bad that she publicly declared she intended 'to invoke vengeance' against him through the means of a black fast.[1]

What had caused the spat between Elizabeth and Edmund is unclear. The court records only note the charge, relevant evidence and people involved:

the past relationship between the litigant and the defendant was rarely of interest to officials. Perhaps Elizabeth had found out that Edmund had been the one to inform on her about her tax evasion a few years earlier. As one of the principal inhabitants of the Bowland area, it was his duty to report the misdemeanours of his neighbours when the court assembled. Equally, the bad blood could have stemmed from another, much more personal incident. Whatever had passed between them, it was clearly serious enough for Elizabeth to employ extreme measures. 'Fasting upon' a person meant trying to cause extreme discomfort for the intended victim. It could even be used to kill them.

Despite its sinister name, the black fast was an orthodox Christian practice—indeed, it is still performed by some observants today. Normally undertaken on Ash Wednesday and Good Friday, it is an extreme form of fasting where the devout eat nothing during daylight hours and drink only a little water. The aim is to encourage the worshipper to focus on their spiritual rather than corporeal self, and to meditate on the sacrifice made by Christ for the salvation of humanity. The idea of bringing oneself closer to God through bodily mortification was very popular during the medieval and early modern periods, and fasting took on particular significance. It was thought to bring other benefits as well. For example, it was popularly believed that fasting on the feast day of St Mark the Evangelist (25 April) would grant protection from harm in the following days, and if one fasted on the same day of the week as that of the Feast of the Annunciation (25 March), one would be immune from sudden death all year.[2] Black fasts in general, therefore, were not unusual or controversial, especially before the Reformation. The problem was that Elizabeth was harnessing their power for nefarious purposes. Turning the black fast into a form of sympathy magic, she wanted to project her own suffering onto Edmund. While her body experienced pain, his would feel the same, yet magnified tenfold. As she became weak from lack of sustenance, he too would sicken and begin to waste away.

My guess is that Elizabeth chose to undertake the black fast because she felt she had no other way to redress whatever wrong had been done to her.

Although we know very little about either magic-worker or intended victim, it is clear that the power dynamic between them was skewed. Edmund was male, seems to have had a lot of family in the area and enjoyed enough authority to make presentations to the local Church court. Elizabeth was female, widowed and, when asked to produce six neighbours who could speak in her defence, was unable to do so. This last point may not mean she was entirely without friends, however: all that the six testifiers were required to do was to honestly say that Elizabeth hadn't planned to perform the black fast. If she had publicly declared that she would do so, as Edmund claimed, the fact that she could not find six people to say the opposite simply means that no one was prepared to commit perjury. Even so, Elizabeth seems to have been relatively isolated, either because she did not have many allies or perhaps because she was known as one who could harm her neighbours. Put simply, she was at the end of the social spectrum, where seeking justice through judicial or social means was difficult. She must have felt that her only option was to get revenge, and the best means for her to do so was through magic.

Elizabeth was far from the only person to try and cause harm in this way. Twenty years earlier and almost 300 miles away in Maidstone, Kent, the cunning woman Alice Havyn was investigated for 'celebrating the fasts of Saints Ninian and George', to punish someone for stealing one of her client's goods. St Ninian (sometimes known as St Trinian) was an early Christian missionary to Scotland, whose feast day on 16 September was associated with absolute fasting. Similarly, in 1507 a woman from Folkestone, also in Kent, was presented to court for 'fasting a certain fast called a *blakke fast* for vengeance against enemies'.[3] It is notable that all of these fasters were women. Although inflicting magical harm was not solely a feminine activity (as evidenced by John Harry in the previous chapter), it makes sense that the majority would be. As in Elizabeth's case, revenge magic is generally the recourse of those who feel disempowered or at the end of their tether: people who have no other options, or who doubt that their complaints will be respected or heard. The pervasive misogyny inherent in medieval and early modern society means that more women would have felt this way than men, and the temptation to turn to a less orthodox power must have been strong. The act of fasting itself is also a particularly feminine activity; research has suggested that because medieval women were generally in charge of food management and preparation, regulating one's diet became a central means of asserting control—whether within their community, their household or their own life.[4] For this reason, fervently religious women often chose fasting as a method for expressing devotion. It seems logical that those who found themselves in dire situations might resort to the same practice when seeking supernatural redress.

What may be more surprising, however, is that none of the women mentioned above was indicted for witchcraft or even punished particularly harshly. Elizabeth initially denied the charge that she had planned to undertake the black fast and, as we saw, was therefore given more than a month to present six neighbours who could speak in her defence. This she could apparently not do, so she refused to appear at the next hearing. Although this seems a pretty clear admission of her guilt, the court did not follow up on the case. Instead it suspended her from church services and left it at that. Whatever we may think of church-going today, this was not an entirely toothless punishment at the time: it meant that Elizabeth was unable to take Communion or receive absolution for her sins, get married or otherwise take part in the religious life of her community. However, such exile was not permanent: if she confessed her actions and performed penance, she would be welcomed back into the church family.

Suspensions like this were a standard form of censure meted out by ecclesiastical courts when the person under investigation refused to appear. The previous year the same court had suspended John Stanworth from church services because he did not respond to the charge of fathering an illegitimate child. When Stanworth eventually did submit to the court and admit to 'fornicatory concubinage' with his lover, he was allowed to return to church after doing four weeks of penance.[5] This involved walking ahead of the church procession on consecutive Sundays, 'barefoot and dressed only in linen garments with no more than a gown, carrying a wax candle worth 2d., which afterwards he should offer into the hands of the curate of

Burnley [his local church].* The penance demanded of Elizabeth for her malevolent fasting would have been similar, probably with a variation in the number of days according to the perceived severity of the misdemeanour.

Admittedly one of the reasons that Elizabeth was not punished more harshly was that she committed her offence when she did. Practising magic of any kind was not a secular crime in England in 1519, only a moral one. Whereas the ecclesiastical courts were responsible for policing crimes that tarnished the soul, the lay courts—presided over by the monarch's representatives, rather than those of the Church—were in charge of material affairs, but had little jurisdiction over sorcery. What's more, only lay courts could exact corporal punishment and seizure of property, so as long as no physical harm had been done by her magic, Elizabeth was immune from these penalties. The Church courts largely administered punishments based around prayer (most often, reciting the Rosary), physical exertion (such as carrying two packhorse loads of slate to the local church) or ritualised humiliation (like the processions described above). These punishments should not be seen as light: they could be physically and mentally exhausting, and they affected one's standing in the community. However, compared to punishments like imprisonment, dismemberment and execution, which the secular courts could hand down, they were certainly preferable. Edmund Parker must have known that penance would be the likely outcome of his report against Elizabeth and may well have thought it was lenient, considering what she was trying to do. The public censure and religious correction that Elizabeth would have undergone, though, might have been enough to warn her away from trying to curse people again.

It was only after the English Church broke with the Papacy in the 1530s that magic became a secular crime. As part of the Henrician Reformation, the power of the Church was radically reduced and much of its judicial

---

* Interestingly, a woman brought up on the same charge in the same session was given the same penance—but for only three Sundays instead of four. She likely escaped a fourth week because she submitted to the court for 'correction' immediately, and it is notable that the penance was identical for both men and women.

jurisdiction shrank with it. Although ecclesiastical courts continued to operate well into the nineteenth century, the secular powers started to take on more of their former responsibilities. The first secular Act against Conjurations, Witchcrafts, Sorcery and Inchantments was introduced in 1542, towards the end of Henry VIII's reign. It outlawed a number of magical practices that had formerly been tolerated or only lightly punished. These included many of the activities covered in this book, such as finding lost goods, discovering buried treasure and provoking people to 'unlawfull love' through 'Invocacons or conjuracons of Sprites wichecraftes enchauntmentes or sorceries'. For the first time, each of these incurred the death penalty, alongside the (surely more heinous) act of trying to 'waste consume or destroy any persone in his bodie membres or goodes'.[6] This particular activity had resulted in execution even before 1542, but a death sentence was rarely handed down for the spell-casting itself. When Mabel Brigges was executed for practising the black fast in 1538, for example, it was because she had been trying to kill the king and Thomas Howard, the Duke of Norfolk; it was her treasonous intent that precipitated her death, not the method she employed. In reality, even though the 1542 Act stipulated execution for magic-use, it was never employed to its fullest extent. No one was killed under Henry VIII's witchcraft law; in fact it was repealed five years later, after the succession of Edward VI. But in 1563, under Elizabeth I, witchcraft and magic became a secular crime again.

Elizabeth's 'Act agaynst Conjuracons Inchantments and Witchecraftes' was both harsher and more lenient than Henry's. It restricted the death penalty to those who had been found to have caused harm through witch-craft, while other magic-use incurred a year's imprisonment. However, it was enforced much more rigorously than the previous legislation—perhaps because there was less risk that cunning folk might be killed if they were reported. It is important to remember that service magicians and malevo-lent witches were rarely conflated in the minds of early modern people, or even among judges. While witches were broadly feared and often suffered the death penalty for their supposed crimes—by hanging in England, and by burning in Scotland and parts of the Continent—cunning folk largely were not.[7] It appears that they were spared the excrescences and horrors of the witch trials that swept across Europe in the early modern period. In my research I have found reference to more than 380 service magicians practising in England between 1542 and 1670, many of whom were healers and midwives, diviners and goods-finders. Of these, fewer than five were accused of malevolent witchcraft, and only one was eventually found guilty and executed. I'm sure there are other cases, but even so, the proportions are striking, belying the modern assumption that the witch trials of early modern England targeted healers and other women who professed cunning skills. For most people at the time, there was a difference between the useful magic generally being practised and sold by cunning folk and the harmful, vindictive curses dealt out by witches.

In 1647 John Bonham from Sutton in Cambridgeshire confessed to being a witch. He admitted to having a familiar spirit who took the form of a mole, which he sent to kill Robert Peacock's horses and Charles Freeman's bullocks. It was revenge for Freeman's cattle having trampled a fence that John had only just mended.* Such vindictiveness and what was perceived as uncontrolled emotion comprised a core aspect of witchcraft, according to late medieval and early modern thinkers.

The Dominican friar Heinrich Kramer expounded on this theme at length in his *Malleus Maleficarum*, or *The Hammer of Witches*. First published in 1486 and widely circulated across Europe thereafter, the *Malleus* is perhaps the most famous text on witchcraft. It was not the first or last book of its type, but it is among the most extreme in its views— particularly with regard to its attacks on women. Although not wholly representative of the full genre of witch-finding manuals, it is nevertheless orthodox in its statements regarding witches' fundamental nature. Kramer specified that witches achieved their aims exclusively through the help of demons, and that people who are ruled by their emotions, who are naturally bitter, eaten up with envy and not especially intelligent, are ideal targets for

---

* Due to a lack of compelling evidence, both John and his wife Bridget, who was accused of witchcraft with him, were acquitted at the Court of Assizes in September 1647.

the Devil. Unfortunately, early modern thinkers also tended to associate these traits with women.[8] Demons then managed to convince such a person to turn to witchcraft by playing on these characteristics, offering them vengeance on their enemies in return for their souls. It was believed, therefore, that witches' core motivation was to do harm and to achieve this through diabolical aid. So, had Elizabeth Robynson been observing her black fast a few decades later, her actions might well have been interpreted as witchcraft, leading to her being accused, arrested and potentially executed.

By contrast, while some cunning folk were capable of inflicting supernatural injury, harm for the sake of it was generally not their incentive. If spite *did* drive the spell, it was the spite of the person commissioning the magic rather than that of the practitioner. Moreover, most cunning folk claimed to work through divine forces or at least morally neutral ones; and even those who did purport to use spirits (ranging from fairies to demons) still claimed to be in control of the creatures, rather than being enslaved by them. These distinctions did not convince the likes of Heinrich Kramer or later Protestant theologians such as George Gifford, who remained firmly convinced that even good magic must necessarily be demonic. If it wasn't being caused by God, who else could its source be? Beyond such thinkers, though, many people were happy to accept that cunning folk and witches were fundamentally different. The harmful magic that service magicians occasionally practised was targeted and performed on behalf of a client, rather than a personal diabolical vendetta. And as we saw, magical redress was an attractive proposition to people who felt powerless within their communities and who believed that justice would not be served through the legal system. Still, that distinction between cunning folk and witches was not universally held: some people disapproved of what magicians got up to, especially if they were of a more godly persuasion.

One lawsuit from Ely in 1635 demonstrates the tension between those who trusted cunning folk and those who cast them as witches. In the middle of November that year a woman named Margery Paule was invited into the house of one Mistress Godfrey. According to Margery's neighbours, it was well known that she 'taketh upon her to tell fortunes', as well as helping pregnant women when they were close to labour.⁹ Mistress Godfrey wanted Margery to confirm whether she was with child or not, and Margery was happy to assure her that she was. However, apparently Godfrey's husband Thomas was in the room at the time and wasn't at all pleased about Margery's visit. He paced up and down as the women talked and briefly went out into his orchard, before returning in a rage. A witness testimony described how Thomas 'tooke the said Margery Powle by the shoulder And asked her what shee did there you witche, And kicknige [*sic*] her once or twice did ffling her against the threashould'. Margery picked herself up and ran out of the house, with Thomas' death threats ringing in her ears as his wife cried at him 'to be patient and to hould his hand'.¹⁰ Margery limped home, her thigh already swelling from the assault.

On the surface, this brutal episode looks like a straightforward case of hatred towards cunning women, and perhaps misogyny. But reading the rest of the Assize record, it is more complicated than that. In his own deposition, Thomas claimed that Margery wasn't there to diagnose whether his wife was pregnant: she was there to tell Mistress Godfrey when her husband would die. According to Thomas, Margery said that he would pass away soon, and that Mistress Godfrey would quickly move on and marry someone better. Of course this doesn't justify the assault, but it does give useful context. More importantly, the reason this record survives at all is because Thomas Godfrey was tried for attacking Margery: it was the witch-hater on trial, not the cunning woman/supposed witch. Her neighbours and friends all testified that Margery was a cunning woman, but that didn't justify the beating she had received at Thomas' hands. Thomas admitted the assault; and although we have no record of the outcome of the case (verdicts were normally recorded separately from the depositions and rarely survive), we can be fairly sure that he was punished for his violence.¹¹

This case dates from 1635, when puritanical Christianity was building towards its zenith and knowledge of witchcraft was widespread. That a cunning woman and her supporters were able to bring someone to trial in this environment tells us something about the distinction most people held in their minds between magicians and witches. Clearly the boundary was fluid for some people, but for many others there was a clear difference.

◆

In 1589 Mistress Dewse visited the magician Richard Birche. She was eager for Birche's help. She had learned of the cunning man's skills through a prisoner at Newgate whom Birche had often advised—although exactly what sort of advice he offered is not specified. On finally making Birche's acquaintance, Dewse told Birche that 'she had heard of him & longe soughte for him', for she was certain that he would be able to exact revenge on her enemies.[12] Dewse was clear about how she wanted to get this revenge. She demanded that Birche make images of her enemies so that she could 'pricke them to the harte, or els that by his arte they mighte all dye'.

Wax dolls like the ones she requested were not unusual. Sometimes called 'mommets' or 'poppets' in England, they were found all over Europe in one form or another. The technique for making and using them varied, but a fifteenth-century magic book called the *Liber de angelis* (*The Book of Angels*) offers a good example of one method. The spell is dramatically labelled the *Vindicta Troie* (Vengeance of Troy), and instructs the practitioner to make a likeness of one's enemy out of wax taken from funeral candles. The magician should then write the name of the victim on the doll's forehead and the symbol of Saturn (♄) on its breast and between the shoulders. The doll should look as disfigured as possible, with limbs arranged in an unnatural pattern and the face contorted. It should then be held in the smoke resulting from the burning of a range of noxious substances, such as bones and human hair, wrapped in a funeral cloth and buried face down in fetid earth. As if this were not grisly enough, if the practitioner really wanted to ensure the death of the victim, they should insert a needle into the doll's spine.[13] All of the above should be performed on a Saturday to further invoke Saturn, which was believed by astrologers to be an unlucky planet. Most people probably did not go to this much trouble with their cursing, although the dolls would always be personalised in some way. That could be by adding some of the target's hair to the poppet or by placing it in the victim's house—buried in front of the doorstep was a popular option. Spells like this were shockingly cruel, and anyone who undertook them would have been either extraordinarily desperate or extremely bitter.

Dewse likely fell into the former category. The men whom she wanted to kill included one Justice Younge, the wealthy merchant and former Lord Mayor of London, Sir Rowland Heyward, and a man named 'Sye', possibly a local sheriff. Apparently these men had made Dewse's life, and that of her husband, a misery; indeed, their behaviour towards the Dewses had been so awful that it would 'greatly please God' if Birche did them harm. According to Birche's surviving testimony, his client described Younge as a thief who 'lived by robbinge papistes'. The Catholic population of England was suffering during the later years of Queen Elizabeth's reign. Since the execution of Mary, Queen of Scots on Elizabeth's orders in 1587, diplomatic relations with the Catholic nations of Europe had declined dramatically. Catholics, both at home and abroad, were judged to be a threat by the English government, which was understandable, given the various assassination attempts against Elizabeth, as well as the attempted invasion of England through the Spanish Armada of 1588. While in the early years of Elizabeth's reign Catholicism had been tolerated—so long as observants practised their religion discreetly—from the 1580s adherents of the 'old religion' were increasingly penalised by both the law and their neighbours. Recusants (those who refused to attend church) were fined £20 for every month they were absent (more than £4,000 today), while being found with Catholic devotional items such as rosary beads could lead to forfeiture of land and goods, and Catholics were not allowed to attend university or hold most state offices.

Mistress Dewse was presumably one of the many recusants in England, and her life was becoming more and more difficult. Justice Younge had been responsible for the arrest and harassment of many of her acquaintances, and petitions to the Lord Chancellor for fair treatment had fallen on deaf ears. Her house had been raided, on Younge's and Heyward's orders, and her maid arrested. Now the pair were conspiring to make Dewse's husband 'lose his office, w[hich] woulde bee both her and her childrens undoinges'. Faced with a justice system that was licensed to discriminate against her and her family, and likely having witnessed the execution of some of her fellow worshippers and friends, it is little wonder that Dewse sought drastic measures.

She was well aware of the risks associated with her request for harmful magic: even Birche warned her 'that her practise was perilous & daungerous'. But Dewse was not to be deterred. She offered to pay him whatever he wanted, if only he would help her kill her enemies. She promised him £60 (the equivalent of over £12,000 today) and said that she had even procured the wax needed to make the images. Birche was cautious and may have even been working to entrap Dewse, if his later testimony is to be believed. He claimed that he could not make the dolls himself 'for that hee was lame', but agreed to 'stande by her & tell her if shee did amisse' while Dewse made them herself. Under his direction, she made wax dolls of all three men and stuck them with needles. She put one through Mr Younge's heart. On Heyward's doll she pushed needles into the heart and under the ribs. On Sye's, she thrust them into his eye sockets. Once done, she stored these effigies in a cupboard and waited for the magic to take effect. It seems that she was at least partially successful: she later told Birche that 'shee thanked God some of the pictures did worke well and so she hoped would all the reste'. As payment, Dewse sent Birche a sugar loaf, two lemons and a capon (a cockerel that had been castrated to make the meat more tender) along with her unending thanks. He had rejected the £60 she had originally offered him, saying that he would do the spell out of courtesy, not for money. Perhaps he really did sympathise with her cause, or maybe, like several other cunning folk, he felt that accepting payment in kind would make his involvement harder to prove if things went wrong.

Dewse's conspiracy was eventually exposed; Birche might even have reported her himself. His testimony is the only one to survive in the State Papers, and he was careful to declare that he did not perform any magic himself and that he had even warned Justice Young about Dewse's intentions. Perhaps Robert Birche was a government spy who sought to entrap

Catholics this way—or maybe he simply got scared and decided to turn king's evidence while he had the chance. My guess is the latter. Dewse herself was apprehended, but there is no mention of her in the documents after Birche's initial deposition in January 1590. Both parties would have qualified for execution under the Act against Conjurations, so did they feel the full force of the law? We don't know. I, for one, hope they were spared.

◆

Not all attempts at revenge sought the victim's death. Often practitioners and their clients simply aimed for retribution that was in proportion to the slight they had suffered—in short, to make the punishment fit the crime. This is probably why so many jilted lovers opted for impotence spells as their punishment of choice. Like female infertility, male erectile problems were recognised as a medical condition in the medieval and early modern periods, so of course not all such cases were put down to magic. The idea that impotence could also have a supernatural cause dated back to antiquity, though, and was well recognised by Christian theologians and law-makers from at least the eleventh century. It was thought that jealous ex-lovers might use spells to disrupt their partner's new relationships. Thomas of Cobham's *Summa Confessorum*, a confession manual for priests written in the early thirteenth century, related one such incident in France:

> ... it is well known that often, when men deserve it, the devil binds some man in his members so that he may not have intercourse, as it happened once in Paris that a certain sorceress impeded a man who had left her so that he could not have intercourse with another woman whom he had married. So she made an incantation over a closed lock and threw that lock into a well, and the key into another well, and the man was made impotent.[14]

The reference to men who 'deserve it' regards the sin of fornication (sex before or outside marriage) rather than abandoning one's mistress, but it is still noteworthy that clerics recognised that a jilted woman might seek a kind of rough justice. The lock-and-key motif seems apposite, symbolically separating the male and female genitals and impeding the opportunity for penetration. Other methods also relied on a sympathetic link, such as hiding the testicles of a rooster under the newly-weds' bed or tying the intended victim's name to the penis of a wolf (presumably once it had been detached from the wolf?). It was believed that most of these spells could be undone again; for example, one recipe in the thirteenth-century *Liber Antimaquis* explains how to both cast and reverse the spell:

> In the climate of Saturn, to bind someone take the blood of a wolf, the brain of a cow, and the blood of a black cat, and mix them in equal amounts. And if you give it to a man or woman, they will not be able to have intercourse. The cure is made through the help of Venus or Mars. Take equal amounts of the castor-oil plant, the bile of a black cat, a wolf's eye and also a female gazelle's [there may be a lacuna in the text here] and mix in the same amount of bat's blood.[15]

The spell-caster might lift the impotence out of mercy or once the ulterior motive, of breaking up the new relationship and getting their lover back, had been achieved. Love, desire, anger and heartbreak were just as powerful emotions in the fifteenth century as they are today.

Indeed, supernaturally punishing sexual misconduct and errant lovers is not a practise confined to the pre-modern period. The Museum of Witchcraft and Magic in the village of Boscastle, Cornwall, contains an array of curse objects, including a collection of poppets. Most of them date to the mid-twentieth century and show a remarkable level of continuity with their fifteenth-century predecessors. The malevolence that radiates off these dolls is palpable: even the hardened sceptic with whom I once visited the museum felt a chill as they peered through the glass display case. Most of the surviving poppets are made of clay—perhaps because those made of wax would have melted or otherwise fallen apart long ago—and the majority are stuck through with pins. One particularly brutal example is of a man made in reddish-brown clay, with well over a hundred nails stabbed into his torso. The museum's founder, Cecil Williamson, recorded in the catalogue that the doll was made in France, by 'a woman to be revenged upon a restaurant proprietor who had caused her daughter's pregnancy'.[16] That the pins in this doll are stuck all over the man's chest and abdomen, rather than targeting his heart or face, might relate to the maker's desire for him to suffer pain akin to that of pregnancy and childbirth.

Resorting to supernatural harm is generally what people do when they have no other option left: when they cannot get their lover back; when their attempts at reconciliation have failed; or when justice is simply not to be found. All that is left in such situations is bitterness and a desire for revenge. Poppets like this are disturbing for exactly this reason. Although the realism of the figures and the violence done to them is unnerving enough, it is the sense of helplessness, anger and hatred that the practitioner must have felt while making them which makes them truly frightening. It is not surprising that sometimes curses like these worked: the psychological effect of knowing someone wishes you serious harm can be devastating—sometimes even fatal. Fear and chronic stress can have enduring effects on the body's nervous and endocrine systems, leading to symptoms ranging from high blood pressure, migraines and disrupted sleep patterns, to skin complaints, breathing difficulty, disrupted menstrual cycles and stomach problems. These physical complaints can layer on top of the psychological toll that stress takes, which is associated with poor concentration, memory loss, low mood, anxiety and a pervasive sense of dread.[17] So imagine knowing that one of your neighbours was performing a black fast upon you, or finding a curse doll buried in a shallow grave beneath your doorstep. Whether or not the spell had any power in itself, the stress and fear alone of knowing that you were viscerally hated by someone could be sufficient to make you suffer. Revenge magic was genuinely dangerous.

Even so, we know of fewer cases of cunning folk offering these services than there are of any other kind of magic. The absence of such records, particularly in the sixteenth and seventeenth centuries, might indicate that they feared being cast as witches, and thus kept such activities quiet. It might also be that most practitioners simply refused to take commissions for harmful magic, specialising instead in more benevolent services such as finding lost goods. There are certainly far more cases of magicians using their powers to heal than to harm. Given the fragility of our bodies, perhaps this fact shouldn't be surprising. I like to think, though, that the preponderance of magical healers also reflects the desire of most cunning folk to turn their powers towards good causes—even if this, too, could mean risking their own lives in the process.

CHAPTER 5

HOW TO SAVE LIVES

FERDINANDO STANLEY, THE FIFTH EARL OF DERBY, WAS thirty-five years old and in rude health. He spent the Easter week of 1594 in the north of England, dining sumptuously and taking part in vigorous activities like riding and hunting. Although life was not entirely perfect—Ferdinando had recently been implicated in a plot against the ageing Queen Elizabeth I, which had left him on the outer fringes of courtly life—he had reason to hope for a bright future. He was a skilled poet and patron of the arts, supporting the careers of such famed authors as Edmund Spenser, Robert Greene and possibly, through his performance troupe, even Shakespeare. He had succeeded to his father's lands and titles less than a year before and, if his Easter activities are anything to go by, was enjoying his new wealth and status immensely. Most significantly, Ferdinando enjoyed blood ties to the Tudor dynasty: he was the great-great-grandson of Henry VII and was named as a hypothetical heir to the English throne in the will of Henry VIII. As courtiers jostled for position around various possible contenders for the crown, it was unlikely that Ferdinando would be shunned by society for very long.[1]

But Ferdinando's sunny outlook changed on 5 April, when his health took a turn for the worse. At first it seemed that he might merely have overdone it. At around five o'clock in the evening he started vomiting a russet-coloured bloody fluid, which, though obviously alarming, could perhaps be explained by all the hunting, feasting and drinking he had partaken of over the past four days. Early modern medical knowledge was largely based on the Galenic idea of the four humours, which dictated that the human body was made up of blood, yellow bile, black bile and phlegm. The balance of the humours was affected by factors such as diet, age, gender and activity levels, and when they were unbalanced, this could lead to various illnesses. Ferdinando was in his mid-thirties and was therefore judged to be on the cusp between youth and the prime of life; as such, he would naturally have a higher balance of blood in his system. Wine and rich foods would only have exacerbated this inclination, and the heating properties of exercise were likewise thought to stimulate the body's production of blood. Altogether it was really no surprise that his health was out of balance after a few days of living to excess. That he was vomiting blood might be optimistically explained as the body trying to restore its own equilibrium by removing the surfeit.

Even so, the experience was unpleasant, and the next day Ferdinando returned to Lathom House, his ancestral home east of Liverpool. Despite being careful to rest, and undergoing a 'glyster', or enema, to flush out his system, his symptoms only got worse. On day three of his illness he reportedly vomited 'above seven pintes' of the same 'grosse and fattie', iron-coloured liquid.[2] There were no professional doctors nearby, so a local cunning woman was called in to help, while a messenger was sent to Chester to summon a group of university-trained physicians. The journey would have involved traversing the Mersey, a tidal river that at this time had only a few crossing points. Even travelling at top speed, therefore, it would likely have taken two days for the doctors to reach Ferdinando's bedside.

Meanwhile, the cunning woman got to work. The illness of Ferdinando Stanley was widely reported on, so we know for certain that she was there; but at no point do we hear her voice, or even learn her name. What we do know is that she seemed to do some good. Aside from the vomiting, Ferdinando was also jaundiced, had a 'swelling and hardnesse of his spleene' and suffered from violent hiccupping. At times, though, he was much more at ease and his fits subsided. The cunning woman seemed to be achieving these moments of respite through some sort of sympathy magic, for 'so long as hee was eased, the woman her selfe was troubled most vehemently in the same manner, the matter which she vomited, being like also unto that which passed from him'.[3] There is no elaboration on how she did so, but by all indications she was attempting to cure him by drawing the illness into herself.

When the physicians finally arrived, they found the cunning woman sitting in Ferdinando's room. She is derogatorily described as 'A homely woman, about the age of fiftie yeeres . . . mumbling in a corner of his honors chamber . . . tempering and blessing (after her maner) the juice of certaine herbes'.[4] What herbs she was using is not specified, but we know that Ferdinando drank a tonic of rhubarb and 'Manna' (a plant gum extracted from various trees, thought to have a laxative effect) boiled up in chicken broth before the physicians arrived. It seems likely that the wise woman was the one who gave this to him. Whatever she was preparing now, she was given short shrift by the professionals. Upon spotting her, one of the doctors marched over and dashed the pot of herby juice out of her hands, then chased her from the room. As she left, she promised to keep doing what good she could from a distance, though she claimed there was little hope for him as he was strongly bewitched. In the following days the physicians would come to agree with her, but for now it was their turn to try their cures.

Medicine before the modern period had very few of the structures and regulations that we're familiar with today. Italian cities were among the first in Europe to try to regulate medical practice, with the foundation of guilds or colleges that would train, examine and license their members. The College of Physicians of Venice was founded in 1316, and Florence followed suit by forming a Physicians' Guild in 1392. London's College of Physicians, meanwhile, did not gain a charter until 1518. Licensing and regulating medical practitioners was both sporadic and highly localised: none of these institutions held any authority outside the boundaries of their respective cities. Apothecaries, who mixed and sold medical ingredients, and barber-surgeons, responsible for everything external to the body, from hair-cutting to tooth-drawing and amputations, had a similarly patchy history of regulation, with each forming regional guilds and offering training through apprenticeships. That there was limited motivation to control medicine reflects the state of healthcare at the time: formally trained, professional doctors like those summoned by Ferdinando were few and far between. In fifteenth-century England there were only about sixty university-trained physicians, and although this number had risen to several hundred by Ferdinando's day, there were still not enough to serve the entire population. Such physicians also tended to charge high rates that were well beyond what most normal people could afford, so they were largely the preserve of the nobility or wealthy merchants. Most people had to rely on their own house-hold cures, barber-surgeons (who were less expensive and exclusive than physicians), experienced locals and, of course, cunning folk.

In practice the difference between licensed physicians and unlicensed practitioners could be slim, but the main point of distinction was their knowledge of the humours. Humoral theory and attendant concepts like the *complexio* or temperament—whether something had hot, cold, wet or dry qualities—were incredibly complicated. These ideas originated in ancient Greek medicine, had been preserved in the Arabic-speaking world for much of the medieval period and only arrived in western Europe, where they were translated into Latin and shared in handwritten tracts, in the eleventh and twelfth centuries. To know about the humours, therefore, meant that one had to have a functional grasp of Latin. This precluded most men and almost all women from reading these texts, which in any case were relatively rare and expensive to buy. Although by the sixteenth century many of the concepts had filtered into the vernacular and were being popularised by cheap print, the Royal College of Physicians still tested practitioners who claimed to be licensed by asking about the properties of different cures. This explains something of the tensions playing out between the physicians and the cunning woman in Ferdinando's sickroom. It also explains the uncomfortable treatment plan on which the doctors now embarked.

On reviewing Ferdinando's symptoms, they surmised that his disease was caused at least in part by 'a surfet' of food and 'a most violent distempering himselfe with vehement exercise'.[5] At first they prescribed bloodletting to rebalance his humours: a common enough procedure that formed a major part of healing well into the nineteenth century. For reasons that are not entirely clear, Ferdinando rejected this advice, but did consent to further enemas. These gave only temporary relief. Next he was given powdered bezoar stone and unicorn's horn—yes, you read that correctly—in large quantities. Bezoars are small stones of undigested material that appear in various animals' stomachs, but were most often harvested from ruminants. From antiquity well into the seventeenth century, they were thought to be a sort of panacea for various ailments and particularly for poisons. Unicorn horn was an ancient medicine too, first written about in Europe by the Greek physician Ctesias in the fifth century BCE.[6] With the advent of Christianity, unicorns began to take on religious significance and their horns were seen as a symbol of the unity between Christ and God the Father. The unicorn was also associated with a Christ-like innocence: it was said that only virgins could touch or capture unicorns, because the animals were repelled by anything that had been sullied. This inherent purity was why unicorn horn, usually sold ground up into a powder, was highly prized as an antidote to poison or disease: it would drive any corrupt matter out of the body.*

Unfortunately, neither the bezoar nor the unicorn horn was effective in Ferdinando's case and his condition continued to deteriorate. Next the physicians suggested that the patient eat some of his own vomit, on the reasoning that 'thereby the bottome of his stomacke might be scoured and cleansed'.[7] The advice was based on the principle of 'like curing like', working

---

* 'Unicorn' horns, when sold intact, were probably actually taken from narwhals, whose long, spiralling horns do look like they could have come from a mythical creature. What powdered unicorn horn consisted of is anyone's guess, but I would hazard at ground-up bones.

on the same idea as taking the 'hair of the dog that bites you'. Before the phrase came to mean drinking more alcohol as a hangover cure, it was a means of protecting oneself from contracting rabies: if an infected dog bit you, then taking some of the dog's hair and either ingesting it or using it to make an ointment for the wound was meant to counteract the venom of the bite. Despite the logic, though, Ferdinando refused to comply with his physicians and did not eat his own vomit. He was given medicine to make him sweat instead, as well as poultices to place on his stomach.

After six days like this, Ferdinando lost the ability to urinate. His stomach bloated and the pain worsened; he began falling into fits that left him paralysed for hours. The surgeon at his bedside tried everything to get his bladder working, eventually resorting to inserting a catheter, which on 'being conveied into his bladder, was strongly sucked by the Chirurgion'. The attempt failed. By this point the physicians were fairly convinced that the cunning woman had been right and that it was witchcraft that was making Ferdinando suffer so terribly. And so was the patient: he cried out that the doctors 'laboured in vaine, because he was certainly bewitched'. It was now remembered that Ferdinando had rejected a woman's petition just a few days before he got sick, 'to assigne her a dwelling place neere unto himself, that she might from time to time reveale unto him such things . . . which God revealed unto her for his good'. Her proposal was rejected as a 'vaine' idea, but perhaps that in itself had been folly: could this illness be some form of revenge, either invoked by the bitter woman or even by God Himself? Whatever the cause, it was too late. The cunning woman had concluded there was nothing anyone could do. The curse upon Ferdinando was too strong, and all she could ever have done—at great pain to herself, it is worth adding—was ease his suffering a little. On 16 April, after eleven days of agony, Ferdinando died.

The historian Judith Bonzol suggests that Ferdinando Stanley was poisoned. That his physicians largely ignored this possibility and alighted instead on witchcraft as the ultimate cause, Bonzol posits, can be explained by the fact that the situation was politically sensitive.[8] Stanley was a real contender for the throne once the unmarried, childless Queen Elizabeth died, and his ambiguous religious persuasion—no one was entirely sure whether he was Catholic or Anglican—made him a potential candidate for different factions to rally around. He had already entertained the idea of a Catholic plot that would unseat the queen and make himself king, though Ferdinando ultimately rejected the proposition and denounced the instigator to Sir William Cecil, Elizabeth's right-hand man. There were therefore plenty of people who might wish to see Ferdinando dead, not least the queen herself. Perhaps Bonzol is right, therefore, that the doctors saw a safer option in naming witchcraft as the cause of death. Even so, they had their reputation to consider. That the physicians would side with a cunning woman's diagnosis and agree it was a curse that killed Ferdinando shows that they must have believed the conclusion to be credible—particularly after a wax doll with hair 'like unto the haire of his honors head, twisted through the belly thereof' was found in Ferdinando's bedchamber.[9] It also means that, despite the obvious snobbery they carried with them when they entered Stanley's sickroom, the doctors held at least some respect for the cunning woman by the time they left.

In some ways the Earl of Derby's case is an unusual one. Most nobles would not have had a cunning person at their bedside; and as is clear by the way this wise woman was treated, physicians would have discouraged such a practice. The wise woman had been called for practical reasons: Ferdinando's regular healers were not close by, and so a cunning person was summoned in the interim. Still, the fact that she was drafted in—and so quickly—is significant. People within Ferdinando's household must have known about her and trusted her sufficiently to put their lord in her hands. That Ferdinando consented to be treated by her in turn implies that she was recommended by someone whose advice he respected, perhaps one of his servants of the bedchamber or someone else who had intimate access to his person. Such positions, which required very close proximity to the lord—including sleeping at the foot of their master's bed—were necessarily built on a firm foundation of trust. That a servant of the bedchamber was responsible for the cunning woman being at Ferdinando's side is my conjecture, for someone in the household clearly knew her and respected her reputation. And it seems that this respect was well deserved: whether or not her cures actually comforted Ferdinando, from the reports of her trying to help even after she was cast out, and from the way she suffered while performing her healing, it is clear that she gave the job her all.

◆

This level of dedication was not unusual. Most magicians would have firmly believed in their abilities and thus took their responsibilities seriously. We've just seen that healing magic could be an incredibly intimate process, taking an emotional and often physical toll on everyone involved. This level of effort was not solely reserved for noble clients. The sincere effort some healers invested in their patients is made apparent in the example of Elizabeth Page, a Somerset cunning woman who was called in to heal a sick infant in the mid-1550s.

Elizabeth Wryte, Page's neighbour, had a young daughter. The diocesan record that mentions the case does not specify how old the girl was, but we do know that she was little enough to still be sleeping in a cradle. She had been healthy for most of her short life, but then she started to ail for no apparent reason. Her mother was understandably worried. The child kept slipping in and out of a trance-like state and stopped feeding. At a loss for what to do, Wryte turned to Page, begging her to come and give her opinion as to what was wrong. Page does not seem to have been a midwife or trained in childhood diseases, but the fact that she was Wryte's first port of call would suggest that she had a reputation as a healer. When Page obligingly visited the child soon afterwards, Wryte must have looked on with a mixture of anxiety and relief as she checked the girl over. Yet any relief at receiving help must have turned to alarm when Page left without comment. Two days passed and Wryte's daughter continued to fade, seemingly wasting away before her mother's eyes. We can only imagine what Wryte was going through. Frustration, helplessness, fear and guilt would be my guess at some of the emotions she felt. Having waited long enough for Page to return, Wryte sought her out again. Dreading the answer, she asked outright whether her daughter was bewitched.

Page's reply went some way towards explaining why she had left in such a hurry after her initial consultation. Yes, she said, the child was definitely bewitched. Indeed, she was close to death. Page wanted to help, but she knew that in order to do so, she would have to become 'as ill a case as the said child then was'. In short, she would have to risk her own life if she tried to heal the child. Presumably what she meant by this was that she would use sympathy magic to take the curse into herself, thus purging it from the infant. Like the cunning woman who helped Ferdinando Stanley, Page would experience all the symptoms of her patient and, if she was not strong enough, then she herself would die. Given the circumstances, perhaps it's no surprise that Page took a couple of days to think the situation over.

We don't know what Wryte said to convince her that it was worth the risk, but Page eventually agreed to help. She accompanied Wryte home and went straight to the girl's cradle. She knelt down beside it, tenderly 'crossing the forehead of the said child'.[10] She then 'spoke certain words over' her, but what those words were, Wryte could not tell. When Page stepped away, she looked determined. She told the mother 'to be of good comfort and her child should be well'. Wryte had to be patient, Page told her, as she could not do anything just yet, but once her husband had gone to bed, she would immediately rise and begin her spells. All that Wryte had to do was take the child to bed with her that night. Around midnight the child would recover.

Wryte did as she was told. Bundling up her daughter, she took her from her cradle and held her close in the dark. I imagine it is unlikely that she slept, but perhaps she did: after days of worry, maybe there were moments of fitful sleep, half comforted by the knowledge that someone else—someone with knowledge of how to handle such terrible illnesses—was at work. What we do know is that the child did improve, not at midnight as promised (no doubt causing her mother new anxiety), but by 1 a.m. Wryte's deposition tells us that, although the girl had been 'lying by this deponent [Wryte] all the night (being as it were in a trance), [she] recovered and took sustenance'. The little girl fully recovered and lived for a long time afterwards.

Meanwhile, the spell took as much of a toll on Page as she had feared. She survived the ordeal, but now openly declared the girl to be her daughter, saying, 'This is my child, for she had been dead, and I had not been.' She had given life to her like a mother, gifting her a future that she would not otherwise have had. We don't know how Wryte felt about this claim, but by risking everything to save the girl, Page had clearly forged a powerful bond with the child. So proud was she of her success that she could not help boasting about it in her community. Indeed, sharing the story widely might be what eventually caused the case to reach the ears of the ecclesiastical authorities, which is why we have a record of it today.

The story reveals a number of things about the work of cunning people. It was the principle of transference that underpinned the methods of both Elizabeth Page and the cunning woman who cared for Ferdinando Stanley. Taking the sickness out of the patient and putting it into another living creature was a common approach in magical healing, particularly when it came to dealing with supernatural diseases. It might take its precedent from the New Testament story of Jesus and the Gadarene demoniac, in which Jesus exorcised demons—called 'Legion, for we are many'—out of a possessed man and cast them instead into a herd of swine. The pigs, driven mad by the spirits, charged straight into the sea and drowned, thus destroying Legion's hosts. The man who had been possessed made a full recovery. Before, he had been constantly tormented, wandering 'among the tombs and on the mountains, he would howl and gash himself with stones' both night and day. After Legion left him, though, he was once again able to dress himself, speak and consort calmly with other people.[11]

It is a moot point to try to determine what diagnosis he would receive through modern medicine: our healers in the sixteenth century would have agreed with the Gospel writer that he was possessed. What is important is the fact that they replicated Jesus' actions by using the same basic formula. Page and the unnamed wise woman both thought their patients were bewitched, believing that they had a devil or demons inside them, sent by a malevolent sorcerer. The cunning women chose to use their own bodies as vessels within which to trap the spirits and would have then looked for a way to purge it from themselves. This might have been through prayer—essentially performing an exorcism—or by transferring the demons on to something else, often to an animal. Using animals as repositories for disease was a common practice among cunning folk in the sixteenth and seventeenth centuries. Apparently the favoured method of Katherine Thompson and Anne Nevelson, two healers from Northumberland, was to put the bill of a white duck to a patient's mouth and recite charms until the disease was drawn out.[12] Others would take a bewitched patient's urine, mix it with flour, then feed the resultant 'urine cake' to a stray dog. The curse would thus pass out of the human and into the animal: if the spell was successful, then sadly the dog would die, but the patient would recover.

The other interesting thing we can learn from Page's case is that, although she clearly had a reputation for healing, it seems that her husband didn't approve of her activities. The detail that she had to wait until Mr Page had gone to bed before starting her spell suggests that either he was a demanding spouse who required her to work until gone midnight, or that she had to hide from him what she was doing. Given that this episode occurred in the mid-1550s, by which time the idea of malevolent witchcraft had become firmly entrenched in European society, perhaps Mr Page disapproved because he feared his wife might be accused of witchcraft. However, as we saw in the previous chapter, Henry VIII's Act against Conjurations had been repealed in 1547, so there was no secular punishment to fear. Furthermore, Page was not exactly subtle about her actions once the spell had succeeded. Perhaps the secrecy from her husband was necessary because he worried about her health: knowing how much these spells demanded of her, maybe he did not want to see her suffer.

While the reasons why Page's husband tried to stop her from practising magic are largely guesswork, it is abundantly clear that Elizabeth Wryte felt strongly about the life of her daughter, and that Page felt enough compassion to help. Tenderness and love were very real emotions for people in the past. The medieval historian Philippe Ariès suggested in the 1960s that pre-modern families withheld affection from young infants, as they were reluctant to emotionally invest in children who might quickly pass away. This assumption is based on estimated mortality rates at the time of 40–50 per cent for children under ten. With such high figures— which could be driven even higher during times of famine or epidemic disease—it would be understandable if people became inured to death. Emotionally shutting off parts of yourself until there was a decent chance that a child would survive perhaps makes sense; indeed, it is a survival technique.

However, the story of Wryte and Page suggests that such theories are wrong. Even in a world of endemic precarity and sickness, people were still human: they loved and cared for one another, even when there was a risk they might lose each other at any given moment. We have enough records of anxious parents turning to magic to heal their children to confirm that people would have had the same feelings and affections that we have today.[13] In 1538 a father named Hamper from Rye, in Sussex, asked his local curate for help because his child had the 'chyne' or whooping cough.[14] The curate was reported for irregular practice as a result, but it did not stop him giving the child holy water from the church's chalice three times. And John Wade and his wife undertook a twenty-mile round trip from Coggeshall to Colchester in 1590 to consult a cunning man about their sick baby. Apparently the magician, a Mr Shereman, gave them a recipe for a magic ointment that would help. We also have evidence that some cunning folk specialised in children's diseases, suggesting that there was a steady stream of worried carers to make such expertise worthwhile.

◆

Alongside affection, there is a strong scent of desperation around these cases. Although understandings of the human body became more sophisti-cated in this period, there were still plenty of diseases that defied explanation or treatment. The most effective medicines relieved symptoms rather than cured the underlying cause, which meant that while it might be possible to soothe a feverish patient or ease convulsions, ultimately it was a case of hoping that the body would fight off the ailment itself. People would often find themselves looking on helplessly as their loved ones suffered, so it should not surprise us that people searched for magic cures.

After seeking care for their children, someone going to a cunning person for healing most often went on behalf of their spouse. We have encountered some unhappy marriages in this book, but whether or not there was affection between a husband and wife, they still needed each other. Indeed, the death of a spouse could mean physical hardship for the person left behind. Traditional divisions of labour in Europe largely saw women confined to the household, performing domestic work and engaged with cottage industries like brewing or spinning; meanwhile men would do business or heavy farming outside the home. Although restrictive, these divisions did have practical reasons behind them. The labour-saving devices that we take for granted today simply did not exist for people in the past. This may seem like stating the obvious: in a time before electricity, of course there were no vacuum cleaners or washing machines. But we should be thinking about the absence of infrastructure that was far more basic than that. Water was not piped into houses: it would have to be collected from nearby streams, wells or lakes. It was not possible to heat houses or ovens at the drop of a hat: fires had to be lit and maintained in open hearths, and food cooked over them. The fuel that fed those fires had to be gathered, whether it was through chopping wood, cutting peat from the ground or collecting and drying animal dung. Food would rarely arrive in a household ready-prepared; chickens, for instance, if they had not been raised at home from chicks, would be brought home live, then killed, plucked and cooked. Grains like wheat and spelt had to be taken to the nearest windmill or water mill to be ground into flour; if such technology wasn't available locally, it would have to be ground by hand. And let's remember that these grains had all been sown, grown and harvested by hand.

What this means is that someone on their own could realistically do little more than subsist in our period. Some religious men and women decided to live a very basic life in solitude, but even they would rely on the alms of travellers and penitents to keep body and soul together. For most people, the way to survive was to band together in households and family units. The 'women's work' of feeding, clothing and tending to the family was a full-time, strenuous job, and it was essential labour without which their husband, elderly parents and children could not survive. Likewise, 'men's work' of ploughing the fields, tending to heavy livestock and constructing and repairing buildings was vital. To lose a spouse, then, would—almost literally—have felt akin to losing an arm. A household without someone skilled at spinning or sewing, keeping the fire going or raising crops and animals risked failing altogether.

We don't know, therefore, whether it was love or practical need that drove John Shounke to consult one Father Parfoothe about his sick wife in 1585. We do know, though, that he did not regret it. Parfoothe had a reputation as a healer and blesser of both livestock and humans and, if John's testimony is anything to go by, seems to have been good at his job. Although John did confess himself to be 'hartelie sorie for sekinge mans helpe and refusinge ye helpe of god', when ordered to by the archidiaconal court in Essex, his contrition was not entirely sincere.[15] He openly admitted that he had asked for Parfoothe's help in saving his wife, and proudly declared that he would do so again. We can be fairly certain that he wouldn't have made such a statement if whatever advice Parfoothe had given hadn't worked. The fact that Parfoothe was still being consulted about sick cattle seven years later likewise suggests that he was successful in the services he offered.

It is worth lingering briefly on the point that Parfoothe healed both humans *and* animals. Of course animals were as vulnerable to disease as people, and their sudden deaths could be as devastating to a household as that of a family member. There was also a widespread concern that cattle, horses and even chickens could become sick or infertile as a result of a witch's curse or some other misfortune. It seems that Father Parfoothe was one of the many practitioners who could be called on either to perform pre-emptive spells to protect animals from harm or to provide cures if they were already suffering. 'Healing' enchanted items was also under some cunning folk's purview. In the 1640s one Elizabeth Stothard was consulted by a milk-maid about a cursed milk churn. Elizabeth advised the woman to carry a stick of rowan when she milked the cows in future, which would drive away any ill-willed spirits. In a sign of well-meaning follow-up care, a few days afterwards Elizabeth called on the milkmaid to see how things were going. Apparently the milk was churning as well as it had ever done previously, producing beautiful cheese again.[16] In many villages, cunning folk would have been the frontline defence against witchcraft and mischievous spirits, and no doubt the milkmaid was grateful to have Elizabeth to call on.

Unfortunately, not all those who professed healing powers were so honest or, indeed, successful. The fear and desperation triggered by a severe illness made families easy targets for charlatans. Usually those offering healing magic were established in their communities and enjoyed a reputation that they had carefully built up over several years. Especially if they didn't overcharge for their services, the cunning person could be fairly confident of a steady income from their skill; meanwhile their clients knew where to find help, and would perhaps even return to the magician for further advice if the initial cure failed. Such familiarity—and security—was absent if a magician was itinerant, though. These practitioners could possess a certain allure: they could pass themselves off as well travelled, and thus as keepers of skills and knowledge that most local healers were not privy to. If they were unknown by their patients even by reputation, they would also not be tainted by any past failures in their craft. More importantly, they could disappear before their patients realised that the cures they had been sold were bogus.

Roger Clerk may have been this type of cunning man. Living in Wandsworth in the early 1380s, he is known to us because he appeared in court for deception on 13 May 1382. Apparently Clerk turned up at the door of Roger atte Hache's house on Ironmonger Lane in London the day after

Ash Wednesday. How he had come to hear about Roger atte Hache's sick wife is not entirely clear, but hear of her he did and decided to try his luck.

What kind of person did Roger atte Hache encounter when he opened his door to Clerk's knocking? We know from the trial account that Clerk 'gave the said Roger . . . to understand that he was experienced in the art of medicine', and some signifiers in the way he was dressed would have helped to make this claim convincing. What people wore was an important marker of identity at the time, so much so that it was regulated by law. Dress was used to distinguish such states as gender, class, religion, marital status and vocation. While this could be useful for identifying another person at a glance, it also facilitated discrimination. Thirty years before Roger Clerk was visiting, for example, London had ruled that sex workers must wear striped hoods out of doors, with 'vestments neither trimmed in fur nor yet lined with lining . . . that so all folks, natives and strangers, may have knowledge of what rank they are'.[17] In the case of this ruling, the aim was ostensibly to preserve the modesty of 'respectable' women—though no doubt it also made it easier for clients to locate the sex workers being regulated. Physicians and other trained medics also had a dress code, which was similarly used both as an advertisement and as a marker of rank. This normally consisted of a distinctive hat (usually soft and squashy, similar to a doctoral cap) and long academic-style robes. Characteristic tools of the trade, like the fluted glass flasks used to collect and inspect urine, might also be openly carried on the way to consultations in order to show off the profession.

Perhaps, then, this was the sort of outfit Clerk sported when he went to visit the atte Haches. He must have been impressive enough for Roger to let him in, or perhaps Roger was just desperate for help. Either way, he invited Clerk to the bedside of his wife, Johanna. Clerk found her 'lying ill with certain bodily infirmities', the worst of which was a raging fever. 'Fever' is something of a catch-all term that describes a symptom rather than the disease, so there is no way of telling what exactly was making Johanna sick. Needless to say, though, fevers are dangerous in their own right, and the underlying cause might have been even more so. Clerk assured Johanna's fretting husband that he was quite skilled enough to cure her—for the right price. Roger atte Hache handed over twelve pence as a down-payment for Clerk's services, with the promise of more when Johanna recovered. Clerk's fee would have amounted to about two days' worth of an ironmonger's wages (given that atte Hache lived in Ironmonger Lane, we can safely assume this was his occupation). In return for this sum, Clerk 'then and there gave to the said Roger atte Hacche an old parchment, cut or scratched across, being the leaf of a certain book, and rolled it up in a piece of cloth of gold, asserting that it would be very good for the fever and ailments of the said Johanna'.[18] Clerk instructed that the package should be tied around her neck as a sort of amulet and from this she would soon derive some relief.

It didn't work. It is unclear whether Johanna died—hopefully not—but the surviving record does state unequivocally that 'in no way did [the charm] profit her'. Given that the case was heard in court some three months after Clerk's consultation, Roger atte Hache's anger seems to have festered; if she had not passed away, we can probably assume that Johanna was still sick. Perhaps atte Hache could have forgiven Clerk for this failure—after all, there were plenty of diseases that could not be cured—had it not quickly become clear that the magician was a cheat. He had lied, not only about his knowledge and skill, but even about the charm itself, which was nothing like what he had claimed it to be. Atte Hache brought the parchment and cloth of gold along for the court to see, and Clerk was asked to describe its contents. He had claimed that it was a charm against fevers, with the words *'anima Christi, sanctifica me; corpus Christi, salva me; in sanguis Christi, nebria me, cum bonus Christus tu, lava me'* (soul of Christ, sanctify me; body of Christ, save me; blood of Christ, drench me; as thou art good Christ, wash me).[19] If this had been the amulet's inscription, it would have been impressive. It would have shown that Clerk was literate and had the ability to read and write Latin. What's more, the adjuration was also frequently used by conventional medical practitioners: calling on Christ, the Apostles or other saints as part of healing was condoned by both the Church and learned physicians, unless it was done in a clearly blasphemous way. A common charm for curing toothache, for example, involved relating a story about how Jesus cured St Peter's sore mouth. The episode does not appear in the Bible, but was part of medieval culture, and that particular healing charm was in circulation in England from at least the Anglo-Saxon period.

If Clerk's parchment had been inscribed with these words, therefore, perhaps the case would have ended differently. But it was not. When the scroll was opened, the court recorded that 'not one of those words was found written thereon'. The parchment was cut and scratched, but that was all that could be said for it. The court concluded that Clerk was 'in no way a literate man', and declared that 'a straw beneath his foot would be of just as much avail for fevers'. This latter charge might be a reference to a custom in which men stuck a piece of straw between their foot and shoe, signalling to others that they would be willing to perjure themselves during a trial for the right price. In short, the court was calling him the worst sort of unscrupulous liar—and Clerk agreed with their summation. For me, this detail of the case is crucial. Unlike John Chestre, the cunning man practising in London around the same time, whom we met in Chapter One, Clerk did not try to defend himself or his abilities. Whereas Chestre gave examples of people whom he had helped with his magic, Clerk could offer no such evidence. While Chestre acknowledged that what he was doing was illicit, he held fast to the fact that his magic *worked*. Clerk, meanwhile, acknowledged that his cure was fake and was worse than no good.

The fact that Clerk lived out in Wandsworth is also an important point. He travelled into London to ply his trade, a good distance away from his community and the people who knew him. Perhaps he went from door to door in different streets across the city, offering his services when he found a household where someone was lying sick. Demanding at least some payment in advance, he could be confident of making a living, whether his cures actually worked or not. If they did, all to the good: he might get the other half of his fee. If they did not, he may have relied on the fact that his client was unlikely ever to see him again.

Clerk was punished for his actions. Found to be 'ignorant of the art of physic' and an 'infidel', to boot—there is no explanation as to what exactly the court meant by this—he was sentenced to ritual humiliation. He was led bareback on a horse through the middle of the city, with the parchment hung around his neck alongside a whetstone, the symbol of a liar, and a urine flask, the sign of a physician. The accoutrements would have clearly signalled to passers-by that he had lied about being a physician. To make sure that his humiliation was noticed by everyone, Clerk's ride was accompanied by musicians blasting pipes and trumpets. The people of London were thus duly warned about Clerk's fake cures; Roger atte Hache no doubt felt that Clerk got what he deserved.

But I wonder whether this interpretation of Clerk as an opportunistic scoundrel is perhaps unfair. He clearly understood what words *should* have been written on the parchment he gave Johanna, suggesting that he had some knowledge of Latin, even if he lacked the ability to write it down himself. Maybe he was also intimidated by the court and, faced with a sick patient that he had failed to help and a blank piece of parchment, felt that any attempt to defend himself would only make matters worse. Over the following centuries, more cases like that of Roger Clerk were reported. Sometimes we catch glimpses of truly immoral characters who took advantage of the scared and the desperate, but more often the stories have to be taken with a pinch of salt. When the surgeon William Clowes wrote a tirade against quacks and magical healers in the sixteenth century, he included a cautionary tale about charlatans that must surely be fictional. It involves a 'lewde woman' who had a reputation for healing 'men, women, children, and beasts by a certayne charme' and charging a loaf of bread and a penny for her services. When forced to reveal what the charm consisted of, she admitted that it said, 'My lofe in my lappe, My penny in my purse, Thou are never the better, Nor I am never the wurse.'[20]

These stories reveal that there was a widespread fear that magical healers were taking advantage of the sick. As the case of Roger Clerk shows, magical healing could be expensive, and if a family only had enough money to consult one healer, they might fear they were wasting it on the wrong practitioner. Tirades like William Clowes' also tell us that, as medical practice became increasingly professionalised, there was a concerted effort to vilify unregulated healers. In fairness, these efforts were not limited to cunning folk; and of course the unregulated nature of healing did mean that some truly dangerous 'medicines' were sold across Europe.[21] Approaching cunning healers with caution—especially ones who travelled to offer their services and had no proven track record—was probably advisable.

◆

Prayers and religious charms often featured within learned medicine, particularly before the late fifteenth century. Gilbertus Anglicus, an English cleric who was also the trusted physician of King John, wrote a medical textbook in the 1230s. The *Compendium medicinae* demonstrates the authority and learning of its author, drawing on the ancient wisdom of Greek and Arabic healers like Galen, Haly Abbas (the Latinised version of Ali ibn al-Abbas al-Majusi) and Avicenna (Abdallah ibn Sina), and guiding the reader through the different parts of the body and what might ail them, before listing useful cures. We might not expect to encounter verbal charms or amulets to heal the sick in such a scholastic work, but Gilbertus lists ten charms, including two to stop bleeding, three to heal poisonous bites (plus one aimed specifically at dog bites) and one to aid conception. Many of them include a prayer to accompany the magic words spoken. One of the charms against poisonous bites begins with the recital of the Paternoster and the Kyrie eleison, before instructing the healer to use the incantation '*Poto pata Zene Zebete*' over the wound.[22]

This may feel a little surreal to us today: how did a university-trained cleric and physician justify the incorporation of such charms in his work? Gilbertus and other physicians and surgeons like him categorised these charms as *experimenta*. This term was used to describe rituals or actions that carried powers unexplainable through their natural qualities. Physicians at the time were aware that many things worked despite lacking an obvious explanation; for example, magnets drew metal towards them, even though most rocks of a similar colour, size or shape did not. Such oddities were understood as falling somewhere between what was natural and what was supernatural. The power was assumed not to come from angels, demons or any other supernatural intervention; but as there was no obvious cause, they were essentially put down to being preternatural or 'occult'. Gilbertus would have interpreted his charm against bites in a similar way: the sound and shape of the words *Poto pata Zene Zebete* seemed to be effective at curing diseases, even though it was not clear how or why. The cause and effect of the Paternoster that also featured in the remedy, meanwhile, had a clear rationale: it was drawing on the power of God to aid the patient.

This is where the line between magic and religion becomes rather blurred. As we saw earlier, cunning folk drew readily on the power of Christ and the saints to heal the sick. So did monks and priests. Today we may wonder whether there really was a difference between these two practices—or whether it simply hinged on the practitioner's identity and whether or not they were condoned by the Church. We should look briefly, therefore, at the range of healing options available from Christian shrines, monasteries and churches.

◆

Glastonbury Abbey in Somerset was once one of the richest religious foundations in England. There has been a monastery on the site since at least the eighth century, and by the twelfth it was widely recognised as the burial place of King Arthur and Queen Guinevere. This connection to the legendary hero of England drew royal patronage from successive monarchs, including Henry II, Edward I and even Henry VIII, before he ordered the abbey to be dissolved in 1539 during the Protestant Reformation. Even more important than these royal accolades, the abbey claimed to have been founded by Joseph of Arimathea. St Joseph was the follower of Jesus who took care of his body after the crucifixion, and a long-standing tradition claimed that after Christ's ascension Joseph travelled to England, bringing Christianity to the country and burying the Holy Grail at Glastonbury. Among other evidence cited to support this claim is the marvellous spring that has run close to the abbey's grounds for centuries. The water that streams from it is rich in iron, tangy to taste and leaves red stains where it courses. Its flow also remains consistent, even during severe droughts. From such miraculous properties, it is no great leap to conclude that the cup that contained the blood of Christ was buried nearby.

All of this made Glastonbury a preferred destination for pilgrimage during the Middle Ages. Rich and poor, old and young would come to pray, venerate the saints and beg forgiveness for their sins. They would also come seeking healing, and the monks were happy to sell small bottles of the blessed spring water to pilgrims to drink or bathe their wounds, as the little of Christ's blood it contained was believed to heal their ailments. Yet closer to the sorts of magical healing we have already encountered in this book was what happened in the crypt of the Lady Chapel, the central space within the abbey. It was here that the sick would gather in the hope of a miracle.

Pilgrims would have descended the steps into the crypt slowly, careful not to trip as their eyes adjusted to the gloom underground. Those with damaged legs or painful joints would have moved even more slowly. As they entered, the first thing to hit them would have been the smell. The air was filled with the reeking, suffocating odour of tallow, and the sound of murmured prayers would be underlain with the steady drip of wax falling from ceiling to floor. Indeed, each pilgrim would enter clutching a little wax figure, moulded into the shape of whatever limb or organ they wanted healed: a leg, a hand, a heart. Looking up, they would see dozens of figurines like theirs suspended above their heads. Repeating prayers and supplications, they would look along the stone arches that formed the ceiling of the crypt to find an empty hole bored through the beams, from which to hang their wax body part. Once it was found, the patient (or their carer or a monk, if they were unable to do it themselves) would hang up the wax body part, calling on the Virgin Mary to take pity on their plight. Depending on the complaint, they might also pray to a relevant saint, such as St Apollonia, the patron saint of toothache, or St Willibrord, who was believed to be able to cure epilepsy. Perhaps the pilgrims would stay a while, or more likely they would leave quickly to escape the stench of disease. Resurfacing into clean air, they might immediately have felt a little better, although most wouldn't have expected a sudden cure. The disease would take as long to leave their body as the wax of their little effigy, in the warm, stale air of the crypt, would take to melt. It could take days or even weeks, but with the sacred power of the Lady Chapel and the prayers of the Glastonbury monks on their side, most would have felt optimistic about recovery.

Many other Christian practices bordered on the magical, particularly before the Reformation. St Peter's Church in Westminster, for example, used to house a girdle apparently worn by the Virgin Mary, which was loaned out to royal women in childbirth. A long belt made of parchment, it would be wrapped around the expectant mother's waist when she went into labour. The hope was that the Virgin's power would keep both mother and child safe and well through the birthing process. Although the Westminster girdle was reserved for the highest elite—such a sacred item could not be given to just anyone—enough birthing girdles survive from the time to suggest this was a widespread practice. While most of them would not lay claim to having been worn by a saint, they were sacred objects nonetheless. One such girdle, made in the late fifteenth century and now in the Wellcome Collection in London, is ten feet long and made up of four sheepskins. The entire length is covered with words and images: prayers to Sts Quiricus and Julitta, Jesus and the Virgin Mary; drawings of the crucifix and the side-wound of Christ (in medieval iconography Jesus is often depicted as literally giving birth to the Christian Church through the gash). There are also dice—perhaps because childbirth was considered to be a gamble and dependent on good luck? Recent biochemical analysis has found that the belt is stained with cervico-vaginal fluid as well as honey, milk and herbs, which were often used in childbirth remedies.[23]

After the Reformation, however, such girdles, alongside votive offerings and other prayer-charms, were rebranded as magic in most Protestant countries. The reformers' aim of stripping Christianity back to focus solely on what was recorded in the Bible called for the removal of all the apocryphal stories and rituals that had accrued in Catholic tradition. Many of these rituals were seen as unhelpful distractions from the core of the Christian faith. But there were also those who believed that they were part of a satanic ploy to trick people into worshipping beings other than God—a notion that most Catholics would have rejected. All this demonstrates that magic is never easy to define: in many cases what counts as magic and what does not is ultimately a matter of perspective.

◆

Medicine in the medieval and early modern periods was complex. Life was dangerous: a simple cough could rapidly develop into a fatal fever; family members and friends could be lost overnight. The birthing girdles show how, in times of mortal danger, any and all methods were embraced to keep people alive. Magic blended with religion, and both were used along-side practical measures like herbal poultices and nourishing foods. It would be easy to deride such methods if it were not for the fact that they are a testament to how fiercely people tried to care for each other. We have only recently emerged from a global pandemic—surely we can sympathise with the fear and confusion people must have felt when they went down with an unexplainable illness. Looking for someone to blame—as Ferdinando Stanley's physicians and cunning healer did—is also not alien to us: for examples of this behaviour, we don't need to look further than the conspiracy theories about where Covid-19 came from and how it spread.

Magic could not solve everything of course. By and large, cunning folk restricted themselves to curing particular ailments, even specialising in a single condition. Some practitioners would only cure fevers or stomach worms; others would limit their help to children or animals. The reason for this is probably largely practical: if they knew only one incantation and it specifically referred to one kind of illness, it would make sense to focus on that affliction alone. Roger Clerk, whether he was a charlatan or not, was adamant that his cure was good for fevers. Maybe he was simply making that claim to reassure his customers, or maybe he only knew how to treat fevers. Often the important thing was not to overpromise. It was better to be honest about one's skills than mislead clients and risk retribution. We see this hesitancy in the case of Elizabeth Page: though she did ultimately cure her neighbour's little girl, she thought carefully about how and when to do so.

Healing was among the most common services that cunning folk were called on to provide, second only perhaps to divination. This is not only a testament to how difficult life could be, or to the dearth of other medical practitioners. Most of the magicians we encountered in this chapter were clearly trusted, enjoying long-standing reputations and having clients repeatedly returning for their services. There must have been something in what they did. Whether it was experience gained through observation, practical skill or the ability to fortify a patient through comforting words, cunning folk were an essential part of the medical landscape. The desperation with which people sought magical aid is also in evidence in the next chapter, where we will consider the financial scrapes that some individuals found themselves in.

CHAPTER 6

HOW TO GET RICH QUICK

My lord, I know that you are far in debt, and know not which way
to pay the same; also that you have lost much money by play, and
daily do . . . But yet, if you will follow my counsel, I can devise such
a way for you whereby you may both recover your loss and also win
as much as shall pay your debts, and have enough to serve yourself
besides from time to time . . .[1]

THE ABOVE WORDS WERE MUSIC TO THE EARS OF HENRY,
Lord Neville. He was twenty years old in 1544 when his servant approached
him with this offer, and despite his tender age and aristocratic lineage,
Henry's life was pretty miserable. Caught in a loveless marriage since the
age of twelve, he had at least three children to support and an ancient
family title to live up to. Although he had recently been knighted by the
king in recognition of his support at the First Siege of Boulogne, upon his
return to England, Henry felt rather flat. To escape the demands and expectations of his household, he began to frequent the gambling dens and
brothels of London.

Within months, Henry was deeply in debt. He was not a professional
gambler and quickly fell prey to the tricks that swung play in his opponents'

favour. Paying for sex also did not come cheap, and no doubt many of the venues that catered to disillusioned nobles like Henry charged inflated prices for their various entertainments. Henry's father, Sir Ralph, the fourth Earl of Westmorland, was exasperated by his son and heir for wasting the family's fortune. No doubt Henry's wife, Anne, also strongly disapproved: money and feelings aside, her husband risked exposing her and any future children to the so-called 'French Pox', or syphilis, which was now spreading throughout Europe. The servants in the Neville household of course knew of their young lord's vices, which is why one day in mid-November one of them, Ninian Menville, suggested a solution.

As you might expect by now, the solution was of a magical nature. Henry was bad at gambling, so the obvious answer was to draw on some sort of supernatural aid that would tip the balance towards him instead of the card-sharps. Although not a magician himself, Ninian knew that there were practitioners in the city who could make special rings that brought luck to the wearer. If Henry had such a ring, he could pay off his debts, make enough money to stay in credit and even carry on with his favourite hobby. Henry eagerly asked how he might go about finding the right wizard. Another servant in the Neville household knew just the man, Ninian replied. And so Gregory Wisdom, physician and accomplished magician, arrived early the next morning.

The reason we know about this case is because, in 1546, Henry ended up in prison for commissioning sorcery and other assorted crimes. We will soon see that Wisdom was a fraud and Ninian his abetter, but let's not judge Henry too harshly for being taken in. After all, the finest minds in Europe at the time were busily exploring the same kinds of magic that Henry was buying into—so who was he to doubt the two men?

Before things went sour, Wisdom seemed like the answer to all of Henry's woes. He cut a good figure in his fine clothes, looking both 'wise and wealthy', according to Ninian. Well versed in astronomy and astrology, Wisdom confirmed that he could indeed make rings that brought luck to their owner. But in order to make better sense of the story, we first need to take a brief look at the practice of astrology. Although we tend to think of it as semi-magical today, in the medieval and early modern periods astrology was treated as a science. It relied on precise calculations of what the seven 'planets'—the Sun, Moon, Mercury, Venus, Mars, Jupiter and Saturn—were doing, and which constellations they were interacting with at any given moment. It was clearly observable that as hours, days and seasons went by, the planets would move across the sky and pass in front of the various signs of the zodiac (the constellations of Virgo, Aries, and so on). Measuring the regular movements of the planets, therefore, had a practical function first and foremost, as they marked the passage of time and helped to calculate, for example, the annual date of Easter. Yet there was a more occult function too, which was based on the idea that the stars and planets could influence what happened on Earth. Here the premise was that each planet had partic-ular, essential properties. The Moon, for instance, was feminine, cold, moist and associated with mental instability, while Saturn was associated with masculinity, old age and a melancholic disposition.[2] What's more, celestial bodies emitted stellar rays carrying these properties, and when they hit Earth, they affected the world accordingly. It meant that horoscopes could be taken at crucial junctures in a person's life—at birth, before marriage or during times of illness—to predict what might happen to them (we will discuss this further in Chapter Eight).

More importantly for our current purposes, there were those who believed that the power of the stars could be actively harnessed to make things happen. This is the point at which astrologers undeniably crossed the line between natural philosophy—the proto-scientific study of the world—and magic.[3] Among other purposes, astral power could be employed to make protective or lucky amulets. These would normally involve engraving images of the relevant conjunctions into metal or precious stone, drawing down the energy of the stars and capturing it in a wearable item. For good measure, an inscription demanding good fortune for the wearer (or a passage from the Bible or a psalm) might also be added. All this would have to be done at a particular time, when the planets were in the right position. For extra potency, the material chosen for the amulet needed to reflect the qualities of the relevant planet. If it were the Sun's influence that the magician wished to capture, for example, they should make their amulet out of gold; if the practitioner wanted to harness Saturn's power, they should make it out of lead.[4]

Gregory Wisdom's rings were not simply made under the influence of the stars, though; they were also imbued with the power of supernatural beings. The magician gave Neville a choice. Either he could have a talisman made with the aid of demons or—more expensive, but also more reliable and less spiritually problematic—he could produce one infused with the power of angels. Both options were still founded on astrological principles, as it was broadly accepted by scholars that the heavens were regulated and moved by angelic beings. Biblical passages like St Paul's Epistle to the Ephesians also seemed to hint at the fact that demons inhabited either the celestial realm or the lower atmosphere: 'And you hath he quickened, who were dead in trespasses and sins; Wherein in time past ye walked according to the course of this world, according to the prince of the power of the air, the spirit that now worketh in the children of disobedience' (Ephesians 2:1–2). The reference to a prince of the air working for mischief was commonly interpreted as a reference to devils. When one called on the celestial bodies to make a talisman, therefore, it was thought that one could also summon either the angel associated with a planet or the devils who were floating about the atmosphere.

Angels and demons were essentially the same, at least in terms of their age and many of their characteristics.[5] Both had been created by God to do His will, and all had been angelic at the outset. After a war in heaven, however, God expelled Satan and all who had fought on his side; those who had rebelled against God became demons, now determined to tempt humanity away from its creator by making it commit sins. Demons retained some of their powers and much of their knowledge about how the world worked, which could make them useful magical aids as a result. For this reason, many learned magicians attempted to summon devils and trap them temporarily in magic circles, or for longer in gemstones or other receptacles. It was this that Wisdom was offering to Henry Neville—a demon of his own, trapped in a ring, which could influence the dice that he cast or the cards he drew from a deck.

Neville went for the slightly less frightening—and less spiritually compromising—option and asked for a lucky ring made through angel magic. Wisdom congratulated him on his choice, but cautioned that the item would take some time to create. He would have to wait for the right conjunctions in the sky, obviously, as well as procure the necessary materials. For that he wanted four marks (£2 13s 6d) up front, in addition to food and lodging for as long as it took for the ring to be produced. He also demanded a retainer of £20 per annum for life. This was asking for a huge amount of money: the cost of materials alone was worth about £1,500 today. Understandably Henry was taken aback, both by the initial outlay and the idea that he would be responsible for Wisdom's salary ever after. Even so, the temptation was great: Wisdom promised that Henry would have made £2,000, perhaps even £3,000, by Christmas—in today's money, a minimum of £1.5 million in winnings. After some haggling, therefore, Neville agreed. Wisdom would receive £10 a year (roughly £5,000 now) when Henry succeeded his father as the Earl of Westmorland; and in the meantime he would get a share of Henry's winnings. Accommodation and materials would also be provided at Henry's expense. No doubt pleased with the outcome of his negotiations, Wisdom went to settle into his new home.

Why did Henry consent to such extortionate terms? We can only speculate. Perhaps it was a combination of Wisdom's genius as a confidence trickster and the fact that Neville was not the sharpest tack in the box. But then there were plenty of great men and women who had commissioned similar services in the past. We have examples of magic rings from all over Europe, promising to do something miraculous for the wearer. One found in Eltham Palace, Kent, and dating to the fifteenth century, promises good fortune for its wearer. Studded with diamonds and a ruby, it was in all likelihood commissioned by a member of the royal family. Another ring from Italy, probably made in the fourteenth century, is inscribed with two passages from the New Testament: 'But Jesus passed through their midst' (Luke 4:30); 'And the Word became flesh' (John 1:14). It is made of gold and set with a toadstone, which was thought to be effective against poisons: perhaps its purpose was to help its wearer navigate dangerous situations. Europe's nobility clearly laid some store by these items and were prepared to pay good money for them.

On a practical note, how else could Henry hope to make as much as £2,000 in a little under a month? Maybe if he did something spectacular, like save the king's life, then he might be lavishly rewarded, but short of that and selling the family silver, there were few options. For all his faults, he does seem to have been ashamed of his debts and unsustainable lifestyle. In the circumstances, not losing money would, at least, restore some of his self-worth. What's more, the hope of radically changing one's life through an initial cash outlay remains the foundation of gambling today: we all want to win the lottery.

Wisdom was true to his word, and on Christmas morning Henry woke up to his miraculous present. Henry rushed out of the house to try the ring's worth. He was not disappointed. That very day, playing at his friend Myles' house alongside Sir Nicholas Poynes and a man named Thistlethwayte, Henry won £30. He was delighted, having easily made back his initial investment. He was confident there was further fortune coming his way. Unfortunately, though, his lucky streak was not to last—not even another twenty-four hours. On St Stephen's Day, 26 December, he played at 'Domyngoes'—a gambling den perhaps, or the house of a Spaniard living in London—and promptly lost everything he had. Delight now turned to fury. Henry angrily demanded all of his money back from Wisdom, as well as the contract he had rashly signed the day before, which promised Wisdom the £10 annuity they had agreed, but specified that the payments would start straight away, rather than after Henry's father's death. Wisdom claimed that he had only added this clause in case Henry happened to predecease Sir Ralph, though this verbal codicil would mean little if Wisdom called in the money.

As his employer raged and threatened, Wisdom remained perfectly calm. What had Henry been doing that day, besides playing with his friends? he asked. Had he, perhaps, celebrated his new-found fortune by sleeping with a sex worker? Neville looked sheepish. Yes, he admitted eventually: he had. Now it was Wisdom who exploded. Of course the magic had stopped working! It was angel magic: it propitiated the purest beings in the universe and asked them for their help! Neville had cheated on his wife (again), broken the sacred vows of matrimony and sullied himself with base pleasures. In response, the angel who had lent him its blessings had withdrawn its good favour. As such, the ring was now useless.

Brushing aside Neville's spluttered protestations that he wasn't told about this condition, Wisdom proposed a different solution to Henry's now-worsened money problems: he could go treasure-hunting. If magic rings had not given Henry pause, this should have done. Both activities were illegal under the 1542 Act against Conjurations but unlike magic rings, looking for treasure was specifically name-checked in the legislation. Even so, Henry pressed on. Ninian informed Neville and Wisdom that he had heard from a 'blind man which was a Jew born and a practiser of the same art [of magic]' that there was £2,000 buried under a cross in the north of England—in fact, on land owned by the Neville family.

It is likely that Ninian and Wisdom wanted to reassure Neville with these specific details, as they were associated with magic. The Jewish population of England had been violently expelled more than 250 years before, in 1290, and would not be formally allowed to re-enter the country for another century. Even so, *conversi*—Jews who had converted to Christianity—were tolerated in small numbers. Yet there was a strong suspicion across Christian areas of Europe that no conversion was sincere, but was rather a means to survive and thrive in areas inhospitable to Jewish people. Indeed, the Inquisition in Spain and elsewhere had been founded to investigate false conversions. Even without this level of policing, 'New Christian' families were frequently shunned by their neighbours.

On an individual level, though, some people could benefit from the suspicion that they had remained Jews. Many Christians in Europe saw Judaism as intrinsically tied to occult forces and powerful magic. Pico della Mirandola, for instance, a Christian thinker and occultist living in the fifteenth century, asserted that the most powerful language in the world was Hebrew because it was the language spoken by God to Adam and Eve. Jewish mysticism, emerging in the twelfth century in the form of the Kabbalah, was consequently revered as an exotic and ancient form of magic. Many Christians somewhat bigotedly assumed that most Jewish people harboured knowledge of the supernatural, so consulting a man who was 'Jew born' (and assuming that his conversion to Christianity was only a front) added extra weight to Wisdom's claims. The fact that the practitioner was blind only gave him further authority: blindness had long been associated with heightened sensitivity to the spirit world. If a blind Jewish man who was practised in the occult arts claimed there was treasure buried somewhere, Henry would have assumed there was a good chance it was true.

Whether it was the credentials of Wisdom's source or the amount of money he promised to bring back, Henry was convinced that it was worth a try. He laid out twenty nobles (about £3 13s) in expenses, and on New Year's Day Wisdom and Ninian headed north. Three weeks later only Ninian returned and he was empty-handed. They had torn down the cross near 'Portegewes' and dug where the money was supposed to be buried, but had found nothing. Wisdom, fearing Henry's violent and rash nature, had refused to come back to give his client the bad news. At this point we might expect Henry to give up on the magician's ventures entirely, but Wisdom had one more money-making plan up his sleeve. This one was by far the most extreme and truly risked the death penalty for all involved.

Having given Henry several weeks to calm down, Wisdom and Ninian approached him once again in the first week of Lent. Apparently Neville was playing tennis at Westminster at the time—a sport that became particularly popular during Henry VIII's reign—perhaps Wisdom was not confident that he would be let in if he went directly to Neville's house. Either way, Wisdom claimed he had the ultimate solution to all the young lord's woes: he offered to kill Henry's wife. It was a loveless marriage, he argued, and Lady Anne was a good enough woman that she would surely go straight to heaven. Really it would be a kindness to them both. This would free Neville to marry again: someone of his own choosing this time, someone that he loved and someone who would bring a substantial dowry. Perhaps Wisdom also planned to offer Neville the love spell he would need to secure such a match.

It is important to remember that we are relying here on Henry Neville's testimony, given while imprisoned in 1546 for attempted murder. The document claims that Henry was utterly horrified and refused to give his permission for such an endeavour. Maybe this is true, but in which case it seems odd that he would meet Wisdom two further times, apparently by chance, first by Moorgate and later in Moorfields. This in itself is suspicious. Moorfields was, as the name suggests, a marshy area just outside the London walls. It was beyond the immediate purview of the city authorities: though technically regulated by London by the sixteenth century, in practice there was little oversight beyond the city's physical boundary. The area was also known as a site where beggars and patients from Bethlehem mental hospital would congregate. It was not, therefore, a place where a young nobleman would normally spend time, unless he wanted to avoid being spotted by people he knew.

This suggests to me that the meeting was no chance encounter, but was arranged in advance. It seems very unlikely, therefore, that Neville had rejected Wisdom's murderous offer in Westminster—not least because, when the pair met at Moorgate, Wisdom told Henry that the magic had been done. Not only had he cast a spell to kill Anne Neville, but also Henry's father, Sir Ralph. Coming into his inheritance would not only be lucrative and liberating for Henry, but he would also be a much more attractive prospect on the marriage market: in the circumstances, it seems plausible that he commissioned the deaths of his closest family members. But perhaps on hearing the news, Henry regretted what he had set in motion. The subsequent meeting in Moorfields took place the next day and we are told it was with Wisdom's father, rather than with the magician himself. Shortly after getting home, Henry demanded that Ninian help him capture Wisdom and take him to the authorities. His plan was to make Wisdom confess everything to the Duke of Suffolk at the Barbican, before Neville himself was wholly blamed for the coming murders.

Luckily for Wisdom, the Duke of Suffolk was unwell the day Henry marched the magician over to the Barbican, giving Wisdom enough time to scare Henry out of saying anything. After all, everything from the angel-filled ring to the treasure-hunting and the murder-magic was illegal and carried the death penalty under Henry VIII's new law. Did Neville want to risk hanging as a common felon, Wisdom asked, just because he was angry with him? The answer, clearly, was no.

Fortunately for everyone involved, Wisdom's spell did not work. Both Anne and Ralph continued in good health and may have been blissfully unaware of the attempts on their lives. Eventually word got out anyway, of course. Exactly how is a mystery, but it may be that, in 1546, Henry's creditors called in his gambling debts. (Wisdom had conveniently disappeared long before.) He was committed to the Fleet Prison—a dingy place largely reserved for debtors—and maybe the story came out there, while he complained bitterly about how magic had failed to fix his problems. When it became known quite how immersed in sorcery he had been, though, Henry seems to have been genuinely afraid for his life. He wrote panicked letters to Sir William Paget, a member of the king's Privy Council, confessing everything and begging him to intercede for his release. It took several months, but eventually he was freed. Both Sir Ralph and Lady Anne pleaded on Henry's behalf, though whether out of affection or to preserve the family reputation is debatable. Luckily the Privy Council did not judge Henry to have been a genuine threat to the realm and, as no one had actually died, there was room for leniency. It may also have helped that Henry VIII had passed away in January 1547, while Neville was in gaol. When his son, Edward VI, took the throne, a whole swathe of laws was repealed, including the 1542 Act against Conjurations. Neville clearly benefited from the new government's reduced concern about magical activities in England.

How foolish was Henry Neville? And how unusual is his story? It is certainly rare to find such a detailed record of events, and he may well be unique in pursuing such a range of money-making schemes in under six months. In itself, though, the way he scrabbled to get rich was not particularly out of the ordinary. He is an archetypal example of many young nobles crowding into the royal courts of early modern Europe, trying to sustain a lavish lifestyle they could barely afford. The traditional ways of making money—raising taxes on the lands they owned or governed, for example, or hoping for gifts from a benefactor higher up the social scale—worked only if one had control of the land in question, or if one was well liked. Many members of the aristocracy (particularly young people who had not yet come into their inheritance) could claim neither. Like so many others we have come across, Neville's story is one of desperation. Not the sort of visceral fear that people must have felt when their children got sick or when they lost all their worldly goods, but a gloomy situation nevertheless. Neville must have felt he was heading in a downward spiral, falling deeper and deeper into debt while alienating himself from his family. Any escape—even if it was illegal, dangerous and expensive—must have looked attractive.

The sorts of magic that Henry bought were also quite common. We have already seen that lucky rings and other talismans were a part of the nobility's wardrobe: Neville was neither the first nor the last to put store by such measures. Nor was he the only one to consider murdering his family. Killing one's spouse was something that many people dreamed of doing and at least some attempted; indeed, in the next chapter we will encounter patricide, as well as fratricide and filicide, by ruthless people determined to get ahead. Of all Neville's get-rich-quick schemes, though, treasure-hunting was perhaps the most conventional. It may even have been the most effective, for reasons that will become clear as we turn to our next tale.

◆

It was not only the social elites, of course, who were preoccupied with money worries. Even those who had taken vows of poverty needed a cash boost from time to time. This was true of William Stapleton, whom we first meet in 1527. William was a monk, but he didn't want to be one. Being a lay priest—who lived in a parish and ministered to his own flock—would have been all right, but the monastic life was certainly not for him. Ideally his days would not involve getting up at three in the morning to pray, or being punished when he failed to do so. He was tired of his vocation and wanted to leave—preferably as quickly as possible, as William had overslept again and was due to do yet more penance.

Unfortunately, joining a monastery in the first place was an expensive business, and his parents (presumably) had paid a hefty fee for him to become a member of St Benet's Abbey in Norfolk. The only way he could give up his habit was to buy his way out of holy orders: a difficult task, given that he had renounced all worldly possessions. To his credit, William went by the book, at least to start with. He explained his situation to his superior, who granted him a licence to leave the abbey for six months. At the end of that time William should either come back with the money for his dispensation to leave the monastic order or 'return again to religion'. Having thus gained his liberty—albeit temporarily—William travelled to see his friend, Denys of Hofton.

In his letter to Thomas Cromwell, who was at the time still in service to Cardinal Wolsey, William explained that he hoped Denys might 'help me towards the purchase of my dispensation'.[6] Regrettably, Denys did not have the money to lend, but asked whether William had enjoyed the books he had recently borrowed. The books in question were the *Secreta Secretorum* and the *Thesaurus Spirituum*, texts containing 'experiments' and purported secrets of the universe of the kind that Gregory Wisdom would claim to be familiar with. The *Secreta* purported to be a letter written by the philosopher Aristotle to Alexander the Great, imparting all sorts of knowledge about the universe, including how to manipulate various spiritual forces to one's will. Copies of the book had circulated in Europe from at least the twelfth century, and it was widely known among intellectuals by the sixteenth century. As a monk, William would have had the training to both read Latin and understand the theory behind the various spells contained therein. Yes, he had read the books, he told his friend, and he had liked them very well. Denys was pleased, for, 'if you be minded to go about anything touching the same,

I will bring you to two cunning men that have a placard [a licence?] for treasure-trove, by whose means, if [William] had any cunning, [he] might the better help [himself].[7] Thus began a surprisingly lucrative few months, which would take William all over the south of England in search of buried treasure.

Treasure was buried all over Europe. Ancient inhabitants left their marks on the landscape in many ways, including sacrificial deposits and burial mounds, which sometimes contained large amounts of precious metals. Bronze Age peoples across the British Isles seem to have had a tradition of 'sacrificing' valuable items to rivers, lakes and the earth. The Duddingston Hoard, discovered just outside Edinburgh in the 1770s, contained dozens of metal items that, more than 3,000 years ago, had been deliberately burned and broken before being deposited in Duddingston Loch. No one is quite sure why more than fifteen pounds of useful metal were abandoned like this, but current theories include that it was an offering to a water deity or a sacrifice in celebration of a successful battle. The famous Anglo-Saxon ship burial at Sutton Hoo, Suffolk, gives us an idea of what treasure-hunters might find beneath the Earth's surface. The site was raided long before it was formally excavated in the 1930s, but from what remained we can tell that the graves were lavish, filled with beautifully decorated weapons and armour that were intended to accompany their owner into the afterlife.

There were also deposits from more recent times waiting to be discovered. Centuries of war and turmoil had blighted the land, from the Viking invasions of the eighth century to the Norman Conquest in the 1060s, not to mention the skirmishes and battles of the Wars of the Roses, which had come to an end only a generation before William Stapleton was born. Civilians were caught up in these conflicts, resulting in murder, burned crops and plundered homes. People fleeing unsafe areas carried what they could and buried the rest, in the hope of recovering it later. Even if they were unable to leave, families might still hide valuables so that they would not be discovered by an army passing through the region. One of the safest places was in the ground: even in the sixteenth century most houses were built from flammable materials such as thatch and wattle-and-daub, too easily destroyed to act as safe long-term hiding places. As a result, caches of buried coins, jewellery and other prized items were dotted across the landscape, many of which would, sadly, never be recovered by their original owners. Some of these stashes would hold hugely valuable items. In 2009 a detectorist discovered 6.5 kg (14 lb.) of Anglo-Saxon gold in a recently ploughed field near Hammerwich in Staffordshire, a find that became known as the Staffordshire Hoard. (The lucky finder and the farmer who owned the field were rewarded the handsome sum of £3.2 million between them.) Such astonishing wealth should not be expected by all treasure-hunting hopefuls. Nevertheless, the potential for impressive finds is there, and after the news broke about the hoard there was a brief surge in metal-detecting as a hobby.

Today, metal detectors and skills like reading the topography of ancient settlement sites can significantly improve one's chances of striking gold. Pre-modern people too looked for telltale features in the landscape, but used magic as their version of a metal detector. The first thing to do was try to identify a likely site, and here two features were seen as especially propitious: roadside crosses and earth mounds. Crosses, particularly if they were old and carved from stone, were a good bet for simple practical reasons. As clearly identifiable, long-standing landmarks, they were a choice site for people to bury their goods and find them easily again afterwards. Perhaps there was also a perceived apotropaic aspect to the crosses: God would protect the goods until the times were stable enough for them to be recovered. The connection between treasure and roadside crosses was so entrenched by the mid-sixteenth century that it was singled out in Henry VIII's Act against Conjurations of 1542:

> Divers and sundry persons unlawfully have devised and practised invocations and conjurations of spirits . . . to understand and get knowledge for their own lucre in what place treasure of gold and silver . . . might be found or had, in the earth and other secret

> places . . . and giving faith to such fantastical practices have digged
> up and pulled down an infinite number of crosses within this realm.[8]

Although 'infinite' might be a bit of an overstatement, it was clearly a
trend by the time Gregory Wisdom was offering to pull down a cross on
behalf of Henry Neville.

The other place to search for treasure was barrows. These human-made
earth mounds, sometimes containing hollow chambers in the centre, still
sit, squat and immovable, in fields and on hilltops across western Europe.
Most long barrows (so-called because they are long and thin, in contrast to
circular round barrows) belong to the early Neolithic period, and by the
sixteenth century their builders were long forgotten, as was their original
purpose. They came to be associated with fairies and other earth spirits, and
legends sprang up about the unique powers that the barrows possessed.
Wayland's Smithy, for example, a long barrow in Oxfordshire, has a long
tradition of being the home of an invisible blacksmith. The legend goes that
if your horse casts a shoe on the road, you can take it to Wayland's Smithy,
leave the horse and a coin at the entrance and shortly afterwards the animal
will be ready to take away, freshly shod.[9] What the barrows were best known
for, though, was being the site where fairies kept their treasure.

So far, so good. But with more than 40,000 tumuli scattered across
western Europe, and hundreds (if not thousands) of roadside crosses,
knowing about these sites in general did not narrow the field much for a
treasure-hunter. This is where magic came in. During William's escapades,
he teamed up with a range of different cunning men, 'shewers' and 'boy
scryers' whom he hoped would help him identify where best to dig. Shewers
(or show-ers) and scryers were terms for people who were particularly adept
at seeing spirits and hearing the messages they wished to communicate to
the company. While cunning folk would do the magic to conjure the spirit
in the first place, the scryers would actually be able to see them once they
appeared. Often the scryers would be prepubescent children, mostly boys.
This was based on the assumption that children were more malleable and

receptive to the supernatural, as well as on the importance of their perceived innocence: angels especially would be attracted to children's virgin purity and thus more inclined to answer questions.

Together, the cunning folk and the scryers would summon a spirit and speak with it. The spirit could be angel, devil or fairy, depending on the practitioner's preference and/or what spells were contained in the book they were using. Binding the spirit in a magic circle, they would adjure it to tell them where treasure was buried. If a demon had been summoned—and even if a spirit appeared looking like an angel, there was a chance it was a devil in disguise—the magician would force it, through magic words, to tell the truth. Often this incantation would be the names of God or the archangels, as God's power trumped that of Satan. If the magician had done his job in the right way, and if the child relayed the messages correctly, the spirit would divulge the treasure's location.

Once the location had been identified, the next step was to dig, but it had to be done carefully. Treasure was not just hidden; it was well known that many troves—especially those hidden in barrows—were guarded by further spirits who might attack unwelcome fortune-hunters. As demons were thought to dwell underground as well as in the air, it made sense that one might encounter them when digging deep enough, especially when one was digging from greed, as devils were keen to corrupt people.[10] There was also a strong connection between the ground, valuables and death. As mentioned above, graves often held valuable goods that might be raided by later generations, and many of these would be the barrows that pre-modern people associated with fairies and ghosts. Medieval and early modern fairies were not small creatures with wings and wands; often human-sized, they could be powerful entities that turned malevolent if they felt they had been mistreated (or simply if they were bored). Stealing the treasure they hoarded in the tumuli they called home was an obvious way to upset them.

Unlike fairies and demons, ghosts on the other hand could actually be quite helpful when it came to recovering riches, as they were thought to actively want people to find it. A ghost would normally be attached to treasure as a form of penance: perhaps it was wealth that someone had accumulated in life through unethical means, or they had chosen to hoard it rather than give it to a good cause. Either way, the person's avarice had cursed them to walk the Earth until their sin had been expiated, which could entice them to help someone who was pure-hearted to find the treasure. Paradoxically, therefore, a haunted trove could be a very good thing, and could even provide a moral justification for treasure-hunting in the first place. Nevertheless, as they could not be sure exactly what creature they were dealing with, prudent magicians would take steps to protect themselves before they started digging.

There were various means of doing this. The most obvious, but also the most complex, was to summon the spirits out of the ground and magically bind them, hoping that the spells were powerful enough to hold them. This seems to be what William Stapleton and his accomplices attempted on one of their treasure-hunting expeditions, when they tried to summon the spirit Oberion. Apparently Oberion appeared to the group, but refused to aid them because, amusingly, he was already bound to Cardinal Wolsey (we will explore Wolsey's rumoured magical activities in the next chapter). An alternative method was to try to avoid the spirits entirely: treasure-hunters in the Duchy of Württemberg, in modern-day Germany, would wear amulets and dig in complete silence to protect themselves.[11] If these methods didn't work, the consequences could be severe: medieval morality tales relayed instances of people being viciously attacked by demons, barely escaping with their lives. The more common weapon of these demons was raising violent storms. A man named William Wycherley, who seems to have been an extraordinarily active cunning man in the 1530s, was apparently battered by wind and a fierce storm that appeared from nowhere when treasure-hunting in Sussex. Likewise when the famed astrologer William Lilly publicly looked for buried treasure in Westminster Abbey in the seventeenth century, a freak storm blew through the building so powerfully that it almost ripped the roof off. If he had not quickly dismissed the demons, Lilly claimed, there might have been serious injuries.

Despite the dangers, treasure-hunting was a popular get-rich-quick scheme, especially among highly educated men.*

William Stapleton, armed with the knowledge garnered from his religious training and supplemented by his magic books, joined this group of intellectual elites. Over the course of 1528 and 1529 he undertook at least seven treasure-hunting operations. In his letter explaining everything to Thomas Cromwell, he claims that he never found any treasure. His first attempt failed before it even started. William and his little party of cunning folk and scryers arrived at Sidestrand in Norfolk and were about to 'make search of the ground where we thought the treasure should lie' when a servant of the local landowner, one Lady Tyrry, 'forbade us for meddling in her said ground'.[12] Undeterred, William then teamed up with a duo of a cunning-man and a scrying-boy in the Norfolk town of Felmingham. Despite searching the surrounding land, though, they didn't find any treasure. Next they were invited to a man's house in Norwich, where it was guessed that money might be hidden, 'whereupon we called the spirit of the treasure to appear, but he did not, for I suppose of a truth that there was none there'.[13] And this is how William's story continues throughout his long and rambling letter to Cromwell: even if he sometimes succeeded in summoning spirits, he never managed to find any money.

William may or may not have been lying when he said this. Technically, all found goods, if they had been abandoned, automatically belonged to the Crown, so he might have been hiding his successes in case he was forced to give up his new-found wealth. Moreover, he had a strong reputation for treasure-hunting, for someone who was apparently so bad at it. William freely admits in his letter that word got round about his skill, and so he started to be housed and employed by a succession of acquaintances, all wanting to exploit his talents. It was these new contacts that helped William to finally escape the rigours of his monastic order.

---

* There are occasional references to women and girls using magic to find buried riches, but the bars to female education—especially in Latin and religious ritual—made it a mostly masculine pursuit.

Following his third treasure-hunting expedition in Norwich he met one Richard Thony who, along with his friends, raised 46s 8d to buy William's dispensation. This afforded William the right to be a hermit rather than a monk, thus giving him the freedom to roam the country instead of being tied to a particular abbey. Stapleton used his new role to continue his spirit-raising, hoard-finding pursuits among even more acquaintances, and to collect more books on magic. Eventually his reputation grew to the point where he caught the eye of one Lord Leonard, with whom he stayed for some time. To his relief, Leonard was the one who 'sued out my capacity for to be a secular priest', thus freeing William from his ascetic obligations once and for all. From there he was employed by Thomas Howard, the Duke of Norfolk, as an exorcist, because the duke was concerned that he was being vexed by a malignant spirit. This in turn led Stapleton to enjoy regular contact with the most powerful men in the land, including Thomas Cromwell, whom William petitions for clemency for his rule-breaking. Even if treasure-hunting did not directly bring forth the riches he expected, therefore, William did eventually get what he wanted. Indeed, he even achieved more than he had hoped for, as his skills brought him some extraordinarily powerful contacts. Clearly there were ways to make the idea of treasure-hunting pay, even if the digging itself was not always successful.

◆

Profiting from one's reputation as a fortune-finder may explain John Dee's petition to William Cecil, the Lord Treasurer, for a treasure-hunting permit in 1574. The controversial but undeniably brilliant court mathematician, astrologer and magician Dr Dee claimed that, along with his astronomical knowledge and his skills for conjuring angels, he could find the queen a fantastically lucrative gold or silver mine. In return, Dee solicited the rights to all the buried treasure in England. This was a breathtaking request and was quickly refused by Cecil. Perhaps it was little more than a publicity stunt.[14] Nevertheless, Dee might well have been confident in his ability to make good on his offer, if only it had been accepted.

What Elizabeth's government was more sympathetic to, though, were Dee's experiments in alchemy. As with other elites across Europe, Elizabeth and her courtiers were fascinated by this branch of natural philosophy. Like astronomy, alchemy has its roots in antiquity, eventually reaching western Europe via Muslim and Byzantine sources in the twelfth century. And like astrology, it sits on the cusp between magic and science. The main aim of alchemy is to transmute base metals like lead into purer metals—ideally, gold—and it relies on the Aristotelian idea that all substances are made up of four basic elements: earth, air, fire and water. This means that all matter can be reduced back to these four elements, if one knows the right method. Alchemy takes this principle and runs with the idea that, if all metals are made from the same elements (just blended in different proportions), it should be possible to adjust them sufficiently to change them into gold. This was thought to be possible if the alchemist could create the transmuting agent often called the 'elixir' (from the Arabic *al iksir*, meaning the 'potion' or 'cure-all') or the philosopher's stone.

Elizabeth I was well known across Europe for her exceptional learning and interest in the sciences. The historian Glyn Parry suggests that she was first introduced to alchemy's potential through John Dee's *Monas Hieroglyphica*, a book published in Antwerp in 1564, which claimed to be able to unlock the deepest secrets of nature. The potential of such a discovery was deeply attractive to both the queen and her treasurer, William Cecil, who were keen to find a way to rectify the epidemic of debased coinage that was racking the country's finances (about which more later). Theorem XXI of the *Monas* claimed to expose the 'great secret' sought by alchemists, suggesting that if Dee received the right patronage, he could make gold for his master or mistress. Elizabeth's support for Dee was sporadic (as we will see in Chapter Eight, she relied on him for astrological guidance at certain times), but she certainly patronised a range of other alchemists during her reign. These included Cornelius de Lannoy, a gentleman alchemist from the Low Countries; William Huggons, who ran the distilling houses that Elizabeth founded at Hampton Court; and Millicent Franckwell, who was granted £40 a year to conduct her alchemical experiments in Elizabeth's Privy Chamber.[15]

Like ritual magic, alchemy was expensive. Its practitioners claimed extensive learning that was available at a high price and required a lot of equipment. Over time, the method for creating the philosopher's stone became increasingly elaborate, involving successive distillations, both to take the materials used back to their most basic elements and then to amplify their potency. Incidentally, refining purification techniques in this way and developing the various instruments needed for distillation laid the groundwork for chemical experiments that would form the basis for modern chemistry. Of course, alchemists could also demand a lot of money from their patrons, because the potential rewards were so great. Cornelius de Lannoy claimed that he was able to make £33,000 worth of gold per annum through his elixir (roughly £11 million today), as well as creating precious stones such as rubies, emeralds and even diamonds.

But the philosopher's stone could do far more than this: it could restore health and prolong life. Alchemy worked on the same principles as the bodily theory of the four humours, adjusting the elements of a substance until they were in the right balance. If one were able to make an incorruptible, completely pure substance, then that substance would have the capacity to clear all corruption and disease from the body. Is it any surprise that those who could afford it would invest their money in creating such a wondrous item?

Not all alchemists enjoyed royal patronage, or were skilled enough to even attempt making gold. Some knowledge of alchemical processes could help people accrue a small amount of wealth at a pinch, though. John Buckley, a university student at New Inn, Oxford (now incorporated into Balliol College), and William Bedo, a stationer, were among those who experimented with such low-level alchemy. According to William's deposition, he met John in 1569 when he was asking around for someone skilled in discovering lost goods. John was recommended as being well known in Oxford for goods recovery—although John vehemently denied it in his own testimony to the court—and the two quickly became friends. After spending some time together, John revealed that he had acquired a copy of the polymath Giambattista della Porta's book, *Magia Naturalis*. Like the *Secreta Secretorum*, *Magia Naturalis* laid out many of the purported secrets of the universe. Unlike the *Secreta*, though, its focus was much less on moral questions and advice, and far more on practical experiments to achieve such diverse ends as breeding hybrid animals, propagating new plants, 'beautifying women', 'changing metals' and 'counterfeiting gold'. In return for a 'Tablett of gold' worth £4, John offered to translate into English for William relevant passages of the text that explained how to 'lighten' or 'diminish' 'any sylver coigne in the wayght not hurting the prent therof'.[16] In short, John taught William how to extract precious metals from coins, debasing the currency without damaging the money's surface.

A 1658 English translation of the *Magia* summarises the technique:

> Some [diminish gold and silver] with *aqua fortis*, but it makes the work rough with knots and holes; you shall do it therefore thus: Strew powder of brimstone upon the work, and put a candle to it round about, or burn it under your work, by degrees it will consume by burning; strike it with a hammer on the contrary side, and the superficies will fall off, as much in quantity as you please, as you use the brimstone.[17]

Essentially the method outlined here is to spread a small amount of sulphur onto the coin's surface, heat the coin up from beneath with a candle and then, once hot, hit it against a flat surface with a hammer. The silver will have been brought to the top through the chemical reaction and will fall away when the coin is struck. It could then be collected and melted down into a lump of pure silver. Apparently William found this method to be relatively effective and started using it regularly on shillings and sixpences. This was exactly the kind of debasement that the queen and Lord Cecil were worried about, and it was illegal in the 1570s when William Bedo was taken to court.

As part of his defence, William said he had been told that the practice was all right so long as the metal being debased was Spanish. This claim might have been an attempt to appeal to the nationalist, Hispanophobic feelings of the court, as political rivalry between England and Spain was running high at the time. As part of these tensions, English privateers had taken to attacking and plundering Spanish galleons as they crossed the Atlantic, weighed down with South American silver. Although the English State officially had nothing to do with such raids, in reality it was condoned and encouraged by Elizabeth's government. Perhaps William was trying to reframe his activities as a kind of patriotism, by debasing Spanish silver rather than English coins. We don't know whether or not this tactic worked, because only the deposition records—rather than the outcome—survive. William's defence was quite weak, though, and debasement had been a serious problem for the Tudor economy for decades, so it is possible that he was severely punished.[18]

◆

Debasing coins is not really what we would think of as magic today, but it is a good example of the way that learned scholars' interests could blur the line between natural (if occult) philosophy and the supernatural. The metallurgy that John Buckley engaged in was a light-touch form of alchemy and, as previously stated, alchemy was based on a mixture of proto-scientific principles and magic. Those people who claimed to have extensive knowledge of one generally also knew about the other: Buckley's knowledge of the supposed secrets of nature gave him the skills to pursue natural experiments as well as magical ones, which puts practitioners of natural philosophy into a grey area as people who could also work with the supernatural. We see this in the way that William Bedo and Buckley first met. William sought out Buckley because he was apparently skilled at finding lost goods, and he obligingly 'cast a figure' at William's request. 'Casting a figure' could refer to drawing up a horoscope to discover the fate of the missing items or to drawing a circle and summoning a demon. It is notable that many of the practitioners employed to help a client to make money quickly fell into this liminal space of learned-man-cum-magician.

It is also clear that many of the get-rich-quick schemes on offer followed the principle that one needed to spend money to make money. This may be something to do with the dynamic between magician and client. The clients we have encountered in this chapter tended to be wealthy and powerful, from Henry Neville, who was the heir of an earl, to the monarch of the realm herself. The magicians providing the money-making services, meanwhile, tended to come from lower social echelons. All were highly educated—William Stapleton was a monk with a thorough grounding in Latin, and John Buckley was a university student at a time when a tiny proportion of the population received such schooling—but they were usually from the gentry class or lower. As we saw with Gregory Wisdom, the class difference sometimes led magicians to take advantage of the power and influence of their clients, including charging large sums for their services. This does not mean that all clients went away disappointed; again, we inevitably hear more about the failed attempts than we do about the successful ones. Nevertheless, there is a clear trend of money-making schemes requiring a sizeable initial outlay, and of people who were knowledgeable—if not wealthy themselves—providing the magic. We will explore this relationship further in the next chapter.

The principle that one should make some sort of sacrifice in return for the chance to get rich still plays into instant-wealth schemes today. Buying a lottery ticket or placing a bet—basically, any form of gambling—involves a down payment that, both emotionally and economically, invests the gambler in the transaction. There is of course a broader, practical aspect to this investment: lottery tickets rely on a minimum quota of people putting their money in, so that there is a pot to be won. Even so, magical thinking quickly creeps in. Like throwing coins into a wishing well, some may feel that the winnings are *deserved* if a sacrifice is made. And it works the other way too: perhaps this is the reason Henry Neville continued to trust Wisdom after his magic ring failed—he may have believed that by sleeping with a woman other than his wife on St Stephen's Day, his gambling losses were deserved.

Magical thinking, emotional vulnerability and a level of desperation all fed into the attempts to get rich that we have encountered in this chapter.

But they were also calculated risks, which employed supernatural aids and cutting-edge ritual practices to balance the odds in one's favour. No matter how much treasure is buried underground, the likelihood of finding some is small without a means of narrowing down the search area. Sometimes a person might simply strike gold, which was enough to give hope to others and spur them on in their own treasure-seeking pursuits.

CHAPTER 7

HOW TO GAIN A KINGDOM

KING HENRY IV WAS SPENDING THE LATE SUMMER OF 1402 AT his palace in Westminster. According to the *Collection of Chronicles and Ancient Histories of Great Britain*, written about forty years later, Henry was 'engaged in play together with many princes and barons' when he received a letter from his ally, the Duke of Orléans. Expecting friendly words and perhaps important news from the Continent, Henry ordered the herald to read out the letter before the assembled court:

> Most high and puissant prince, Henry King of England, I, Louis, by the grace of God son and brother of the King of France, Duke of Orléans . . . give you to know that by the help of God and the Blessed Trinity . . . looking at the indolence into which many noble men have fallen, descended of royal line, when they have not employed themselves in their youth in deeds of arms . . . I purpose at once to begin the business of arms, so I have undertaken to be at a day and place resolved on as well by you as by me, each accompanied on his side by a hundred knights and esquires, noble in name and arms, all gentlemen without reproach, and there we to fight fairly, one against the other till one surrenders, and the one to whom God shall give the grace of victory shall take his adversary home as his prisoner, to

do his will on him, and we will not carry anything upon us which savours of any charm or of invocation whatsoever which is forbidden by the Church, and there shall be no arrows in our said fight, but each shall help himself with his body as God has it given him . . . And now, most high and puissant lord, send me word and let me know your wishes in this affair . . . and be pleased to shorten the time of communicating your pleasure, for I suppose that you know that in all deeds of arms the shortest way is the best . . .[1]

The audience sat in stunned silence. That a sworn friend would propose raising an army to engage in deadly combat was surprising enough, but on top of this every line of the letter seemed crafted to provoke and insult. Although written in respectful language, it was clear that the Duke of Orléans was suggesting that Henry had fallen into idleness since becoming king in 1399. The specification of what weapons would be allowed in combat implied that Louis did not expect Henry to fight fair. Most provocative of all, though, was Louis' stipulation that neither charms nor invocations be used. The reference hinted darkly at a rumour spreading through political circles: that Henry had dishonourably won the English crown through magic.

Henry Bolingbroke's ascent to kingship had not been straightforward. As the grandson of Edward III, he was of royal blood, but Henry's father, John of Gaunt, was Edward's fourth son. With three older brothers and the tradition of primogeniture in place, it should have been unlikely that Gaunt's line would ever inherit the throne. However, in response to the death of Edward III's eldest son—also named Edward and known as the 'Black Prince'—the king had created an entail stipulating that only his direct male heirs might inherit. This meant that the Black Prince's son, Richard, was first in line for the crown, and indeed became King Richard II in 1377. However, according to Edward III's will, the throne would pass to Henry Bolingbroke, should Richard die heirless.

This created a somewhat strained relationship between the two men. The cousins had been born within a few months of each other in 1366, but otherwise were as different as two people could be. Henry had a reputation for military prowess, was fiercely loyal to his father and became well known for his piety after a pilgrimage to Jerusalem in 1392–3. Richard, meanwhile, was not fond of jousting, tried to disinherit his uncle John of Gaunt on numerous occasions and had a reputation for being easily swayed into making bad (and costly) decisions by his sycophantic courtiers. This latter failing led to a parliamentary coup in the 1380s, in which Richard was forced to remove his closest friends from key positions in government. Among those targeted were Michael de la Pole, the first Earl of Suffolk, who was the son of a wool merchant and was treated as an outsider by the rest of the nobility. He was accused of embezzlement, monopolising the king's time and poorly advising Richard in line with his own interests rather than those of the country. De la Pole was exiled, and others within Richard's circle were executed by the so-called Merciless Parliament of 3 February–4 June 1388.

In fairness to Richard, he had inherited the throne when only a child, and had shown admirable courage at the age of fifteen when he rode out to meet the army of the so-called Peasants' Revolt of 1381. However, he also had a vindictive streak, which meant that his rule became little short of tyrannical. When Parliament intervened once more to restrict Richard's out-of-control spending in the 1390s, he accused the Commons of committing treason and arrested and tried three of his lords for that crime in 1397. Two of the lords were exiled and one died in mysterious circumstances while in custody, but this did little to calm Richard's growing paranoia that there were plans to unseat him from the throne. Aware that his rule was increasingly unpopular after years of heavy taxation, failed wars and corrupt political machinations, he went to great lengths to try to neutralise any perceived threats to his power. It was then that Henry Bolingbroke came into the firing line. As the next but one in the line of succession, Henry was seen as the greatest threat of all, so Richard contrived a way to disinherit and exile his cousin in the winter of 1398–9.

It was during his time in exile that Henry seems to have developed serious designs on the throne. Before this, he may well have been content to remain as one of the principal lords in England, serving his king and, in time, any children that Richard might have. His ignominious removal and the company he kept while abroad, however, changed Henry's perspective. It is at this point that Louis d'Orléans enters the story. When Bolingbroke left England for France, he was welcomed and housed by King Charles VI. Relations between France and England were tense—as they often were throughout the fourteenth and fifteenth centuries—and there were political benefits to having disaffected English nobility at the French court. Louis d'Orléans, as head of the French war party, was keen to weaken England by whatever means available and saw an opportunity in Bolingbroke. He made an alliance with the exiled Henry, in which each undertook to defend and support the other against their enemies. The main purpose of the treaty was clearly to arm Henry and help him to recross the Channel to invade England. This would distract King Richard's forces and give Orléans an opportunity to seize the duchy of Aquitaine, which was at that time under English control. The historian A. L. Brown has suggested that Louis did not expect Henry to succeed in his mission—indeed, he probably counted on it being a failure, although the venture would still allow him to conquer Aquitaine. But it did not fail. Bolingbroke timed his arrival in England to coincide with Richard going on campaign in Ireland. The king took his most loyal lords with him, meaning that although England was theoretically still well defended, the country was more amenable than usual to Henry's arrival. Richard was increasingly unpopular, and Henry—equipped with his glowing reputation and the excuse that he had only returned to England to (forcibly) reclaim his rightful title as Duke of Lancaster—soon amassed a sizeable following.

The initial coup was relatively bloodless. Richard's allies were caught off guard and were quickly forced to retreat west across the country as Henry moved in from the east. Support for Richard ebbed away, and by the time the king arrived from Ireland with reinforcements, there was little to be done. Knowing that he was unable to resist Henry's army, Richard agreed to let his cousin 'assist' him in his rule. The king was captured in North Wales and taken to London, where he was imprisoned in the Tower on 2

September 1399. By the end of the month he had renounced the crown in favour of Henry.

Thus far the situation involved force of arms, battles of personalities and strategic alliances. All of this, though dramatic, cannot be labelled particularly unusual for late medieval politics, and certainly not magical. That, however, was before Richard was pronounced dead in February 1400. Although Henry would never admit it, there was little doubt among the general populace—or among historians today—that Richard was murdered on his cousin's orders. Exactly how he died, though, was open to speculation. One French account, written soon afterwards, claimed that Richard was hacked to death by a knight named Sir Piers Exton. This is almost certainly untrue: Richard's body was exhumed and examined in the nineteenth century and was found to be intact. English chronicles from the fifteenth century mostly agree that he starved to death—either by his own volition or because Henry denied him food.[2] Richard's body was exhibited in London to prove that he really was deceased and thus dissuade any plots to unseat Henry and restore his cousin. Assuming that Richard had indeed starved, he would have looked pitifully emaciated. However, there were other means to kill someone that would leave a corpse looking like that: rumours started to spread that Richard had been murdered either through poison or magic.

There were precedents for such nefarious activities. For example, a plot to murder Edward II and three of his courtiers had been discovered in the 1320s, which involved necromancers making wax dolls of their victims. The conspirators were caught before the king and his followers came to any harm, but Richard de Sowe, a local man whom the magicians used as a test case, was not so lucky—he died in agony after a nail was driven into the head of the poppet made in his image.[3] Poison in particular was regarded as a genuine threat to people in power—the roaring trade in unicorn horn and bezoars is proof enough of that—but it was also seen as cowardly, and was misogynistically interpreted as a feminine method of murder, given that it relied on secrecy and subterfuge rather than strength and courage. The covert aspect of poison, coupled with the fact that it harnessed the hidden properties of plants, animals and minerals, meant that it was also closely linked to sorcery.[4]

Whether Richard II had died through these means or through an actual spell, therefore, the end result was a strong suspicion that Henry had used magic to secure his new kingdom. Murdering anyone, let alone one's kinsman, was reprehensible behaviour. To do so through 'secret' means—at a distance and without prior warning, without allowing the victim a way to defend themselves—was utterly dishonourable. The Duke of Orléans' letter, sent two years after Richard's mysterious death, was clearly taking advantage of these rumours in order to sow unrest among the English people. It is unlikely Louis genuinely thought Henry would take up his challenge to arms, but he did not need him to: the letter's purpose was to keep alive speculation that Henry was dishonourable and cowardly, and that his right to the throne was questionable.

Henry might easily have ignored the letter if the claims were deemed sufficiently outlandish, but he did not. He responded vehemently that, having been insulted by Louis' propositions and his presumption to challenge a social superior to battle—Henry was, after all, a king now, not a friendless exile—all bonds of friendship between the pair were broken. Louis' reply dropped all pretence at cordiality, saying outright that he did not:

> approve of the manner by which you have come by [your royal title] . . . for at the time when I made the alliance above related I could never have thought that you would have done against your king what is evidently clear and what everybody knows that you have done . . . As to the consideration which you have to the dignity that you hold I do not think that divine virtue has placed you there.

These words could be interpreted as straightforward disapproval of Richard's murder, and Louis' conviction that God would not condone it. But

Louis was clearly suggesting more than this, as is shown by Henry's final response. It openly named the crime Louis accused him of:

> Certainly many people speak with their lips, and in their hearts hold and judge others to be such as they themselves are, wherefore I believe that God is all powerful to cause your sentence to turn on yourself . . . it hath pleased Him to give to us that which surely all the *sorcerers* and *devils* could have not known how or been able to give, nor all those who meddle with their arts, and, however, you may doubt it, we doubt it not, but we know and trust in God that we have entered on it through Him and His providence.[5]*

It makes clear that Henry knew perfectly well what people on either side of the Channel were saying about him: he had used the aid of sorcerers and devils to gain his position. Far from being a divinely appointed monarch, he was a usurper who might lead his country into hell.

Indeed, Henry's reign was marred by what seemed like magical setbacks thereafter. In his campaigns against the Welsh king (or rebel, depending on who you ask) Owain Glyndŵr, Henry's armies were repeatedly thwarted by extreme downpours of rain, snow, hail and wind, which seemed to appear from nowhere. Commentators at the time suggested that some 'diabolical art'—either of Glyndŵr's or of the Minorite friars who were said to be his allies—caused the storms.[6] Such events might have been seen as divine comeuppance: there would have been a kind of poetic justice if the tactics Henry used to gain the throne were also the ones that led to him losing a substantial part of his kingdom. Ultimately the Welsh uprising failed, but Glyndŵr's reputation as a powerful magician continued long into the early modern period.

---

* I enjoy the phrasing in the opening sentence of this quote. It sounds like a medieval version of the playground comeback 'I know you are, you said you are, but what am I?' and reminds me that, even in serious matters of state, dialogues could quickly become petty.

Would an aspirant noble really go so far in their pursuit of power? Most historians reject accusations of Henry's magic-use as politically motivated: a wild allegation hurled at a rival in a bid to bring them low. No doubt there is an element of truth to this. Orléans was writing in the hope that he could destabilise England's ruler, not out of concern for Henry's immortal soul (the attempt failed: France didn't regain Aquitaine for another fifty years, long after Louis' death). Likewise, the chronicles that record Glyndŵr's supernatural abilities are mostly hostile accounts. However, this does not mean the rumours were entirely fabricated. Magical assassination attempts were clearly something that medieval and early modern rulers feared, and for good reason—there were certainly enough proven attempts against their lives and crowns. Hugues Géraud, Bishop of Cahors, admitted attempting to fell the leader of western Christendom in 1317, when he confessed that he had tried to murder Pope John XXII through sorcery. One hundred years later, the Archbishop of Canterbury, Henry Chichele, ordered prayers to be said across England to counteract the 'superstitious operations of necromancers, especially such as (according to report) have lately been devised by some persons for the destruction' of King Henry V. Magic was taken seriously as a potential threat to the realm long before it became a secular crime in the sixteenth century.[7]

Louis d'Orléans was himself the victim of treasonous rumours, specifically that he wanted to kill his royal brother, Charles VI. The French king had suffered severe bouts of mental illness throughout his reign, and his subjects debated whether they might be cured by magic or caused by it. A range of magicians and necromancers were employed alongside physicians to try to heal Charles, but accusations periodically broke out that those closest to the monarch were actually trying to prolong his illness or make it worse.

Contemporary chroniclers recorded an extraordinarily detailed account of the magic performed by wizards in Louis' employ, in the village of Montjay. The rumours purported that Louis commissioned an apostate monk and others to perform necromancy that would kill Charles. The ritual involved the monk stripping off his clothes and kneeling within a magic circle in front of a ring, a sword and a dagger stuck into the earth. Apparently, after performing the required supplications, two demons dressed in green suddenly appeared in the circle, took the ring, then disappeared as quickly as they came. Half an hour later they returned with instructions. The ring, which had now turned bright red, should be placed into the mouth of a hanged man. The sword and dagger should likewise be driven into the corpse, starting at the buttocks and driving upwards towards the chest. The items would be imbued with a demonic power through this process. Once done, the ring, sword and dagger were all apparently handed over to Louis, along with a little bag of crushed bone and pubic hair harvested from the hanged man's body. Louis was told to carry these talismans on his person, which he did until a knight at the king's court publicly forced him to hand over the pouch. How exactly these items were meant to kill Charles is not specified—the confused function of the materials speaks to this being rumour rather than fact. However, there is enough corroborating evidence to suggest that Louis did indeed employ a monk to perform spells for him, and he did carry a pouch in his clothes. As the regent of France when his brother was indisposed (and possibly the lover of Queen Isabeau, Charles' wife), he had motivation enough to keep Charles sick and maybe even hasten his death in order to take the throne.[8]

Magical assassination attempts continued throughout our period. It seems that wherever there was political dissatisfaction or uncertainty about a kingdom's stability, supernatural meddling quickly became an option. Thus, during the reign of Henry VII of England, supporters of the pretender to the throne, Perkin Warbeck, commissioned a malevolent ointment to murder the king. This was in 1496, nearly a hundred years after Louis d'Orléans and Henry Bolingbroke's political intrigues: the English crown had passed through the hands of a further four monarchs and had landed on the head of the first Tudor king. Warbeck claimed to be Prince Richard, one of the ill-fated 'princes in the Tower' who had disappeared after their uncle, Richard III, took the throne. Henry ap Tudor had overthrown Richard III and claimed the crown for himself in 1485. Some of those who were unhappy about this turn of events backed Warbeck, who (if he were , truly Prince Richard) would restore the York line to the throne.

As part of this manoeuvring, a faction led by John Kendal, Lord Prior of the Knights Hospitaller in England, hatched a plan to kill the king through magic. The assassination was intended to be brutal, killing not only Henry but also his mother, children, confidants and advisers. The conspirators were going to achieve this through an ointment that would be smeared on a doorway just before Henry walked through it: as he did so, the friends accompanying him would be compelled by some irresistible force to murder him. Magicians with the skill to make such an ointment were apparently rare: some of the plotters travelled all the way to Rome to commission the astrologer who created it. By the time the envoy, Bernard de Vignolles, returned to England, both he and his co-conspirators had got cold feet, however. They disposed of the ointment and confessed everything to the king. Henry VII took a personal interest in the case—his handwriting is found at the bottom of the deposition—and although the plotters were pardoned, he obviously took the matter extremely seriously. The king knew that his young dynasty was in a precarious situation; although he had legit-imately won the crown through combat, nevertheless his connection to the royal bloodline was tenuous. If he was to retain hold of the kingdom and pass it on to his heirs, he needed to keep people onside. Appearing vengeful or tyrannical, like Richard II a century earlier, was a sure-fire way of alien-ating support and encouraging further attempts at usurpation. Leniency should not be confused with levity: Henry was being careful not to make too many enemies through wanton brutality, but he still recognised that the threats were serious.

Assassination by magic was one way of gaining a kingdom, but it was a risky, dangerous route to the throne. Creating a power vacuum at the very top did not guarantee that the right person would fill it, and if the attempt failed, then there was a good chance that the person commissioning the magic (and perhaps the practitioners too) would be executed. What's more, killing a monarch to take their throne works only if you can claim a right to be the next ruler—bloodline was an important factor. Fortunately for those without blue blood, there was another, more subtle way of gaining a kingdom: by becoming the power behind the throne.

◆

Being a royal favourite had its own hazards. The never-ending struggle to climb the social ladder meant that whoever reached the top rungs was bound to be resented by those underneath. This was especially true if the favourite was an outsider. It was even more true if they were seen to wield too much influence. This was the case with Alice Perrers. Although she was probably not of quite such a low station as was claimed by the chronicler Thomas Walsingham—who described her as the daughter of a thatcher and 'mistress of a man of Lombardy' who was 'accustomed to carry water on her own shoulders from the mill-stream'—he was probably right that she was not of noble stock.[9]

Historians believe that Alice came from a family of London goldsmiths and married a jeweller who served the royal household.[10] Despite her relatively humble origins, she transformed herself into the most powerful woman in England when she became Edward III's mistress. Their affair began in the mid-1360s, when Alice was roughly eighteen and Edward was about fifty-five. Although Edward's wife, Queen Philippa of Hainault, was still alive, this arrangement did not cause the marital strife that one might expect, and Alice's new position at court was largely accepted. Edward clearly doted on her, lavishing his lover with expensive gifts (including a selection of Philippa's jewels after her death) and giving Alice control over considerable tracts of land. More than this, Alice became confidante and adviser to the king, particularly after his queen passed away in 1369. As Edward became older, he increasingly relied on her judgement, and Alice started to act as gatekeeper between the king and his courtiers. She was extremely astute at shoring up her position: she had continued managing her husband's jewellery business after his death and understood very well how to handle money and negotiate. However, the more successful she became, the more resentment she bred among the nobles she had usurped. It seemed unreasonable to many that a woman of low birth should have so much influence over the king; to their minds, something suspicious must be going on.

The chronicles of Thomas Walsingham provide one of the more extensive—and excoriating—sources we have about Alice Perrers' life and of activities at court. Walsingham was a monk at the abbey of St Albans and has traditionally been seen as an unreliable narrator, due to his overt misogyny and his abbey's dispute with Perrers over land rights. More recent scholarship, however, suggests that although Walsingham clearly disliked Perrers on a personal level, his chronicle was broadly accurate. It is he who tells us in detail that Alice used magic to gain her position.

As was the case with many wealthy people, Alice employed a friar to act as her confessor and spiritual guide. We have seen previously that many clerics dabbled in the supernatural, either for their own sakes or for that of their clients. It appears that the Dominican friar whom Alice kept on retainer was no exception. He had 'been a long time kept in her company', according to Walsingham and, as her confessor, was privy to all her secrets. Who better to trust with the task of permanently securing her position at the king's side? The friar fashioned figures made of wax for Alice, representing herself and Edward entwined and inseparable. He also distilled certain powerful herbs 'for the sake of venality', which 'restored all strength to the weak'—meaning that it imbued Edward with an unnatural vigour and lust. The 'excessive, wanton sexual couplings' that resulted, Walsingham remarked with distaste, 'ended his life the sooner because of his excess'.[11]

Finally, to make absolutely certain that Edward remained committed to Alice, the friar made her so-called 'rings of oblivion and of memory'—items that were said to have first been created by Moses, the leader of the Israelites. The story went that Tarbis, the daughter of the King of Egypt, fell in love with Moses and begged that he would not leave her. Moses, not feeling the same way about Tarbis and possessing advanced skills in astrology, made two rings. One ring would cause the wearer to forget, while the other would ensure that the wearer would always remember. Moses gave Tarbis the ring of oblivion as a supposed love token, which made her forget all about him, whereas he kept the ring of memory for himself.[12] Alice Perrers was said to use her rings in the opposite way, ensuring that Edward would wear the ring of memory and would thus always have Alice on his mind. Walsingham does not specify what Alice used the ring of oblivion for—perhaps she slipped it on Edward's finger whenever they argued, so that he would promptly forget all about it?

By all accounts, her methods worked. Despite increasingly vocal complaints that Perrers had too much influence, including that she was meddling in affairs of state when she had no right to, Alice remained Edward's favourite until the day he died. There was a brief interval in 1376 when Edward was forced to send her away from court on the insistence of the so-called Good Parliament, but this period of exile lasted only about six months. Edward invited Alice back as soon as was politically viable, and she maintained her status in his sexual and political life until the end.

It is tempting to see Walsingham's account as nothing more than the vindictive jibes of a sniffy cleric, but I think his stories have some merit. He goes into great detail about what Alice's friar did for her, and about the precedent that existed for rings and potions of this kind. While the story of Moses is not recounted in the Bible, it nevertheless circulated in medieval Europe and was clearly taken seriously by some churchmen. Walsingham was aware of this history and, with his ecclesiastical background, he himself may have known the method of how to make such rings. What's more, a young woman like Alice Perrers, who found herself unexpectedly in the favour of one of the most powerful men in Europe, would inevitably be afraid of losing her new-found position. Even if she did not use magic to secure Edward's affections to begin with, would it really be surprising if she used spells to maintain the king's love?

Alice was not the only person at court believed to use such methods to gain control over a king. One of the factors that made Richard II so unpopular was that he elevated unworthy men to positions of power and allowed them to run rampant throughout the kingdom. We have already encountered Michael de la Pole; now let us meet Robert de Vere, the ninth Earl of Oxford. Robert was Richard's closest companion for many years, and Walsingham, ever the commentator on royal affairs, implied in his chronicles that the pair had a sexual relationship. Although same-sex acts were disapproved of by the medieval Church, this was not the issue that most commentators seem to have had with the bond between the two men. The real problem was that the king was blind to de Vere's faults, accepted his (generally poor) advice and allowed him to get away with corruption and bribery on a grand scale. When Richard made de Vere Duke of Ireland, a considerable promotion, his enemies felt that it was particularly ill deserved. Here too the king's inexplicable indulgence was suspected to have magic at its root. In one of his many passages about Robert's poor behaviour, Walsingham recorded in exasperated tones that:

> He is favoured in all these things by the King, who is unwilling to constrain him in any direction, or rather, as it is said, not being able to, because of the sorceries of a certain Friar Robert, [because of which] the king was unable to follow what is good and honourable.[13]

As with Alice Perrers, the suspicion was that de Vere's helping hand came from his household friar. Indeed, friars were frequently involved in political conspiracies in the fourteenth and fifteenth centuries. Edmund, the Earl of Kent, was tried and condemned for employing a friar as part of his bid to unseat Edward III from the throne.[14] Joan of Navarre, stepmother of King Henry V, was imprisoned for employing her confessor, Friar Randolph, to murder the king through 'sorcery and nigromancy'.[15]* Friars had dubious reputations because of their unusual level of independence. While monks

---

* Nigromancy refers to black magic here, from the Latin *nigrum*. Medieval parlance made a distinction between this and necromancy—from the Greek *necromantia*—divining by evoking or summoning the dead.

were bound to religious houses and overseen by their abbot, friars were itinerant and lived in the secular world, taking confession and performing religious services for anyone who needed them. Although they took vows of poverty and chastity, friars were difficult to control and sanction. If a friar caused problems in a community, they could simply leave: there are numerous medieval tales of friars arriving in a village, getting young women pregnant and vanishing shortly afterwards. Their reputation might explain why so many nefarious magical dealings were attributed to them, but it is unlikely to be the only reason. As we saw with Alice Perrers, confessors were held in an extraordinarily high level of trust by their employers. Confessors to nobles would normally only administer to that one person or their close family and would be privy to all their transgressions. Even more importantly, the confessor had the authority to judge the gravity of the sins and administer the necessary penance. Add to this their advanced knowledge of divinity and diabolism, and friars were in a powerful position. In return for their services, they (or any other magician on retainer) would enjoy the protection of their noble master or mistress.

What stands out in these stories, though, is that many of those accused of using magic to gain power were people judged not to deserve that influence. Indeed, rumours about magical aid dogged most low-born royal favourites throughout our period. As we touched upon in Chapter Two, when Elizabeth Woodville unexpectedly became the wife of Edward IV she was widely thought to have gained her advantageous position through spells cast by her mother, Jacquetta. Cardinal Thomas Wolsey, the son of a butcher who rose to become adviser and confidant to Henry VIII, was said to be advised by spirits under his control. Meanwhile George Villiers, who began life as the son of a minor gentleman and ended it as the Duke of Buckingham, was known beyond doubt to have a pet magician, in the notorious John Lambe. Lambe made no secret of his magical prowess: while working as a teacher at Westminster School he would sell spells to his aristocratic students, and he publicly boasted of his supernatural ability to control people's actions. When Lambe came into the employ of Villiers, Londoners openly griped about the moral corruption sitting at the heart of Britain's government. In a few short years Villiers had gone from a political nobody to becoming the favourite, first of James I and, later, of Charles I. Magic in general—and John Lambe specifically—was thought to be behind much of Villiers' success, and Lambe became known as 'the Duke's devil'.[16] Chants rang out in the streets of London voicing the people's concerns about the situation:

> Who rules the Kingdom? The King.
> Who rules the King? The Duke.
> Who rules the Duke? The Devil![17]

Not perhaps the catchiest of tunes, but the point being made is clear enough.

Because these favourites were outsiders before they rose to power, and because much of our evidence relies on contemporary rumours, historians have generally treated power-gaining magic with scepticism. The rationale is that the rumours surrounding royal favourites were little more than spiteful accusations to discredit people who were disliked. But perhaps we should think again. As we have seen throughout this book, magic pervaded pre-modern society: it was employed for everything from recovering stolen goods to restoring cashflow. The idea that it *wouldn't* be used to gain a polit- ical edge seems unlikely, therefore. Moreover, it was not just outsiders who were said to use magic for this purpose. Joan of Navarre, who tried to assas- sinate Henry V, was of royal blood and at the centre of government throughout the reigns of both her husband and her stepson. Likewise, Frances Throgmorton, whom we met in Chapter Two, enjoyed a prominent social position when she was accused of magic-use. While it is true that the rumours around unlikely royal favourites were shared more vocally, this may reflect the extent of their political influence and the importance of gossip at court more than it does the reality of spell-casting.

Many aristocrats used magic to gain favour and influence, and although such practices were technically illicit, fellow courtiers generally turned a blind eye. This might change, though, once someone's position began to wane, and political rivals started to call attention to the individual's previous deviant behaviour in order to bring them low. It is perhaps easiest to think of this in terms of a corrupt modern state: bribery and embezzlement are officially illegal, but everyone knows that they take place. If an individual becomes unpopular, though, or is seen as being too powerful, the law can be invoked to rein them in. Never mind that the accusers themselves also accept bribes—the individual under scrutiny is clearly guilty of breaking the law and is punished accordingly. The condemned royal favourites all fit into a similar pattern, in which deviant activities are indulged until they aren't.

Thomas Walsingham suggests that Alice Perrers used magic right from the outset of her relationship with Edward, which began sometime in 1364. However, her friar was only arrested for his services some twelve years later, in 1376. The arrest coincided with the Good Parliament, when Edward's own power was waning, and Alice's along with it. Her gatekeeping, acceptance of bribes and employment of magic were all used to condemn her when they had previously been tolerated. The same is true of George Villiers. Although he enjoyed protection from his enemies while his patron, Charles I, was powerful, Villiers' safety became less certain as the king lost his grip on Parliament and the country in the late 1620s. This, in turn, meant that he was less able to protect members of his own household. John Lambe, who had long been feared and disliked for his arrogance, immorality and flagrant abuse of power, now quickly became the target of the London mob. One day in 1628 he was stalked through the streets of the capital and was brutally murdered in broad daylight. His killers met no repercussions, and his patron, George Villiers, was assassinated shortly afterwards.[18]

In Villiers' case there can be no doubt that he was employing magic and astrology to maintain and extend his political influence. Whether Perrers and de Vere did the same is more difficult to ascertain, but I see little reason to doubt it. Affection magic was a well-known and powerful means of gaining influence over someone; that courtiers would use it on the king, and thus gain considerable power themselves, makes sense. As with employing sorcery to sway the monarch in a trial, they were taking risks, but in the short term—or as long as the magic worked—the rewards could be worth it. Insinuating one's way into the monarch's good graces was not the only route to gain power, though. Sometimes it was enough to wait and be prepared for when the right moment presented itself. This was the approach adopted by William Neville in the 1530s.

◆

Sir William Neville, second son of the second Baron Latimer, was young, ambitious and, according to the magician who denounced him in court in 1533, not very bright. The product of an ancient noble line that could trace its origins back almost to the Norman Conquest, William clearly expected great things for himself. Frustratingly, primogeniture dictated that his status as the second son prevented him from succeeding to his father's lands or titles. He was not particularly popular at the royal court, his personal land-holdings were relatively small, and his marriage to the widow Elizabeth Greville had brought him only a modest additional income. Something had to change if he was to gain the recognition and prestige he thought he deserved.

Unlike the other (unrelated) Neville we met in the previous chapter, William was not prepared to kill anyone to advance himself—at least, not directly. He did plot, though, to benefit from several people's deaths. According to the treason investigation in 1533, the whole affair began around Christmas time two years earlier, when William got to know a man called Nashe of Cirencester, who claimed to be skilled at telling the future.*

Nashe had good, if tasteless, news for William: his wife would shortly die. This was definitely a positive thing, he assured his new client, because once

---

* The scholar and folklorist George Lyman Kittredge wrote in the early twentieth century that William and Nashe met when the former consulted the latter over some stolen spoons. I have not been able to find a record that confirms this, but if true, it forms a pleasing link between clients of high and low birth. Like Mabel Gray, whom we met in the introduction to this book, William Neville also missed his cutlery.

widowed, William would marry 'one of Graystoke's kindred'—presumably meaning a relation of Baron Graystock, a magnate in the north of England and a substantial landowner—thus significantly elevating his status in political circles and growing his wealth, to boot.[19] Even more encouraging was that, shortly after William's remarriage and if he played his cards right, Nashe predicted that Neville would inherit his family's baronial title of Latimer. If the court testimony of Thomas Wood (we'll meet him in a minute) is to be believed, Neville was delighted at the news and not particularly troubled about the death toll that such a bright future would require. Nashe recommended that Neville visit one Richard Jones or Jonys (the spelling is inconsistent) in Oxford, who was more skilled at fortune-telling and could give further details about how it would all come about.

From Neville's confession, it seems that Jones was a scholar at Oxford University and was particularly interested in astronomy and ritual magic. A surviving letter from Jones to Thomas Cromwell, offering to make a philosopher's stone for Henry VIII, indicates that he also practised alchemy. He certainly had all the equipment. When Neville walked into Jones' chamber, he was astonished at the number of 'styllatoryes, alembykes, and odre instruments of glasse' that littered the room. Distillers and alembics were necessary but expensive tools for alchemical experiments: Jones was clearly invested in his craft. More useful to William at that moment, though, were the skills Jones employed for the conjuration of 'the four kings'.[20]

In their later testimony, neither Neville nor Jones tried to disguise the fact that the 'kings' they were summoning were demons. Neville described them as 'king devils' that Jones could 'so bind them that they shall not lie'. These devils were clearly powerful, for they took the magician on an extraordinary journey 'into a tower, and showed him there the picture of the said William Nevyll standing in a robe of velvet and a cronall [coronet] on his head'.[21] Presumably this only happened in Jones' mind—the records don't tell us that the demons physically carried Jones out of the window and into the sky—but the image the magician painted was sufficiently vivid to convince Neville that it was genuine. The picture of William standing in velvet represented, so the devil kings claimed, the future: a future in which

Neville would be the Earl of Warwick. Not quite the same as becoming king hereafter, perhaps, but assuming the rule of a significant swathe of England was more than William could otherwise hope for. Most helpfully, the devils explained how this would come about. Great change was soon to rock England—Henry VIII would travel overseas and not return. What's more, no heir would assume the throne: according to the devil kings' prophecy, the Tudor line was about to be usurped completely, either by a surviving descendant of Edward IV or by James V, king of Scotland. There would be three fierce battles fought along the length of England, during which William's older brother, John, would be killed. In the interests of safety and the continuation of the Neville family's power, it was essential that William be ready to seize Warwick Castle in the ensuing confusion. William might have told himself that, by becoming the next Earl of Warwick and taking on John's role as Baron Latimer, he was really doing the country a favour by maintaining some order and continuity during all the chaos.

William immediately started to plan his moves after the supposed upcoming battle had been lost and won. He wrote to his brother explaining why he should be exempt from fighting in the northern wars when they began, thus keeping himself away from any danger. He also set about identifying the men he would recruit to manage his estates, telling Thomas Wood that he would appoint 'Roger Wynter, John Walsh, Wm. Gower [all] gentlemen of Worcestershire, and Ric. Sheldon, to be his officers and of his council, John Morgan to be his marshal of the hall, and Thos. Wood to be master of his buckhounds and of his parks'.[22] In his deposition, Wood did not sound particularly enthused about becoming master of the buckhounds, but maybe he was keener on the position in private. None of the investigatory records detail how Neville planned to benefit directly from Henry VIII's apparently impending death, but the fact that the 'kings' claimed that either the King of the Scots or an (unknown) descendant of Edward IV would succeed him is significant. If Neville genuinely believed this prediction, then it would have been sensible to make overtures to the known quantity: James V of Scotland. Currying favour with the potential successor to the throne was standard behaviour among courtiers, and Neville clearly thought he was in possession of advance information that would secure his future, if he acted wisely.

Alongside garnering such politically sensitive knowledge, William also requested from Richard Jones a magic ring 'such as my lord Cardinal [Wolsey] had'. This request echoes wider rumours that were circulating about how Thomas Wolsey had managed to become indispensable to the king; clearly Neville wanted a share of that supernatural power. It is important to note that Neville had also witnessed the seemingly inexorable rise of the underdog Thomas Cromwell, which may have inspired him to pursue magical aid. Cromwell began his political career in Wolsey's household, where William had also been in service in his youth. William noticed that during that time Cromwell 'did haunt to the company' of an astrologer-magician 'and shortly after [there was] no man so great with my lord Cardinal as Master Cromwell was'.[23] There were claims that Cromwell used a magic ring to gain influence over Wolsey, just as the cardinal had used one to gain the confidence of the king.

What makes this case particularly compelling is that, unlike Alice Perrers or Robert de Vere, both of whom were accused of commissioning sorcery by their enemies, William was not important enough to be the victim of concerted political sabotage: no one wanted to make up such rumours. Indeed, Neville confessed to these activities of his own volition. What's more, although William was obviously envious of Cromwell's position—by 1531 Cromwell had replaced Wolsey as the king's closest adviser—he wasn't interested in bringing him down with his activities. He wanted to share in the success of Cromwell and others by using the same methods they had used. It is also a significant case because there is no doubt that Neville really did commission these spells. He admitted employing Nashe and Jones, as well as his chaplain, Edward Legh, another cunning man called Wade and Thomas Wood to practise magic for him.

William's activities might never have come to light, were it not for the fact that, in December 1532 when the investigation began, Henry VIII was in a politically unstable position. The king had formally proclaimed himself head of the Church of England the year before and had been eroding papal rights and privileges ever since. This scandalised Catholic Europe and made an enemy of Rome. The threat of excommunication hung over the king's head. If that happened, any Christian ruler would have been morally justified in invading England and deposing Henry. To compound this risk, Henry had made an enemy of Spain through his treatment of his first wife, Catherine of Aragon. As a result, the government was on high alert against potential threats to the Crown. Neville's habit of openly boasting that he would soon be rich and powerful as a result of Henry's impending death, therefore, touched a nerve. If it had not been such a fraught moment in the reign, William's activities, despite not being at all subtle, might have passed without comment.

It is worth spending some time considering the investigation itself, as it sheds light on the relationship between Neville and the wizards he employed. Four people gave testimony about the affair: William Neville, his younger brother George, Richard Jones and Thomas Wood. Wood's deposition is the most detailed of them all. Not only is he the one to list the people whom William planned to appoint when he was earl, but he also names Neville's accomplices. He details William's excitement at the idea that the king would shortly die, and how he stationed a servant in London so that he would hear the news of the monarch's death as soon as possible after it happened. Wood conceded that he had played a part in all this: it was he who explained to William how magic rings worked and sent letters on Neville's behalf to find a sorcerer with the skill to make one. Still, he did his best to distance himself, claiming that he had warned Neville about taking the prophecies seriously. He regularly stated in his deposition that Neville was a fool: all of his services to William were made in jest, and the letters he sent were 'to make pastime to laugh at'.

These claims would have been more convincing if Wood had not finished his address by offering 'to make for the King the philosopher's stone within twelve months', saying that he was 'willing to be kept in prison till it is done'.[24] Bringing up the philosopher's stone, and thereby echoing Jones' own letter to the council, would indicate that he knew very well how alchemy and natural magic worked. It seems, therefore, that both Wood and Jones were perfectly prepared to abandon their employer to his fate. Like John Lambe, their safety waned with the power of their employer. With Neville also detained and under investigation, Wood could not hope to be rescued from prison. The only option was to discredit Neville as much as possible, and make overtures to someone more powerful. While William could hope for some level of protection through his noble status and intercession from his family, Jones and Wood had to rely on their wits to secure a new patron and, with it, their liberty. It is unlikely, though, that the king took either magician up on their proposal.

As we know, Henry VIII did not die in 1532/3, and he and his heirs reigned for a further seventy years. What ultimately happened to Wood and Jones is not recorded: maybe after the political situation had become a little more stable they were released without further investigation; maybe they were exiled and ordered to leave off their conjuring. William did not become the Earl of Warwick or increase his political status. In fact there is very little record of what he did up until his death, in or before 1545. His chaplain, Edward Legh, denounced him once again for using magic in 1533, evidently trying to distance himself from William's ongoing obsession with gaining power, but otherwise William disappears from view. Neville's main mistake, other than putting his trust in soothsayers who clearly weren't up to the task, was speaking so openly about his plans. His boasting about his prospects, informing others that he would take care of them when he was earl and dispensing unsolicited advice—including not to sow crops, as they would be destroyed by war, and to keep cash ready for emergency use—all made him vulnerable to investigation for magic and treason. But we can understand why he did these things. Courtiers grouped around individuals who looked as if they were going places: advertising the fact was part of making it true. Just as broadcasting that you had visited a cunning person about stolen goods might aid in their recovery, so telling your friends that a wizard had predicted you would soon be rich might have a positive effect. It seems that magic and psychology intertwine in cases like this.

◆

Magic rings, prophecy, the power of suggestion and good old-fashioned (secret) murder: these were all ways of getting ahead in medieval and early modern political life. Because such tactics only ever came to light when they were noticed and sanctioned, we will never know the extent of their use—or how many of these attempts succeeded. How many courtiers donned special jewellery before they went for an audience with the monarch? Carrying charms on one's person was a common practice, and the so-called SATOR AREPO square was thought to have magical qualities that made the owner likeable. The square was a collection of palindromes made of anagrams of the words 'Pater Noster', which conjured the power of God to secure general good fortune:

```
S  A  T  O  R
A  R  E  P  O
T  E  N  E  T
O  P  E  R  A
R  O  T  A  S
```

How many courtiers had these letters scrawled on a slip of paper and hidden about their clothes?[25] How often did they scry the future of their social superiors or even their own family members, so that they could reap the rewards of another's fall? Certainly more than we have a record of. The court was a dangerous place where fortunes could change overnight. Being charming and indispensable to the king or his family might lead to titles, land and fabulous wealth. Having a ring that could help conversation flow more easily, or a friar who could cast spells to make the ruler well disposed towards you, might speed up your success.

Being able to predict the future was invaluable too. Not only did it offer prestige if the predictions were in your interests, but it could also deliver an early warning to get out of the way if things were about to go wrong. When Alice Perrers' friar was arrested as part of the 1376 campaign against her, one of her servants apparently jeered that the confessor should have foreseen his fate. The friar replied that he had foreseen it—just not *when* it would take place. Stories like this appeared frequently as a moral reminder that magic was not to be trusted; indeed, that it did not have all the answers. In a way, William Neville's experiences can be read like this as well: he ultimately stymied his chances at court by taking his magicians' predictions seriously. But such warnings were largely overlooked: the desire to have some knowledge or control of the future was too strong, as we will now see.

CHAPTER 8

HOW TO TELL THE FUTURE

IT WAS A RAINY NIGHT IN EARLY OCTOBER, AND COLDER
than John Crok was used to. Autumn's advance meant that the sun had set
hours ago and John was grateful for the dark. He splashed down the muddy
street in Southwark, attempting to look inconspicuous while trying just as
hard to keep his precious belongings dry. The bag he was carrying was
heavier than he had anticipated when he first took possession of the
package and he was looking forward to getting inside so that he could put
it down. He had travelled a long way over the past few days and had only
stepped off the boat back onto English soil that morning. Crok was tired,
but also exhilarated—he couldn't wait to get to work. Southwark was the
perfect location for his endeavours, a place he knew well and where no one
asked too many questions. It was a far better choice than travelling into
London, even had the gates on London Bridge been open at this time of
night. But perhaps Southwark was not as discreet as he thought: up ahead,
he found someone was barring his way. The borough's bailiff was staring
right at him, and he wanted to know what was in Crok's bag.

This is my best guess at what happened shortly before John Crok
appeared before Edward III in Westminster on 4 October 1371. He had been
arrested by the Southwark bailiff, John Typet, and Crok's bag was the main
focus of the ensuing investigation. No wonder; as the records state, it had

'the head of a dead man contained within it.'[1] When questioned about whom the head belonged to, where he had got it and, most importantly, why he carried such gruesome cargo, John replied that it was 'the head of a Saracen', that he had procured it in Toledo, Spain, and that he bought it 'in order to shut a spirit up in it so that the said spirit would answer questions'. He was also found to be carrying a certain book of 'experiments' that would help him complete his grisly project.

Surprisingly, John experienced very little in the way of reprisals for his actions. Because it was 'not found from the examination of John Crok or in any other way that he had done any deceit or evil to the king's people with the aforesaid head', he was only asked to swear on the Gospels that he would never attempt such a thing again.[2] As soon as he had done so—and promised not to act in any way that contradicted the faith of the Holy Church—he was given his liberty. The head and book, however, were confiscated and burned. The court did not look for explicit signs of remorse for desecrating a fellow human's remains: from the perspective of the justices of the peace, the only point of concern was whether any harm had been done to the public. The fact that John had intended to tell the future through complex, profane and potentially demonic means was of no particular interest. But it is of significant interest to us.

Divination, or the art of fortune-telling, is perhaps the most common of all forms of magic. Methods like the one John Crok planned to employ were relatively unusual, but the essential desire to know the future was widespread. People used divination so that they were able to plan for times of hardship or get some reassurance that things would improve; they sought it so that they might avert disaster or put themselves in the most favourable position to reap future rewards. Or they might have had their fortunes told just for the simple comfort of knowing that there was some order in the world.

We will explore a range of divination methods in this chapter, from passive observations that presaged good or bad luck, to advanced means of seeing the future in detail. We will learn that, unlike other forms of cunning magic, divination was something that could easily be done at home by non-specialists, although more knowledgeable individuals were still called on if a more comprehensive understanding was sought. And while fortune-telling is still very much part of our culture today, the origins of some of the most popular modern methods, like horoscopes and palmistry, can be traced back to the medieval period or even further.

But first let us return to John Crok and the unfortunate, unnamed man's head. This episode throws up a lot of questions. The most obvious is why John specifically sought out the head of a 'Saracen', then transported it a thousand miles before attempting to perform magic. Unfortunately, the Court of King's Bench did not seek any clarification in this respect, but we can make some educated guesses. It probably goes without saying that travelling to central Spain would have been time-consuming, expensive and difficult. Crok was English—apparently originally from Tetworth, near Cambridge—so it would have been a round trip of about 2,000 miles, undertaken both overland and by boat.[3] His profession is not specified, but it is possible that he was a merchant who travelled to the Continent regularly. Equally, he might have made the trip specifically to buy the head. Either way, the decision to make the purchase in Toledo must have been a deliberate one; it was certainly not the most convenient option.

'Saracen' was a blanket term used by medieval Christians to refer to Muslims, largely regardless of ethnicity, and Toledo had strong Islamic connections. Most of what is now Spain and Portugal had been conquered by the Umayyad Caliphate in the eighth century and remained almost exclusively under Islamic rule until the early eleventh, ruled from the Andalusian city of Córdoba. When the Caliphate of Córdoba began to decline, the so-called *Reconquista* (Reconquest) by Christian monarchs began, and in 1085 Toledo was captured by Alfonso V of Castile. By the mid-thirteenth century the area of Iberia directly under Islamic rule had been reduced to the Emirate of Granada in the far south. Despite the increasingly zealous tenor of the Reconquest, reaching a zenith in the Spanish Inquisition of the fifteenth century, some religious diversity remained in Toledo. The extensive

Arabic libraries were preserved, and the city became a cross-cultural hub of Muslims, Christians and Jews.[4] Indeed, as Arabic and Hebrew texts were translated into Castilian (a forerunner of modern Spanish) and thence into Latin, the city acted as one of the main access points for Middle Eastern knowledge to enter Christian Europe. Alongside texts on medicine, astronomy and navigation, books of magic were also translated.

It was probably here that John Crok bought the book that he was found with, but why he specifically looked for a Muslim person's head as well is a matter of conjecture. Perhaps he thought that a spirit would live more comfortably in a supposed infidel's head than in a Christian one. It was well known that invoking Christ repelled demons, so the logic extends that perhaps they might also have been repelled by a faithful Christian's remains. It could also have been a tactic to avoid repercussions: maybe Crok judged that the Christian authorities would be less likely to condemn his activities if he did not use the head of a Christian. In any case, bringing it to England from abroad meant it was impossible to trace and identify the dead person. Or it could be that the head was already prepared for magical experiments by some sort of specialist before it left Toledo. We cannot say for sure, and it remains an unusual case. I have not come across any other verifiable incidents of people trying to make a human head speak and predict the future.

Although Crok's activities are singular, there were some precedents for this method of divination. In Norse tradition, the All-Father Odin consulted the severed head of Mímir, famed for his wisdom and, according to the *Poetic Edda*, the guardian of the well of knowledge that pools under the roots of Yggdrasil (the 'world tree' that connects the nine realms and acts as the meeting place of the gods).[5] More relevant to the fourteenth-century Latin-Christian context in which John Crok was acting, Gerbert of Aurillac, who held the papal throne as Sylvester II from 999 to 1003, was widely thought to own a head cast out of bronze that could answer any question put to it. Significantly, Gerbert had studied logic in Spain before becoming Pope; tradition states that he studied in Toledo, although this seems to be a later embellishment.[6] Other great thinkers and writers purportedly gained their wisdom through miraculous talking heads, ranging from the Roman poet Virgil to the German Dominican friar Albertus Magnus (d. 1280) and the English scholar Roger Bacon (d. 1292).[7] Crok's intentions therefore aligned with some of the most impressive figures of the age.

What Crok expected to learn from his magic head is a mystery: it could have been anything from how the universe worked to whom he might marry. The latter may sound spurious for such formidable magic, but most fortune-telling was, and is, concerned with everyday questions. The mysteries of the world were of far less interest to most people than what happened in their own lives, and it was for this reason that divination was so popular. People wanted to know everything from whether their businesses would succeed to the sex of their unborn children; from when would be the best time to set out on a journey to whether their family would make it through the winter. Importing body parts from abroad or casting magical heads out of expensive metal was very much the elite end of the spectrum for answering these questions, though; most people employed much quicker and cheaper ways to get answers.

◆

The farmer took a deep, smiling breath as he looked out upon the road. He had slept well in the wayside inn and, having risen just before dawn, he was now ready to set off in the glow of the rising sun. He would arrive at the annual fair in good time, ready to sell his wares and, hopefully, bring back a healthy profit. But as he picked up his pack and stepped out, he heard something rustling in the hedgerow. Suddenly a hare shot out of the bushes, running directly across his path. The farmer swore as he watched the animal bound away, its long ears streaming down its back as it disappeared into the grass. A cloud passed over and the man let out a resigned sigh. It was clear that he would not be going to market today.

This was the kind of passive divination that most people used across medieval Europe. The idea that signs of the future were hidden in nature was widespread and led to a belief in various omens. A hare crossing one's path was thought to presage bad luck in the thirteenth century, as was meeting a monk on the road. Spotting a toad, on the other hand, was interpreted as a positive sign, as was finding an iron key or a horseshoe when out walking. The fourteenth-century monk Ranulf Higden recorded the popular belief that if a magpie landed on the roof of a house, a visitor should be expected. (This omen may be a precursor to the 'One for sorrow, two for joy' prognostication poem first recorded in the eighteenth century, which still circulates in the English-speaking world today.) Meanwhile the sound of a dog howling inside a house meant the death of an inhabitant would shortly follow.[8]

Such interpretations of everyday phenomena were not officially sanctioned by the Church. Following the writings of St Augustine of Hippo in the fifth century, most preachers adopted a naturalistic point of view. Whereas there were some clear signs of things to come in nature—heavy grey clouds signified rain, for example—there was no reasonable link between a hare going about its business and a man falling into a ditch later on. But such reasoning did not dissuade people from noting portents; indeed, there were plenty of divinatory rituals that seemed to hold an internal logic, if such a thing was required. A practice called the *sortes biblicae* involved opening the Bible at random and reading the first passage one's eyes fell upon. It was believed that through divine inspiration this passage would be relevant to the situation at hand and would impart some prophetic meaning to the reader. Virgil's *Aeneid* had been used in a similar way by ancient Romans, and the combination of pious intention and received wisdom gave this practice a level of respectability.

We encountered similar practices, including the 'sieve and shears' and 'book and key', in the context of thief-finding in Chapter One, both of which invoked God and the saints to intervene. As we saw, they seemed to answer binary questions—did Geoffrey steal my horse?—so it was natural to apply them to a range of other conundrums. One Mistress Wilcockes, from the parish of Cressing in Essex, apparently used the sieve and shears both to discover lost goods and to tell pregnant women whether they would have girls or boys.[9] In 1641 a Lancashire labourer's wife was investigated for similar activities, but she was focused on whether her clients were pregnant rather than on the pregnancy's outcome.[10] It is notable that the sieve-and-shears method was mostly employed for finding lost goods and questions about fertility, especially when the practitioners were women. Indeed, it was a particularly feminine practice, perhaps because it employed readily available domestic materials, and perhaps also because female clients were more comfortable consulting cunning women than men about their pregnancies. Still, nothing would have precluded the sieve and shears being employed for other forms of divination.

Future-telling practices were so common in the period that Church depositions rarely specify what method was used, or what the practitioner wished to find out. Instead they might merely state that the accused person practised divination or 'sortilege', and were warned not to do so again. When the records do go into greater detail, there is normally a reason—for instance, that the practitioner had achieved some notoriety, or that their magic effected an extraordinary outcome. The latter surely applies to the case of Alice Breede of Whitstable in Kent.

Alice was a dedicated mother, albeit a bit of a worrier. She had one child that we know of, possibly more, and she was keen to know what the future held for them. I'm sure parents today can sympathise with this: people want the best for their children now, as they did then. So in 1492 Alice went to a soothsayer. The child was only young and infant mortality was high: would the child survive the most dangerous years and make it into adulthood? If so, what would happen next? Would they be happy and successful in life or was there suffering ahead? The magician that Alice visited is not named, nor is it specified what kind of magic they performed. We do know, though, that Alice received the worst possible news during her consultation: she was told that the child would be hanged.[11] When and where was unclear: the soothsayer was vague about that part. But it was certainly not a future that Alice could wish for her child. She left the magician stunned and unsure what to do. Like many others, she had wished to know enough about her child's future so that she could plan for it and avert any disasters, if she could. If Alice had been told, for example, that they would be particularly vulnerable to fevers in winter, then she might have stocked up on medicines to help them survive. But protecting a child from execution seemed an impossible task.

What Alice did next must have been done out of love, desperation and the particular logic that derives from attempting to cheat fate: she decided to hang the child herself. If she were to carry out the deed, then the prophecy would be fulfilled—and, crucially, she could ensure that the hanging was not fatal. We don't know how she went about it, but we do know that, thankfully, the child survived the attempt, though there is no way of telling if the prophecy was broken in the process. It seems likely that her act was reported to the authorities by Alice's neighbours, who would have been shocked by what she had done. Yet as there was no lasting harm to her child, Alice was turned over to the ecclesiastical courts, who made her do penance for believing in soothsayers and acting on their words. Her punishment consisted of walking the streets of Canterbury, carrying the noose she had used in one hand and leading her child with the other, declaring what she had done for all to hear.[12]

Cases like this perhaps explain some of the Church's frustration with supposedly superstitious beliefs. Fortune-telling was a tricky art, and many theologians thought it particularly vulnerable to demonic interference. Alice's actions could conceivably be interpreted as a way for the Devil to claim souls. An innocent might have died in the process of the attempted hanging, and Alice herself would have been damned through the murder—the Devil would thus have claimed two victims. By extension, the soothsayer who made the prediction and drove Alice to such extreme measures could be described as an agent of Satan, whether they wittingly chose to do his deeds or not. Cautionary tales appear throughout medieval and early modern literature warning against these kinds of supernatural ploys. One *exemplum*—a morality story—replicated in several clerical texts describes how a woman heard a cuckoo call on May Day five times. As the day was a special one, the woman assumed the bird was carrying a message, and interpreted it as a warning that she had five years to live. She fell dangerously sick soon afterwards, but was so confident that she would recover and live out her five years that she refused to receive the Last Rites. Dying unshriven, with her soul still tainted by unconfessed sins, meant that the woman was left vulnerable to a longer stint in Purgatory—the fearsome liminal realm where souls were painfully purged of sin before they could enter heaven. Her foolishness might even have condemned her eternally: as she failed to die in a state of Christian grace, her soul could have ended up in hell.

Such disturbing tales were intended to dissuade people from relying on fortune-telling, and perhaps it worked on some. It is clear that no amount of ecclesiastical hand-wringing would ever fully stamp it out, though: our desire to know what is coming and to feel some semblance of control over our lives is far too great. Besides, other divining methods existed that were far more reliable and less open to meddling from demons. The movements of the heavens in particular could reveal much and, if read correctly, could be especially portentous.

◆

As with get-rich-quick schemes, astrology could be turned to for those seeking to get ahead. While capturing the power of stellar rays in magic rings was still largely experimental throughout the medieval and early modern periods, many people felt on much firmer ground when using astrology to predict the future. At its simplest, astrological fortune-telling involved observing the heavens and interpreting the unusual phenomena that appeared in the sky. One of the most famous instances of this comes from the *Anglo-Saxon Chronicle*—an extraordinary set of histories recording yearly events in England up to the eleventh century—which describes the omens that preceded an infamous raid on the abbey of Lindisfarne in 793:

> Here were dreadful forewarnings come over the land of Northumbria, and woefully terrified the people: these were amazing sheets of lightning and whirlwinds, and fiery dragons were seen flying in the sky. A great famine soon followed these signs, and shortly after in the same year, on the sixth day before the ides of January, the woeful inroads of heathen men destroyed God's church in Lindisfarne island by fierce robbery and slaughter.

The weather and 'fiery dragons' were interpreted as a sign sent from God that bad things were coming, probably as a punishment for human sin. It is sometimes suggested by modern historians that the description of fiery dragons refers to a comet, though as far as we know no comet had been passing through the sky that year (though earlier entries in the *Anglo-Saxon Chronicle* correctly record the appearance of a comet in the year 729).[13] The *Chronicle* might have been describing some sort of meteorological event or perhaps the aurora borealis.

Although comets were recognised as a part of the workings of the universe, they were still thought to carry signs of things to come. These were rarely positive. The comet of 729 was interpreted by the Venerable Bede in his *Ecclesiastical History* as warning of the bloodshed that shortly followed, including a 'terrible plague of Saracens [that] ravaged Gaul' and the deaths of both the 'holy man of God, Ecgberth' and of Osric, King of Northumbria. When Halley's Comet appeared around Easter 1066, it was similarly construed as presaging strife. The Bayeux Tapestry depicts people in England marvelling at the heavenly body, and Duke William of Normandy taking advice on whether it was a sign that he should invade the kingdom.[14]

All of these astronomical events were perceived as divine messages and they took on a further significance as the idea of stellar rays became more widespread. This concept—purporting that rays which emanated from the stars and planets had an impact on Earth—first reached Christian Europe in the thirteenth century through *De radiis stellarum*, a text attributed to the Baghdad philosopher al-Kindi (*c.* 801–873 CE).[15] The rays that hit Earth could influence people's lives, it claimed, but they could also affect the natural processes of our world. When a comet appeared in the winter of 1664 and remained visible until the following year, therefore, it was seen not just as signalling the exceptionally virulent plague epidemic that was about to ravage London, but was thought to have actually *caused* it. The theory was that the magnetic attraction of the star might have drawn noxious vapours—miasma—up from the ground, making the air toxic and unbalancing people's humoral make-up. In this sense, at least according to some thinkers, celestial portents were a particularly reliable means of divination because they were actually bringing the events about.

The complexity of the heavens allowed for much more insight than this, however. In the words of the thirteenth-century astronomer Guido Bonatti:

> All things are known to the astrologer. All that has taken place in the past, all that will happen in the future—everything is revealed to him, since he knows the effects of the heavenly motions which have been, those which are, and those which will be, and since he knows at what time they will act, and what effects they ought to produce.[16]

Guido was employed as an adviser to the Holy Roman Emperor Frederick II and, although his confidence is a little over-enthusiastic even for the period, it is a good example of how much potential some people saw in the stars. It is also important to remember that Guido was an exceptionally intelligent man with an excellent grasp of mathematics and the movement of planets. While modern readers may be sceptical of the claims he made, the logic that he applied in order to reach his conclusions was perfectly rational within the context of the knowledge available at the time.

Guido Bonatti's illustrious employers, who included the ruler of Ravenna, Guido Novello da Polenta, and Guido I da Montefeltro, Lord of Urbino, certainly put Bonatti's skills to the test. The information they sought invariably comprised predictions that had a practical application, such as when would be the best time to conduct negotiations with a rival power, or the outcome of a battle. It seems that Montefeltro in particular took Bonatti's predictions very seriously and would follow his guidance on timings for everything, from when to put on armour, to when to mount his horse. Though possibly apocryphal, one story claimed that Bonatti accurately calculated the outcome of the battle at Forlì in 1276, foretelling that Montefeltro would triumph over Giovanni d'Appia, the general who was heading the army of Pope Martin IV, but that he would be wounded in the process. Not only was Bonatti right, but Montefeltro was so confident about the prediction that he apparently sent out reports of the victory before the battle had even taken place.

Bonatti's talents—and the prognostic value of astrology more generally—extended beyond the thirteenth century. His most famous text, the *Liber Astronomicus*, was translated into various languages, including Italian, English, German and French, ending up in various ducal and royal courts across Europe. One version, which also contains extracts from other astronomical works, was gifted to Henry VII of England around 1490.[17] Whether the king personally read the text, though, is difficult to say: it is in excellent condition even today and is largely clear of the telltale glosses, or marginal annotations, which normally signify that a book was meaningfully engaged with. But not reading such works does not mean that rulers therefore ignored astrologers, as is obvious from Henry VII's grandchildren.

Elizabeth commissioned John Dee to create horoscopes for her in April 1555. At this time she was still only a princess, treading a difficult line between being the loyal younger sister to the incumbent Catholic monarch, Mary I—and heir apparent to the throne, should Mary die—and a Protestant figurehead for plots looking to unseat her sibling. It was a crucial time. In

September 1554 it was declared that Mary was pregnant with the child of her husband, Prince Philip (soon to become Philip II of Spain). Come June 1555, when the child was due to be born, there were thus four very real possibilities. If Mary and the infant survived, a Catholic succession would be secured and England would be brought into a closer alliance with Spain and the Habsburg Empire. In this scenario Elizabeth would be sidelined, dropping from the line of succession and becoming largely politically irrelevant. If Mary died in childbirth—not unlikely, given that she was thirty-eight years old and her medical experts perceived her life to be in real danger— but the child survived, new legislation passed early in the year stipulated that Philip would govern England in the child's minority. This was deeply unpopular among certain factions in England: Protestants were obviously not keen to see Catholicism triumph so completely, but some English Catholics also feared that England would never leave Habsburg control. In which case, there was the chance that a coup might be mounted, unseating the child monarch and replacing them with Elizabeth. If the child died at birth or Mary miscarried, the likelihood of another royal pregnancy seemed highly doubtful, meaning that Elizabeth would succeed her sister. The final scenario was that both Mary and the child would die, leaving Philip no foothold in England, and Elizabeth as de facto queen.

All of these options presented great risks for Elizabeth. She was in danger of assassination attempts by members of the Marian faction who wished to neutralise the Protestant threat she represented. Elizabeth also risked being implicated in plots against Mary, which would lead to her being executed for treason. Even if she got the happiest possible outcome and became queen, she needed time to shore up support in case the succession was contested. With so much at stake and with the political ground shifting like sand under her feet, is it any wonder Elizabeth commissioned horoscopes for Mary, Philip and herself?

Dee probably cast a 'questionary' horoscope, which, as the name suggests, was calculated to answer a particular query. Such horoscopes were extremely complicated but were intended to give detailed answers, unlike medical horoscopes, for example, which might only give a broad overview of one's health profile and of particularly dangerous days for bloodletting. As far as I know, the horoscopes that Dee cast have not survived, though we do have records of the large-scale investigation initiated by Mary's government, which was concerned that the predictions were part of a wider conspiracy.[18] This perhaps indicates that the horoscopes foresaw a negative outcome for the royal couple and a positive one for Elizabeth. Whether they did or not, this was not the last time Elizabeth would use such devices to predict her future. Dee was later commissioned to create a horoscope based on her coronation date, simultaneously confirming that the chosen day was an auspicious one and scrutinising whether her reign would be successful. It seems likely that John Dee predicted a long and glorious rule for Elizabeth.[19] Whether this was mere flattery or actually what he saw in the stars, in the end he turned out to be right.

Horoscopes were not only a tool for the aristocracy, though, especially not by the sixteenth century. Astrology was becoming increasingly accessible to all, through both printed almanacs and professional astrologers who would sell their services to anyone. Almanacs in particular were essential to the popularisation of astrology. These cheaply printed texts, varying in length from one sheet to dozens of pages, plotted major events of the upcoming year. The kind of information contained within varied according to what publishers assumed would be of interest for their readers. They might include anything from tide times and interesting news from abroad, to helpful home-made remedies. What underpinned almost all almanacs, though, were astrological predictions. At their simplest, this meant marking things like moon phases and solar eclipses, with commentaries about how these might affect the weather and thus when was the best time to sow crops. But they could also include detailed prognostications of the year ahead, including upcoming battles and their outcome, times of sickness, and bad or good days for business. The historian Bernard Capp estimated that by 1660 roughly 400,000 almanacs were sold each year in England, meaning that one-third of all households would have had a copy.[20] Given the culture of sharing literature and reading aloud in the seventeenth century, many people beyond the original buyers would have benefited from almanacs' wisdom. Thus knowledge about astrology would have been widespread among the population of the time. These almanacs were the precursors of the daily horoscopes that still appear in the backs of magazines and newspapers today.

Professional astrologers were also on hand to answer people's everyday questions, especially in major settlements like London and Paris. William Lilly is perhaps the most famous of astrologers active in the seventeenth century. According to his surviving case notes, between 1644 and 1666 he averaged almost 2,000 consultations a year. His clients were from all social classes and backgrounds—about one-third were female servants, but there were also several members of the nobility. They asked about everything from their fertility and marriage prospects to their future wealth, as well as more specific questions, such as where a prized possession had disappeared to. On top of these regular services, Lilly, who sided with the Parliamentarians during the Civil War that wracked the British Isles in the 1640s, used his fortune-telling skills to advise the Roundhead armies. Some of his predictions were astonishingly accurate. In his 1645 almanac, *Anglicus, Peace or No Peace*, he calculated that 'the tenth or eleventh of June may be casually unlucky to a Grandee of England [i.e. the king] . . . The Heavens frown on our Enemies a while . . . Let us totally unite, there's great reason for it, and then if we fight, a victory steals upon us [the Parliamentarians].'[21]

The Battle of Naseby was fought on 14 June 1645 and ended in a resounding victory for the Parliamentarians. This is often seen as the decisive turning point in the war, from which the Royalist cause could not recover. Lilly predicted in later publications that Charles I would be executed, which again proved true in 1649. He even foresaw the Great Plague and Great Fire that destroyed much of London in 1665 and 1666. It is no wonder, therefore, that his services were so in demand. Of course he did not always get it right. Indeed, Lilly's reputation fell considerably after the Stuart monarchy was restored in 1660, marking the end to the Commonwealth that Lilly had been certain would be a huge success. Even so, his work—and that of his Royalist rival in astrology, George Wharton—had a tangible impact on military decision-making and thus on the course of the Civil War.

While astrology still exists in the modern day, recourse to extensive predictions is now less common. Even so, most surveys conducted in the UK and North America over the past fifty years have found that at least one in five adults believes in astrology.[22] The actual figure may be much higher: the astrologer and historian Nicholas Campion has found that asking outright whether people believe in something—particularly if they know that this belief carries negative connotations—will lead to negative responses. When asked more concrete questions, such as 'Do you know your sun-sign [i.e. star-sign or birth-sign]?' or 'Do you read horoscope columns: (a) every day, (b) once a week (c), once a month, (d) never?', the proportion of people who engage with astrology in some way or other rises considerably. In one (admittedly small) survey, Campion found that 70 per cent of respondents (mostly male, between the ages of eighteen and twenty-one) 'read a horoscope column once a month and 51% valued its advice.'[23] This seems an exceptionally high percentage and may not be reflective of the UK population as a whole, but the fact that the statistics can vary so wildly is evidence in itself that we should not see astrology as a dead art.

There is also anecdotal evidence that the proportion of people using astrology and other fortune-telling methods rises during times of uncertainty. In the early months of the Covid-19 pandemic many psychics reported being busier than ever: the online business-reviews website Yelp apparently saw searches for 'Supernatural Readings' more than double in April 2020, after lockdowns had been announced across the globe.[24] The uncertainty that the pandemic triggered led many to seek answers—as to whether their loved ones would be safe, whether they would survive financially and whether their relationships could cope under the pressure. Psychics apparently saw a similar upswing in demand during the 2008 financial crash.[25] It is notable that the questions asked stay relatively consistent—they concern love, health, relationships and unexpected turns of events—but they take on a new sense of urgency when life feels out of control.

◆

Astrology is only one of many fortune-telling practices that link past prac-titioners to the present. Chiromancy, or palm-reading, dates back at least to antiquity and, like astrology, sat on the border between magic and natural philosophy. Aristotle had stated in his *Historia animalium* that it was possible to tell how long someone might live by the lines on their palm: those with lines stretching all the way across would enjoy a long life, whereas those with lines that did not reach both ends would live a short one. The Aristotelian conception of the universe dictates that the human body is a microcosm of the wider cosmos: it is composed of the same basic elements, works on the same key principles and thus reflects the state of the wider world. As such, it was possible to read someone's destiny through the clues on their bodies.

This logic extended to body parts other than hands: podoscopy and metoscopy—reading the lines on one's feet and forehead—were also prac-tised, the methods for which were explained in *Physiognomics*, a text falsely attributed to Aristotle.[26] Some proponents of chiromancy reached for biblical support to show that it was a legitimate means of fortune-telling. Exodus 13:9, for example, reads: 'And it shall be for a sign unto thee upon thine hand, and for a memorial between thine eyes, that the Lord's law may be in thy mouth: for with a strong hand hath the Lord brought thee out of Egypt.' More sceptical theologians rejected the notion that this was a reference to palm-istry, but as we saw earlier, the essential idea that God would draw signs in nature was conventional enough to allow for such an interpretation.

Despite disagreements about whether palmistry was natural or magical, divinely inspired or demonic, there is no doubt that it was popular by the early modern period. When Johannes de Indagine, a Carthusian monk in the employ of the Archbishop of Mainz in Germany, wrote a treatise on palmistry towards the end of the fifteenth century, it proved so popular that it was reprinted several times, was translated into French and continued to circulate across western Europe for a further 200 years.[27] Other guides soon followed, and palmistry took its place on the list of fortune-telling methods that the Church disapproved of.

It became even more disparaged in some quarters because the practice was closely associated with the Romani people. Called 'Gypsies' or 'Egyptians' in early modern England, due to the misconception that they originally hailed from Egypt, this much-maligned group first appeared in European chronicles in the mid-fourteenth century, with the initial reference perhaps coming from Croatia in 1362. It is possible to track Romani migrations west over the next 150 years. They appear in Germany by 1407, in France in 1418, in Spain in 1425 and in England, surprisingly late, in 1505.[28] Unfortunately many of the records we have about the Romani are external sources, most of which conjure an extremely negative view, based on prejudice and stereotype. Yet it seems clear that they were associated with fortune-telling from an early stage. We have reports that some 120 Romani stayed at La Chappelle, Saint-Denys in Paris for three weeks in 1427. Their palmistry skills were apparently so popular among the locals that the Bishop of Paris felt compelled to ban anyone from visiting them and decree that if someone was caught having their palm read, they would be excommunicated from the Church. In 1608 the English playwright Thomas Dekker wrote a scathing account of 'Egyptians', which was littered with stereotypes and was intended as a warning against trusting itinerant communities. Dekker's portrayal is unjust in most respects, but it does give us some insight into how popular Romani fortune-telling had become:

> The simple country people will come running out of their houses to gaze upon them . . . Upon days of pastime and liberty, they spread themselves in small companies amongst villages; and when young maids and bachelors . . . do flock about them, they then profess their skill in palmistry, can tell fortunes, which for the most part are infallibly true, by reason that they work upon rules, which are grounded upon certainty.[29]

The certainty they are working on, according to Dekker, is that they will tell the querent that there is misfortune on the horizon while cutting their purse—thereby fulfilling their own prophecy.

It is even more difficult to get a clear view of early modern Romani than it is of most cunning folk, as there are so few records written from a more positive, or even neutral, perspective. Nevertheless, the regular bans issued by towns against visiting 'outlandish people calling themselves Egyptians' as they passed through an area show how strong an impact they had on contemporary culture, how suspicious and unwelcoming the local authorities were (and still are today), and yet how keen people were to take advantage of their supposed occult knowledge.

Whereas palmistry performed by Romani was condemned as either magic or a deception, other kinds of the practice were held up as a noble art or even, as in the case of Richard Saunders' *Palmistry, the secrets thereof disclosed*, a 'Science'. This book, first published in 1663, runs to almost 600 pages. Alongside chiromancy, it includes directions on how to learn about a person from their face ('The Symptomes of Audaciousnesse, which is the extremity of Fortitude [include] A Cloudy lowring forehead, Long Eye brows . . . [and] The Nose long, extending near the mouth') and from their posture (if a person is 'Liberal and Benevolent' then their shoulders will be 'well compacted' and the 'Hinder part of their neck erect, goat-like').[30] How different the predictions in this lengthy book were from what more humble cunning folk were prognosticating is difficult to say for certain, but my guess is that there is very little variation.

◆

Some years ago I went to Covent Garden in London to meet a friend for dinner. I had secured funding for my PhD the week before, and I was incredibly excited to immerse myself in historical research into the world of magic. I met my friend outside the Tube station, and together we made our way to the big square outside Covent Garden Market. As we arrived I spotted, in between the market itself and St Paul's Church, a palm-reader's stall. I can't remember her name, but she had erected a temporary marquee that was open on two sides and was seated behind a table that was covered with print-outs of testimonies to her accuracy and other accolades. One framed photograph showed the fortune-teller posing with a famous statesman, clearly having just read his future. Beside that was a slightly smaller frame, sporting a sign that read: 'Long readings £7, short readings £3. NO PHOTOS.'

The queue contained at least forty people and my friend wanted to eat, but I convinced her to wait so that I could get my palm read. I was about to start my research on cunning folk, so I was curious about how consulting a palm-reader on the street today compared to the experiences of clients in the past. By the time I got to the front of the queue, the line ran most of the way around the square. I paid for the short reading, as it's hard to ask for twenty minutes of someone's time when at least a hundred pairs of eyes are impatiently waiting for you to get out of the way. I dropped my £3 in the Tupperware box and felt a quick thrill as I sat down, wondering what I was about to find out.

I have thought about that day quite often since. The reading itself was perfunctory, disappointing even: whether the palm-reader was exhausted from so many customers or aware, like I was, that she had at least another hundred to get through, she gave me short shrift and only two pieces of information, both of which were frustratingly vague. I sometimes wonder what she would have said if I had paid for the longer session; and, in my less kind moments, I question how much palmistry she actually knew. I'm not trying to suggest that modern fortune-tellers (or, indeed, those in the past) are insincere: I have had other readings that have been insightful, compassionate and astonishingly accurate. Why this particular event sticks in my mind is mostly because of the 140 or so people who waited more than an hour to receive two minutes' worth of knowledge about their past, present or future. I have no doubt that, if I had asked them, many in the line would have said they were there for a bit of a laugh. But that excuse begins to ring hollow as the numbers build and the minutes they have been standing there,

instead of seeking out a good spot for dinner, tick by. I realised that they—
we—were walking in the footsteps of thousands, if not millions, of others
who have sought answers from cunning folk.

Despite having very little in terms of magical paraphernalia, everything
about the woman and her stall projected a self-image of confidence and
no-nonsense knowledge, which told her clients that they needed her far
more than she needed them. She was in control throughout my reading,
giving the impression of genuine power and making it very clear when I had
outstayed my welcome. The image that she fashioned for herself no doubt
drew the crowds, just as much as people's desire to have their fortunes read.
We can be sure that many magicians of the past carefully stage-managed
their consultations in a similar way. As we will see in the next chapter, their
image and presence were already sculpted in the early modern period.

CHAPTER 9

HOW TO STAGE MAGIC

IN 1480, OR THEREABOUTS, THE FLEMISH ARTIST HIERONYMUS Bosch painted a work commonly known as *The Conjuror*. It is more subdued than most of Bosch's paintings, which are famed for depicting the fantastical and grotesque: chimera demons, enormous ears wielding knives, and people flying through the sky on fish all feature in his other (religiously focused) works. By comparison, *The Conjuror* is mundane. It portrays a scene in which a magician performs the 'cups and balls' trick for a crowd of onlookers, whose faces display varying levels of interest. A nun in the crowd, with her pursed lips and narrowed eyes, appears to disapprove of what she sees. A noble-woman looks a little more entertained and distracted enough by the trick to ignore the man standing beside her, clearly trying to catch her attention. A smiling man touches his companion's elbow, perhaps amused at the magician's stunt and keen to pass on his jollity. The conjuror, dressed in a floor-length red robe and sporting a tall black hat, is separated from the spectators by a wooden table upon which are placed three upturned cups, a small wand-like instrument and three metal balls. In his hand he holds a fourth ball, which has clearly just been revealed from wherever it had been hidden. At his feet sits a small dog dressed in a horned cap and a belt covered in bells, looking for all the world like a canine jester—or a demon. A hoop leans against the table, ready to be used for some other act. The central figure in the painting, though, is a man who stands open-mouthed in amazement at the trick, parodic in how far he has leaned towards the magician to get a better look. Immediately behind him stands another man, who is stealing his coin pouch.

Several messages and allegories are contained within the painting. There is a frog on the table staring up at the magician, and the hint of another climbing out of the amazed onlooker's mouth. This uncomfortable detail is clearly intentional, and it has been suggested that the frogs are intended to represent credulousness, naïvety or even heresy. The biblical Book of Revelation (16:13) describes how frogs will play a role in the run-up to Armageddon: 'And I saw three unclean spirits like frogs come out of the mouth of the dragon, and out of the mouth of the beast, and out of the mouth of the false prophet.'[1] In Flemish tradition, the frog is also linked to blasphemy. Elina Gertsman has argued that the structure of the painting, which includes an attention-grabbing orator on the right of the image and an assembled, transfixed crowd on the left, is a deliberate parody of contemporary images depicting Christ or saints performing miracles before a devout audience. If this interpretation is correct, *The Conjuror*'s message is that magicians are not to be trusted: they are a subversion of what is good and make a mockery of Christian belief.

The force of the warning, though, hinges on viewers' familiarity with the moment it captures: it can only resonate if they recognise the situation. On its least allegorical level, the painting is a street scene. Personally, I find *The Conjuror* enchanting because it encapsulates so much about the place of cunning folk and magic in pre-modern society. There is a spectrum of opinions and emotions on display, from awe to disbelief, amusement to disdain. There is the suggestion that all magic is a ruse designed to relieve the gullible of their money, but also an admission that people from all walks of life are attracted to cunning folk's skill.

This final chapter is dedicated to exploring how magicians were portrayed within their society—in art, popular entertainment and books—and the various messages that both critics and supporters of magic were trying to communicate. So far we have mostly seen what cunning folk did, but to fully understand the world in which they lived we need to look at the wider culture they inhabited too. This also seems an appropriate way of ending our journey

because it will make us think about how magic has evolved over the centuries. European perspectives inevitably changed over time: they shuttled between tolerance and fear, and magic was variously seen as a source of empowerment or form of entertainment. What was taken seriously by one generation was mocked by the next; what was seen as a useful tool by one sector of society was viewed by another as a dangerous sin. The best way to understand these contrasting views is to explore how magic was presented in popular culture of the period, where we can plainly see cunning folk, in all their ambiguity, engrained in the texture of everyday life.

◆

Magic enjoyed as constant a presence in medieval entertainment as it did in real life. People were fascinated by how it worked, what it might achieve and whether it was acceptable—the fact that you are reading this book suggests that it still holds some of that power. As in modern culture, magic did not always have to be taken seriously or treated with respect. It could be used frivolously and laughed at. Marvellous tricks that were not really magic at all, but were impressive enough to captivate their audience, were common. Magic and magicians also wormed their way into plays and stories, where they were used as a device to speak to wider issues and reveal truths about the world. But before getting into drama and stories, let us return to Bosch's painting and the tricks contained therein.

The performance of the conjuror—despite the moral message of the picture itself—is clearly meant to provide a brief moment of entertainment for the assembled crowd. Given the materials laid out before him, the magician obviously has various tricks up his sleeve. The moment captured seems to be when he has revealed where a little ball has been hiding: perhaps it was under one of the cups resting upturned on the table, or maybe it appeared in the conjuror's hand despite the fact that it *should* be under a cup. Whatever the exact trick, the general pattern is still familiar to us today: 'cups and balls' continues to be performed at magic shows around the world. Indeed it is striking how long-lived some well-known magic tricks are. In 1584 Reginald Scot, a gentleman from Kent and a notorious sceptic, published *The Discoverie of Witchcraft*. The tract is ostensibly a refutation of the power of witches and cunning folk, arguing that neither can really perform the acts attributed to them. To prove this, the *Discoverie* contains several hundred pages of spells and rituals, somewhat ironically making it one of the most comprehensive and accessible handbooks of magic ever written. Whether this was an intentional side effect of the work is debatable: Scot ridicules each of the spells he records, but there is nothing to stop a curious reader trying them out for themselves. One of his more convincing arguments about the deceptiveness of magic, though, describes several tricks and how they are done. It helpfully explains how to perform 'notable feats with one or diverse balls', showing the supposed magic to be sleight of hand:

> Laie three of foure balles before you, and as manie small candle-sticks, bolles, saltsellers, or saltseller covers, which is the best. Then

first seeme to put one ball into your left hand, and therewithall seeme to hold the same fast: then take one of the candlesticks, or anie other thing (having a hollow foot, & not being too great) and seeme to put the ball which is thought to be in your left hand, underneath the same, and so under the other candlesticks seeme to bestow the other balles . . . this doone, some charme or forme of words is comonlie used. Then take up one candlesticke with one hand and blow, saeing; Lo, you see that it is gone: & so likewise looke under ech candlesticke with like grace a[n]d words, & the beholders will wonder where they are become . . . But it will seeme wonderfull strange, if also in shewing how there remaineth nothing under an other of the candlesticks, taken up with your left hand, you leave behind you a great ball . . . the miracle will be the greater.[2]

This explanation clearly echoes the kind of trick performed in *The Conjuror* and expresses the same derision as Bosch towards anyone who is taken in by sleight of hand. The *Discoverie* goes on to 'expose' a range of other feats, including how to make a coin sink through a table, undo a knotted handkerchief using only words, burn a piece of cord and make it whole again from its ashes and 'pull laces innumerable out of your mouth, of what colour or length you list'. Scot makes it clear that most such performances are harmless, as they do not really attempt magic: they are simply mechanical and primarily mean to entertain. Such 'magic' shows, aimed at delighting and amazing an audience through artificial marvels and illusions, were popular throughout the medieval period and, as Bosch's painting intimates, were enjoyed by both the nobility and the general public.

The works of Geoffrey Chaucer give us an idea of the kinds of miraculous entertainment expected by fourteenth-century courtiers. Chaucer was fascinated by astrology and occult sciences: alchemy, physiognomy and astronomy all feature in his works. Although never quite straying fully into the supernatural, he was clearly interested in how seemingly magical items and actions worked. Sometime between 1391 and 1393 he wrote a *Treatise on the Astrolabe*—ostensibly for 'little Lewis my son', although the work is sufficiently complex to be of no use to a young child. An astrolabe is a clever instrument that can be used to calculate the position of celestial bodies in relation to the user's location. It was probably first invented in the Hellenic world around the second century BCE, then was adopted and improved in the Islamic world in the ninth or tenth century, before eventually reaching western Europe via Portugal in the eleventh century. Chaucer's treatise is largely based on Arabic sources translated into Latin, which he then penned in English and attached examples relevant to the longitude and latitude of southern Britain. Astrolabes had an extraordinary range of uses in navigation, time-keeping and astrology, some of which are enumerated in Chaucer's work.[3]

In *The Squire's Tale* Chaucer's interest in astronomy combines with his fascination with pseudo-miraculous objects. In this story, a king called Cambyuskan celebrates the twentieth year of his reign with a lavish feast. As the festivities progress, a knight suddenly rides into the banqueting hall on a fantastic brass horse. The newcomer introduces himself graciously, saying that he is an emissary of the 'kyng of Arabe and of Inde' and bears gifts for Cambyuskan. By far the most impressive is the horse itself which, 'easily and well':

> Kan in the space of o day natureel—
> This is to seyn, in foure and twenty houres—
> Wher-so yow lyst, in droghte or elles shoures,
> Beren youre body into every place
> To which youre herte wilneth for to pace,
> Withouten wem of yow, thurgh foul or fair;
> Or, if yow lyst to fleen as hye in the air
> As dooth an egle whan hym list to soore,
> This same steede shal bere yow evere moore,
> Withouten harm, til ye be ther yow leste,
> Though that ye slepen on his bak or reste.[4]

The brass horse is capable of flight, travelling at extraordinary speeds and following instructions without constant supervision from its rider.

Cambyuskan's courtiers gather around it in amazement, keen to understand how it works. One observer posits that it is like the mythic horse Pegasus, which flew on great wings; another warns that it could be a trick like the wooden horse at Troy and might contain armed soldiers. Yet another whispers to his friend that the whole thing is a lie: the horse is an illusion made 'by som magyk / As jogelours pleyen at thise feestes grete'. All these speculations are wrong, however, as the emissary eventually reveals. He tells the king that:

> whan yow list to ryden anywhere,
> Ye mooten trille [turn] a pyn, stant in his ere,
> Which I shal yow telle bitwix us two.
> Ye moote nempne [name, or tell] hym to what place also,
> Or to what contree, that yow list to ryde.
> And whan ye come ther as yow list abyde,
> Bidde hym descende, and trille another pyn,
> For therin lith th' effect of al the gyn,
> And he wol doun descende and doon youre wille,
> And in that place he wol abyde stille.
> Though al the world the contrarie hadde yswore,
> He shal nat thennes been ydrawe ne ybore [drawn or carried away].
> Or, if yow liste bidde hym thennes goon,
> Trille this pyn, and he wol vanysshe anoon
> Out of the sighte of every maner wight,
> And come agayn, be it by day or nyght,
> Whan that yow list to clepen hym ageyn
> In swich a gyse as I shal to yow seyn
> Bitwixe yow and me, and that ful soone.
> Ride whan yow list; ther is namoore to doone.[5]

Explaining how to make the horse move by turning various pegs, the emissary demonstrates that it is primarily a mechanical device. To those who do not understand the secrets of its movements, however, it seems miraculous, perhaps even demonic. Chaucer here derides the ignorance of such responses and stresses that the horse is pure artifice—even though that artifice is somewhat obscure. The horse's creator is described as someone who knew 'full many an ingenious contrivance', as well as being an observer of the constellations. While to some this would seem like magic, to Chaucer this is the harnessing of natural forces and clever craftsmanship. In his story, the lines between the supernatural and the clever-but-natural have become blurred.

Automata like the brass horse became increasingly popular throughout Europe in the later Middle Ages, and the reactions that Chaucer records accurately reflect those of people at the time. The horse itself is largely fictional of course: although some books did suggest that such things were possible through magic, fourteenth-century technology was certainly not sufficiently advanced to create super-fast flying beasts of burden. The entertainment value of the story stems from imagining that such feats were possible. Nevertheless, real mechanical marvels were a common feature of medieval and early modern courts. The castle at Hesdin in the Pas-de-Calais is perhaps most famous for its automata. Here successive lords installed increasingly elaborate displays to entertain their noble guests. Between 1291 and 1302 Count Robert II of Artois commissioned a set of mechanical monkeys that sat on a bridge in the garden, waving at passers-by. The monkeys were covered in badger fur to look more realistic, and must have been a source of wonder when visitors discovered that the creatures were not alive.

Robert's daughter expanded the project and by 1400, under the direction of Count Philip the Good, there were dozens of surprising contraptions on display throughout the castle and its grounds. There was a book that shot soot into the reader's face and a mirror that covered people in flour, pipes that sprayed water up ladies' skirts and mechanical birds that flapped about in one of the garden pavilions. Most impressive of all was a wooden statue of a hermit, which seemed to narrate the classical tale of the Golden Fleece. As the story ended, the listeners were treated to an indoor thunderstorm that would leave them drenched and terrified, offering a taste of what it must have been like to be travelling with Jason and his Argonauts.[6] Similar marvels graced other noble houses in Europe. Pope Leo X, for example, commissioned a mechanical lion to be made by Leonardo da Vinci as a gift for Francis I of France in 1515. The lion was apparently able to walk over to the new king and present an array of lilies from its chest.

While none of these devices was actually magical, some of the tricks they played were clever enough to make people wonder whether they could solely be artifice. Indeed, the craftsmen behind the creations often gained reputations as magicians: reputations that some—like the fifteenth-century engineers Giovanni Fontana and Conrad Keyser—actively encouraged. Unable to fathom how the mechanisms on some of their contraptions worked, people assumed they had conjured demons and trapped them inside the devices to make them move.[7] This uncertainty continued into the sixteenth century, when John Dee (who, as we have seen, did regularly dabble in magic) terrified the scholars at Trinity College, Oxford with the appearance of an enormous scarab beetle. It was part of a production of the Greek playwright Aristophanes' *Peace*, and appeared to fly up the walls of the college courtyard all the way 'to Jupiter's palace, with a man and his basket of victuals on her back'.[8] This feat was only an illusion achieved through the clever use of pulleys and mirrors, although Dee later blamed the performance for his negative reputation as a conjuror.

◆

While shows exhibiting automata had a limited audience, stories containing magic and magical practitioners were far more widespread. What is most fascinating about these stories, though, is that they evolved in tandem with changing social attitudes towards the supernatural. Whereas in the medieval period the use of magic did not attract too much moral indignation, by the later sixteenth century even the most light-hearted of entertainments were bogged down by ethical and theological questions. Medieval legends of King Arthur, which originated in the historically Celtic lands of Brittany, Wales and Cornwall before being popularised at the English and French royal courts, were riddled with magic of various kinds. It is striking that in these tales magic-use largely comes across as morally neutral: it is the intention of the practitioner that makes them good or bad and not their knowledge of the occult.

This point is perhaps most obvious in Merlin, the cunning-man-cum-service-magician (even if he is never named as such) who uses his extraordinary powers to support and advise Arthur. Explanations of how he got his powers and what he used them for differ in the tales that have survived. One of the earliest mentions of Merlin appears in Geoffrey of Monmouth's *Historia Regum Brittaniae* (*History of the Kings of Britain*), written in the twelfth century. Geoffrey portrays Merlin as the son of a mortal noblewoman and an incubus demon, which, one might assume, would condemn him to be at best a trickster and, at worst, evil. Although his preternatural origins imbue Merlin with gifts of prophecy and magic, the piety of his mother—who is described as a 'nun at the church of St Peter'—draws Merlin away from the dark path and towards using his abilities for good.[9] Geoffrey, despite being a trained cleric, apparently did not see magical power (even if it was derived from demons) as a barrier to being a good person.

We see this attitude applied in other Arthurian legends too. The character of Morgen—variously named Morgana, Morgause and Morgan le Fay, depending on the story version in which she appears—is morally ambiguous. In Geoffrey of Monmouth's *Vita Merlini* she is described as a powerful healer who can shapeshift and fly through the sky on strange wings. She lives on the Island of Apples (Avalon) with her eight sisters, who together rule the isle and practise astrology. Morgen is tasked with caring for the mortally wounded Arthur, and her magical abilities are treated as a positive because she does good things with them. Later versions of the legend paint Morgen in a much poorer light, however. In the fifteenth-century *Le Morte Darthur* by Thomas Malory she is described as having learned magic and *nigromancie* (black magic) in the nunnery where she was raised, and she frequently attempts murder through her arts. Even in Malory's telling, though, it is not the fact that she practises magic that makes her bad. Another female magician, Nenyve (named Nimuë or Vivian in other versions), is as powerful and skilled at magic as Morgen, if not more so, but she is overwhelmingly a positive force in *Le Morte Darthur*.[10] Nenyve learns her spells from Merlin and, though she eventually traps her teacher under a boulder where he is doomed to spend the rest of eternity, she does so in response to his aggressive sexual advances. Once Merlin is trapped, Nenyve takes on his role as royal adviser to Arthur and ultimately guides him far more wisely than Merlin ever did. In Morgen's case, it is not simply possession of magical abilities that makes her bad. Unlike Nenyve, Morgen is a bad *person*, who is driven more by self-interest and jealousy than by compassion or wisdom. But while she uses her powers for evil, it is not the power itself that corrupts her.

Scholars have noted that up until the fifteenth century magic is largely portrayed as morally neutral: it is seen primarily as just another practical tool to further people's desires and ambitions.[11] Whether or not those ambitions are honourable does not reflect the magic employed to achieve them. Medieval romances in particular offer a window into what people from across the social spectrum thought about cunning folk and other magical practitioners. Scholars still debate who they were composed for. Geoffrey of Monmouth wrote in Latin, so his stories would have been read only by a select few, but Malory's *Le Morte Darthur*, written in English, must have reached a much wider audience. Published in 1485, it was one of the first books to be printed in England (rather than circulating in handwritten copies) and remained in print for the next hundred years.

Works like the *lais* of Marie de France, meanwhile, were clearly meant to entertain the aristocracy. A poet living in the twelfth century, Marie de France may have been patronised by Henry II of England. Her *lais* are short, rhyming tales, mostly about love lost and found, and often include fantastical elements such as werewolves and men who can shapeshift into birds. The stories are probably not her invention, but—like the Arthurian legends from Wales and Cornwall—would have been part of a long Breton oral tradition. They would have circulated in different versions at all levels of society, as popular around humble firesides as they were in the great halls of knights and lords. The written versions that have survived will only ever be a snapshot: they are merely one performance caught in time. They may or may not be reflective of the wider story-telling tradition of the Middle Ages; whether people lower down the social strata would have adopted the same position towards the magic in these stories is largely unknown. But given the widespread recourse to cunning folk in general, we can guess that many of the retellings would have viewed such magic in a positive light.

The same overlap between courtly and popular entertainment is evident in the works of Geoffrey Chaucer. The son of a successful London vintner, Chaucer worked as a clerk and emissary to the royal court. He conducted diplomatic missions to Italy on behalf of Edward III and was patronised by both Edward and his successor, Richard II. *The Canterbury Tales* contain a smorgasbord of stories drawn from such diverse sources as the works of Giovanni Boccaccio and Petrarch, the lives of saints and Arthurian legends. Many of these stories would have had folk variants, and the diverse social make-up of the Canterbury pilgrims demonstrates a wide range of views on medieval life.

As you might expect, practical magic appears in several of the *Tales*. One of my favourite stories is that of the Franklin, about the relationship between the Breton knight Arveragus and his wife Dorigen. The couple love each other deeply but, as is the way of the medieval military classes, Arveragus has to leave for Britain to prove himself in arms, and Dorigen is left at home. She becomes obsessed with the sharp rocks that wrap around the coast of Brittany, convinced that Arveragus' ship will be wrecked on them as he tries to return to her. Meanwhile a squire named Aurelius lusts after Dorigen and tries to make her sleep with him. Dorigen, who is committed to staying faithful to Arveragus but is also concerned about making an enemy, sets Aurelius a seemingly impossible task: if he can remove all the rocks from the coastline, she vows that she will be his. Eager to possess her, Aurelius seeks out a magician. A young clerk claims that he is able to perform the miraculous feat required, but in return Aurelius has to pay the extortionate fee of one thousand pounds. The squire agrees, and the magician gets to work. Using the power of astrology, the clerk raises the sea level until the rocks have entirely disappeared. Dorigen is devastated, trapped by a promise she never expected to have to honour.

At this point in the story it is clear that service magicians are bad news. Not only has the sorcerer done a trick that will ruin a loving couple's relationship, but he is so avaricious that his fee will bankrupt his client. However, this is where the story turns. Aurelius—so far portrayed as callous, reckless and unfeeling towards the woman who clearly wants nothing to do with him—finally realises that his desire is not shared by Dorigen. He begins to feel ashamed of his actions and releases her from her vow, before turning his attention to how he will repay the magician. On visiting the cunning man and relating the whole affair to him, the magician in turn begins to feel sorry and agrees to waive his fee. The tale concludes with the question: 'which was the mooste fre [generous or noble], as thynketh yow?'

The Franklin's Tale is not particularly romantic by modern standards. For the fourteenth century, though, it is quite striking in terms of the agency it grants to its female protagonist and its ultimate message that anyone can be kind and noble. What's more, it's not the magic itself that is at fault: it is what Aurelius intends to do with it that makes it problematic.

◆

Such a relaxed attitude towards magic becomes much rarer in the sixteenth and seventeenth centuries, as we can see from the way it is presented on the London stage. This does not mean that portrayals of magicians were overwhelmingly negative: not every play was as pessimistic as William Shakespeare's *Macbeth*, with its 'secret, black, and midnight hags', or Christopher Marlowe's *Doctor Faustus*. What most playwrights deemed necessary, though, was to express a range of views on whether someone who practised magic really could be good, or whether they must, through the very fact of dabbling with supernatural forces, necessarily be evil.

The ambiguous portrayal of cunning folk in the plays that I focus on here is likely a pragmatic decision on the part of the authors. They were writing between 1580 and 1610, a time when witch trials in England were reaching their peak. Public interest in the power of witches and other magical practitioners was therefore high, fuelled both by fear and a penchant for sensationalist entertainment. Playwrights were catering to a diverse, primarily London-based audience who carried differing views on practical magic. Some theatre-goers would have visited cunning folk in the past, and so outright mockery of magicians and those who employed them would risk alienating parts of the audience. At the same time, others would see cunning magic as charlatanry at best, and at worst as a collaboration with the Devil akin to that brokered by witches. For them, a performance that unequivocally portrayed cunning folk in a positive light would be just as alienating. A play's success or failure depended entirely on the audience's approval: if theatre-goers rejected it at its premiere, it was unlikely ever to be performed again—at least without a substantial rewrite. That most plays involving cunning folk present both sides of the argument about the acceptability of magic, therefore, suggests that this was a necessary concession in order to please the punters.

Although the works of Shakespeare and Marlowe now dominate our conception of early modern drama, in their own time they were just two of many playwrights catering to a mass audience who craved entertainment. Hundreds of plays were written during the later sixteenth and early seventeenth centuries, and dozens of them featured magic as a plot device. I'm going to focus on two works here, which were written around the time that Shakespeare was at his most active and which, more importantly, placed cunning folk centre stage. John Lyly's *Mother Bombie* (*c.* 1594) and Thomas Heywood's *The Wise Woman of Hogsdon* (*c.* 1604) were both very successful dramas, performed 'sundry times' in London and perhaps elsewhere, and later printed for people to read and possibly perform at home.[12] The plays engage with questions about how cunning folk operated, whether they possessed the powers they claimed, and whether they were a force for social good or ill. Exploring these plays in more detail gives us an insight into what people thought about service magicians, as the works lay out some of the conflicting attitudes and ongoing debates surrounding sorcery.

Both plays are light-hearted romantic comedies. There are confused identities and conflicting love interests, foolish neighbours and clownish servants, and a big reveal at the close, which results in a happy ending. What sets them apart is that all the characters coalesce around the cunning folk who give the plays their titles. Mother Bombie is a shy, gentle woman, clearly drawn from real life, who is constantly helping her neighbours to solve problems, ranging from a maidservant who has lost a silver spoon to a gentleman's daughter who wants a palm-reading. The Wise Woman of Hogsdon (she is never given an actual name) similarly matches reality, though she is far more bombastic and devious than Bombie. She lives in a house in Hogsdon, a village just north of London that was once popular with day-trippers craving some countryside. She takes advantage of her discreet yet convenient location close to the city to offer a range of services, such as advising a man on whether he will win the woman he loves, and a woman on how many husbands she will have. But she caters to other social needs too, including taking in expectant mothers and quietly finding a home for their illegitimate children once they are born. There is also a hint that she runs a brothel.*

Despite choosing similar material to work with, the playwrights clearly differ in their feelings towards cunning folk. John Lyly's Mother Bombie speaks cryptically but always accurately and honestly. She has her clients' best interests at heart and obviously wishes to avoid any unnecessary meddling in their affairs. It is a largely kind portrayal, highlighting the goodness and homeliness of magical practitioners. Thomas Heywood, meanwhile, strikes a sceptical tone. He calls the Wise Woman's decency and authenticity into question, going to some lengths to stress that, while there may be cunning folk practising all over London, most of them are frauds. Heywood inserts speeches that, like Reginald Scot in his *Discoverie of Witchcraft*, expose the purported tricks that magicians used to con their

---

* Such details are not something that we have a record of among real cunning folk in England, though some interesting research into Italian everyday magic shows that sex workers often sold spells to supplement their income. See Guido Ruggiero, *Binding Passions: Tales of Magic, Marriage, and Power at the End of the Renaissance* (New York: Oxford University Press, 1993). The Wise Woman's fortune-telling services, like those of Mother Bombie, are therefore intended to reflect the activities of real-life magicians and express opinions about who they are and what they do.

patrons. In the following exchange, for example, the Wise Woman explains the secret of her preternatural foreknowledge of her clients' questions:

LUCE: But wherefore have you built this little closet close to the doore, where sitting, you may heare every word spoken, by all such as aske for you.

WISEWOMAN: True, and therefore I built it: if any knock, you must to the doore and question them, to find what they come about, if to this purpose, or to that. Now they ignorantly telling thee their errand, which I sitting in my Closet, overheare, presently come forth, and tell them the cause of their comming, with every word that hath past betwixt you in private: which they admiring, and thinking it to be miraculous, by their report I become thus famous.[13]

This admission occurs early in the play, between several interactions in which other characters accuse the Wise Woman of being a charlatan and a witch. From all of this we can assume that either Heywood held negative feelings towards cunning folk or—and this seems more likely to me—that he was trying to capture the prevalent attitude of his London audience. Having got the sceptics onside, though, the messaging becomes more nuanced as the play progresses. The characters who berate the Wise Woman most severely are portrayed as bad people themselves—most notably the scoundrel Chartley, who is a serial seducer of local virgins and physically beats the Wise Woman. Meanwhile, other more prudent and pure-hearted figures behave respectfully towards the Wise Woman and defend her against the aspersions cast against her by people like Chartley. Furthermore, though the Wise Woman is self-professedly a fraud, she nevertheless manages to help her clients. By the end of the play she has been able, through her various schemes, to resolve all the problems brought to her; and she even ensures that the villains of the piece (most notably Chartley) receive their just deserts. The play ends with the lines: 'Nay, mother midnight, there's some love for you. Out of thy folly, being reputed wise, We, self-conceited, have our follies found.' Its message seems to be that, although there is some scepticism about the ethics of magic and the character of the people who practise it, ultimately they are a force for good in society.

Despite approaching cunning women from a different angle, *Mother Bombie* exhibits a similar uncertainty about whether or not magical practitioners are to be trusted. As with the Wise Woman in Hogsdon, Bombie is visited by a range of clients, from high-born gentlefolk to servants. Sober, sensible characters in the play trust her advice as much as the foolish ones—only the really foolish ignore her words at their peril. Although Lyly is warmer towards cunning folk than Heywood overall, Mother Bombie's clients are portrayed as being unsure whether she is a benevolent force or a malevolent witch. The servants who visit her show a mixture of fear and respect, declaring that Bombie is 'cunning in all things' as they make their way to her house, but as soon as she opens the door they start back, crying, 'Crosse yourselves, looke how she looks. Marke her not, sheele turne us all to Apes.'[14] It seems that the benevolent cunning woman has become a malevolent witch.

That switch can also be detected in another strand of the play. At the outset a character named Serena praises Bombie for her services: 'They say there is hard by an olde cunning woman, who can tell fortunes, expound dreames, tell of things that be lost, and divine of accidents to come, shee is called the good woman, who yet never did hurt.'[15] Her brother Maestius is hesitant, as he suspects that using magic ultimately involves consorting with demons. Serena rejects his arguments and persists in defending the magician, but quickly changes her tune when she hears Bombie's predictions. Bombie prophesies that brother and sister will marry the next day 'by the lawes of God, nature and the land'—something that is surely impossible, and certainly not legal. In response, Serena rails that:

> These doggrell rimes and obscure words, comming out of the mouth
> of such a weather-beaten witch, are thought divinations of some
> holy spirit, being but dreams of decayed brains: for mine owne part,
> I would thou mightest sit on that stoole, till he and I marrie by lawe.

In Serena's mind, Bombie has turned from a wise and well-meaning woman into a witch. She now wishes to see the cunning woman punished for her activities and rejects the idea that her power comes from God. She begins to agree with Maestius that people like Bombie are 'olde hags', whose 'olde lawes . . . are but false fires to leade one out of a plaine path into a deepe pit'.[16] The latter assertion was a long-standing clerical belief dating back to the medieval period: that if people put their faith in magic, they would turn away from God and thus end up in hell. That Bombie is also accused of being a malevolent 'hag', however, demonstrates a changing attitude towards cunning folk in the later sixteenth century. While in earlier periods magic wasn't condemned unless it caused harm, by the time Lyly was writing, English culture had blurred the lines between cunning woman and witch.

As we saw in Chapter Four, it was extremely rare for English cunning folk to be formally accused of witchcraft, and even less common that they would stand trial for it. Even so, scenes like this reveal an ongoing debate about the threat that cunning folk posed, and increasing uncertainty about whether a line could be drawn between benevolent magic and malevolent witchcraft.* Mother Bombie seems to be aware of this danger: when not undertaking predictions for her clients, most of her lines in the play are devoted to defending her actions. When another client called Silena states, 'they say you are a witch', Bombie replies, 'They lie, I am a cunning woman.' When offered payment for her services, she refuses, asking instead that her customers spread 'good words' about her and 'raile not if I tell true', recognising that people do not always want to know the truth. It seems that she needs all the support she can get, as a cunning woman in an increasingly hostile environment.

Shakespeare too participates in the debate playing out in theatres, most notably in *The Merry Wives of Windsor* (1602). In one scene, the

---

* Despite representing both sides, Lyly ultimately shows that Mother Bombie was right in her predictions. It is discovered at the end of the play that Serena and Maestius were swapped at birth, meaning that they are not really brother and sister and are therefore free to marry one another as they wish.

philandering knight John Falstaff dresses up as the 'wise woman of Brentford' so that he can escape the jealous husband of one Mrs Ford. The scene is obviously played for laughs: Falstaff is a comic antihero behaving badly and is regularly tricked and beaten throughout the play as his seduction attempts are thwarted. Even so, the way that Falstaff is treated when dressed as a wise woman is revealing. Mr Ford flies into a rage as soon as he sees 'her', shouting:

> A witch, a quean, an old cozening quean! Have I not forbid her my house? We are simple men; we do not know what's brought to pass under the profession of fortune-telling. She works by charms, by spells, by the figure, and such dauber as this is, beyond our element: we know nothing. Come down, you witch, you hag you, come down I say!

Falstaff is then beaten and thrown out of the house. Mr Ford is clearly of the same mind as Maestius (and later Serena) from *Mother Bombie*: that cunning folk are only one step away from witches and not to be trusted. Other characters are less convinced, however. Mrs Ford is in fact the niece of the real wise woman of Brentford and regularly invites her in, when Mr Ford is away. Likewise, as Falstaff is tripping back to his lodgings still dressed in female attire, he is followed home by the servant of a potential client. The servant pursues Falstaff down the street to ask after the whereabouts of a stolen gold chain and whether his master will marry the woman he wants. Thus Shakespeare too displays the ambiguity towards magic that we saw in the other plays. Although officially cunning folk were meant to be avoided, given that Mr Ford is portrayed as an overly jealous man who often makes emotional rather than rational decisions, it is debatable which attitude towards cunning folk represents the right one.

◆

The intended audience of these plays had clearly not made up their minds about cunning folk. There is much more consistent messaging, though, about gender difference in magical practitioners. Whereas the two cunning women and the dressed-up Falstaff are sometimes conflated with witches, this is not the case with the cunning men who feature in early modern drama. Although male service magicians take on a similar role in plays— they are the means through which love triangles and humorous situations are resolved—they are portrayed as scholarly figures instead of hag-like witches. *The Merry Devil of Edmonton* (*c.* 1600) revolves around the wizard Peter Fabell, and the anonymous author deliberately parodies Christopher Marlowe's *Doctor Faustus* when introducing him. The play's opening scene mimics the final one of *Doctor Faustus*, with a demon arriving to drag the magician's soul down to hell. Unlike Faustus, though, who is trapped by the contract he made with the spirit Mephistopheles, Fabell manages to bully his indentured demon into granting him another seven years on Earth. It is a light-hearted take on a grave subject, but it also exposes cultural ideas about male magicians.

While the Wise Woman of Hogsdon and Mother Bombie are shown as largely illiterate, poor and are suspected to be witches (and thus slaves of the Devil), Fabell is highly educated, wealthy and able to outwit demons. He is a graduate of Cambridge University and is not feared by his neighbours and friends—of which he has many, most of whom are members of the nobility—who gratefully turn to him for help. Even so, he turns out to be a powerful trickster. Fabell claims the ability to draw down mists and raise floods (typical witch-like behaviour) and at one point vows to send 'fellows of a handful high' into a convent to 'make the lady prioress of the house to play at leap-frog, naked in their smocks, until the merry wenches at their mass cry teehee weehee; and tickling these mad lasses in their flanks, shall sprawl, and squeak, and pinch their fellow nuns'.[17] Given that the play was written during a period when England was fairly firmly Protestant and anti-Catholic feeling was at its peak, the play's audience would have been amused by the idea that nuns were susceptible to demons and might easily break their vows of chastity. Even so, the powers attributed to Fabell are ostensibly dangerous ones, which should invite censure. In fact he behaves much more like a witch than either the Wise Woman of Hogsdon or Mother Bombie.

Nevertheless, he is treated with respect and is consistently seen as a ritual magician rather than a malevolent witch.

The same is true of Robert Greene's *Frier Bacon and Frier Bungay* (*c.* 1589).[18] Roger Bacon was a real person, who lived during the thirteenth century and studied at the universities of Oxford and Paris, where he took a great interest in natural philosophy. His experiments in occult forces earned him the title of 'Doctor Mirabilis' after his death, and by the sixteenth century he had an established reputation as an exceptionally learned magus. Greene's play leans into this reputation, depicting Bacon as capable of all kinds of feats. These include being able to see what someone is doing by spying on them through a looking glass, transporting people hundreds of miles in an instant and, most famously, creating a brazen (or brass) head that would answer any question put to it. Despite being written only five years before *Mother Bombie* and being directed at the same audience, Bacon does not face the same fear and critique as the cunning woman. Instead he is lauded by the play's other characters as the best magician in England, who is patronised by Henry III and even enjoined by the king to test his wits against Vandermast, the court magician to the Holy Roman Emperor. It is true that by the end of the play Bacon discovers the error of his ways and renounces his occult practices, so Greene does not wholeheartedly condone Bacon and other practitioners like him. Even so, it is striking how differently male and female magicians are portrayed in these plays. Although most cunning folk were not treated as witches in real life, there was clearly a growing perception in the sixteenth and early seventeenth centuries that cunning women bordered on witchcraft, while cunning men belonged to an intellectual elite.

◆

These plays therefore presented different sides of the debate about magic's acceptability. In doing so, they may have provided an avenue for people to express their concerns and work through them. Most of all, they gave the audience an opportunity to laugh. Laughter is excellent for releasing tension and dispelling anxiety, and presenting comedic versions of cunning folk and their clients onstage invited the audience to make fun both of their fears and, perhaps, of themselves. All the forms of entertainment that we've seen in this chapter—from Hieronymous Bosch's painting to the Arthurian legends, from Geoffrey Chaucer's automata to London plays—served a social function as people grappled with the world in which they lived. Stories help us to make sense of the world and explore ethical, metaphysical and social questions in a safe, theoretical space. The various stories we've encountered here show how English society navigated changing attitudes towards magic over our period. Sometimes it was viewed as a helpful and benevolent force, sometimes as dark and harmful, but most often as somewhere between the two. No matter how widely perspectives varied, though, there is one thing that stayed consistent: practical magic continued to play an important part in people's lives.

CONCLUSION

'All right,' said Susan. 'I'm not stupid. You're saying humans need . . . fantasies to make life bearable.'

REALLY? AS IF IT WAS SOME KIND OF PINK PILL? NO. HUMANS NEED FANTASY TO BE HUMAN. TO BE THE PLACE WHERE THE FALLING ANGEL MEETS THE RISING APE.

'Tooth fairies? Hogfathers? Little—'

YES. AS PRACTICE. YOU HAVE TO START OUT LEARNING TO BELIEVE THE LITTLE LIES.

'So we can believe the big ones?'

YES. JUSTICE. MERCY. DUTY. THAT SORT OF THING.

'They're not the same at all!'

YOU THINK SO? THEN TAKE THE UNIVERSE AND GRIND IT DOWN TO THE FINEST POWDER AND SIEVE IT THROUGH THE FINEST SIEVE AND THEN SHOW ME ONE ATOM OF JUSTICE, ONE MOLECULE OF MERCY. AND YET— Death waved a hand. AND YET YOU ACT AS IF THERE IS SOME IDEAL ORDER IN THE WORLD, AS IF THERE IS SOME . . . SOME RIGHTNESS IN THE UNIVERSE BY WHICH IT MAY BE JUDGED.

'Yes, but people have got to believe that, or what's the *point*—'

MY POINT EXACTLY.[1]

—TERRY PRATCHETT, *HOGFATHER*

DOES THE WORLD STILL NEED MAGIC? THE MODERN ERA WAS once heralded as a time of enlightened, rational thought, free from the superstitions of our ancestors.[2] As we reach the end of our journey, there is no point in trying to deny that our forebears believed in magic. But we can, I hope, challenge the idea that their behaviour was irrational. We can also, I think, question whether there is no place for magic in our lives today.

Throughout this book we have seen people from all walks of life face difficult situations: Elizabeth Wryte, who was forced to look on helplessly while her baby girl sickened; Frances Throgmorton, who was trapped in an unhappy and violent marriage; the monk William Stapleton, who hated the vocation that he might have been stuck in for life. The infrastructure and rules that governed their society meant there were few people who could help them; it would be no surprise if they, like many of those we have met in this book, despaired at times. But instead of succumbing to the hopelessness they felt, they turned to magic—and, in doing so, they chose to hope.

If we are honest with ourselves, how different are we today? Times have changed of course—for example, modern medicine means that we live longer, healthier lives overall, and most countries have at least a basic welfare system. Even so, we still regularly find ourselves in situations that are out of our control. We confront these moments every day: on a personal level, when we grapple with our careers or fall helplessly in love; and on a larger scale, when we are faced with war, pandemics or that greatest of modern existential threats, climate change. It is normal to want to manage our own lives, and it is fundamentally human to hope that there is something bigger than ourselves to which we can turn when things go wrong. For some, that means religion; for others, it is a belief in the goodness of humanity. For many, there is a belief (often barely acknowledged) that there is some intangible power in the universe that we may be able to tap into, and which we might call magic.

In preparation for writing this conclusion, I sent a short message to friends, family and acquaintances. I asked, 'Do you believe in magic, and what role does it play in your day-to-day life?' Some replied with an outright no, others with a firm yes, but most were reticent: they began with a cautious

'What do you mean by "magic" . . . ?' before developing a fuller answer. When I defined magic in its broadest sense—performing actions that, through intangible means, affect the world around us—almost everyone conceded that they had practised magic at some point. One friend, who is in all other ways the staunchest empiricist I know, told me that she taps her fingers in a rhythm as she walks home at night, comforting herself that if she gets the pattern right, then she will arrive at her door safely. Another friend eloquently summarised his relationship with magical thought:

> I think in one way or another most people engage in magical thought on a daily basis. Every time we wish or shy away from an idea because it seems to carry bad luck with it, we engage in the smallest of magical practices. [. . .]
>
> How did you feel or think before your driving test, before an exam, before asking out someone you really liked? There's that little bit that clings on to the hope that somehow your feet are going to pick just the right path to that reality.
>
> Those are perhaps the most relatable examples. But the magic taught by stories permeates the way I behave: I feel uncomfortable being named by anyone except my nearest and dearest; I prefer to voice a nightmare because I struggle to shake the sense it might come to pass in some way, if I don't; and sometimes I spend my time dreaming up storms as if I can brew them.[3]

I don't know how many people will relate to the above: everyone has their own perspectives on how the world works. But the idea that we can shape reality through the force of our intentions certainly has widespread appeal. Rhonda Byrne's 2006 book *The Secret* sold more than thirty million copies worldwide and has been translated into more than fifty languages.[4] Drawing on the 'Law of Attraction', it argues that everyone can live the life of their dreams if they fully visualise it and send that intention out into the universe. The concept is not a new one: it has the same philosophy as that adopted by nineteenth- and twentieth-century occultists and spiritualists, such as Madame Blavatsky and proponents of the New Thought movement. At the end of our journey through medieval and early modern times, we can arguably push its origins further back than that. How different is the thirteenth-century idea of harnessing stellar rays to benefit one's life?

It is even more interesting to see how the concept of the Law of Attraction has evolved since the early 2000s. The 369 Manifestation Method is currently circulating on social media: at the time of writing, the top result on TikTok has more than 1.4 million views. Broadly described, the Manifestation Method involves influencing the world by writing out your intention in multiples of three, in a stepped process. In one version the manifester writes out the name of the person they want to influence three times (Merida), followed by the intention you have towards that person six times (Call me) and finally the overall outcome nine times (Merida and I repair our relationship). Another version involves writing out the whole intention three times in the morning, six times in the afternoon and nine times at night. The timescales for the desired outcome can be vague, unless they are also written into the formula. The variations show that the method is constantly shifting, according to the needs and understanding of the individuals who try out this modern form of magic. Even more exciting—to me, at least—is the advice given out by TikTokkers and others who have used the method and found that it worked. By sharing their tips, they become advisers to their communities, albeit online communities rather than physical ones. Several people have also taken to publishing manifestation journals for those who would rather follow a set method than find their own. Are these authors and influencers modern-day cunning folk? It's perhaps not the term most would use to describe themselves, but there are certainly similarities between their knowledge-sharing and the services that magicians performed in the past.

The Manifestation Method is only one way that magic creeps into our lives. Recourse to astrologers and fortune-tellers remains common, especially in times of personal or global uncertainty. Spell books can still be bought in bookshops—and nowadays they can be bought openly, without fear of prosecution for breaking any laws: most Western countries no longer have acts forbidding sorcery and witchcraft, though legislation (rarely enforced) remains in place against fraudulent and manipulative practitioners. This doesn't mean that magic never creeps into policy decisions, however: sometimes state institutions still bow to the supernatural.

◆

In 2015 Ragnhildur Jónsdóttir brokered a compromise between the Icelandic Road and Coastal Administration (IRCA) and the congregants of Ófeigskirkja—a community of elves. The Administration wanted to build a road north of Reykjavik that would destroy a lump of lava: a very special lump of lava known as the 'elf church', which is believed to house dozens of *huldufólk* ('hidden people'). Jónsdóttir, who has been called 'the elf whisperer', registered with the IRCA the 'hidden folk's' concerns that if their church was destroyed, they would all be displaced. Despite clearly being on the side of the elves, Jónsdóttir was not simply warning the IRCA for their sake. As most Icelanders will attest, upsetting the *huldufólk* will lead to ill-fortune for the humans responsible. Broken equipment, industrial accidents and project delays would burden the IRCA and its employees if they upset the fay folk. Fortunately, Jónsdóttir was able to mediate between the two sides, and the IRCA agreed to move the lava-church out of harm's way. Jónsdóttir ensured that the elves were given warning, so that they had plenty of time to move their altar and other furniture out of Ófeigskirkja before the boulder was moved to its new home. In return for these concessions, the elves agreed not to kick up a fuss or disrupt the rest of the building project.[5]

It might be tempting to write off this episode as a cynical PR stunt by the IRCA in order to maintain good relationships with local people and continue the strong folkloric tradition in Iceland. But if that were the case, why would it have taken three years to reach this truce with Jónsdóttir and the Friends of the Lava environmental group about the boulder's removal? Such an interpretation would also ignore the construction workers who, though sometimes refusing to accept the *huldufólk*'s existence, would still rather keep on their good side. Housing developers experienced similar local resistance—both human and fairy—in Scotland in 2005, and road-building projects in Ireland have also been forced to make concessions to fairy bushes and fairy mounds in recent years.[6]

Pragmatic approaches to the supernatural aren't confined to structural engineers, either. Once, while in Devon, my ferry over the Taw and Torridge Estuary was delayed because the boat had not yet received its half-yearly blessing. Tree boughs were shaken over the little ship as passengers and crew sang hymns and exhorted God (and any other beings listening) to keep everyone safe on their voyage. Afterwards I asked the captain whether he believed in the ritual he had just led. He shrugged good-naturedly and replied that the only year they forgot to do it, two of the boats in the three-vessel ferry service developed mechanical faults that kept them out of use for much of the season. He didn't know whether the blessings worked, but it was best to be on the safe side. In our industrialised, increasingly secular world, that is perhaps the mental space that most of us inhabit.

Why do we still need magic? Is it that belief is part of being human, as Terry Pratchett argues in *Hogfather*, where the falling angel meets the rising ape? I don't know. What I am fairly certain of is that our lives are not so different from those of our medieval ancestors that we can easily leave magic behind. It's tempting sometimes to feel superior to our ancestors, whose technology and access to global knowledge was limited compared to our own. But I would argue that respect and compassion are a far better approach than disdain. Although in many ways we live safer, more comfortable lives than most people in the past, we still grapple with anxieties and rely on hope to see us through. We still need magic because we *want* to believe in something bigger than ourselves—that there is wonder in the world and that we can partake of it. From donning lucky socks before an exam to appeasing unseen creatures, to the industry of psychics and faith healers whom people sought out during the Covid-19 pandemic, we want to indulge in the idea that we live in a magical universe—a universe in which we all have a stake. Even if we laugh at ourselves as we grab our lucky socks, we still put them on, just in case.

ACKNOWLEDGEMENTS

This project was born from a long journey, every stage of which was driven forward by a different person, and they all deserve my heartfelt thanks. First, my mum, who taught me to believe in magic. She also taught me to approach the world with compassion and an open mind: without that lesson, this book wouldn't take the shape it does. The research that forms *Cunning Folk*'s foundations comes from my PhD thesis, which developed under the guidance and expertise of Ronald Hutton and Catherine Rider. Pursuing a PhD was itself made possible through generous funding from the Arts and Humanities Research Council—without support for the arts, we lose our humanity. Thank you to Marion Gibson and Alec Ryrie for being such thought-provoking and constructive thesis examiners. Special thanks are also due to Marion for her continued support—I'm not sure this book would have got off the ground without the fortifying mid-pandemic conversations. I'm very aware that any research stands on the shoulders of giants, so, in no particular order, thank you to Owen Davies, Keith Thomas, Alan Macfarlane, Richard Kieckhefer, Malcolm Gaskill, Emma Wilby, Frank Klaassen, Sharon Hubbs Wright, Brian Hoggard, Sophie Page and Willem de Blécourt among others, for paving the road I've followed.

Cunning Folk would not have entered my head had it not been for my agent, Matt Turner at RCW. Matt contacted me shortly after I'd given what I thought was the worst radio interview in my life—thank you for seeing potential in the story I was telling in such a garbled fashion. I'm grateful for your consistent enthusiasm, and for putting me in the eyeline of the teams at the Bodley Head and Bloomsbury US, who are ultimately responsible for bringing *Cunning Folk* into the world. Thank you to Jörg Hensgen and Will Hammond at the Bodley Head and to Ben Hyman and Morgan Jones at Bloomsbury US for all their support—particularly to Jörg, for his meticulousness and sensitivity during the editing process.

Now for the personal shout-outs. To Mum, again, for being my constant cheerleader. To Nanny, just for being my constant, and to Grandad, even though he's not technically here. To Wyn, for being the best sister I could hope to have, and for creating such impossibly awesome humans that I can only assume magic was involved. Thank you to Ros, Iris and Victor for being my family. James, what are the seven words to make a woman love you? Thank you for saying them every day. Suze and Aaron—my life is better because you're in it. Joan, you're the prefect venting partner; thank you for your bravery and honesty. Caitlin, Lucy, Wilson—your mind-broadening wells of knowledge are amazing, as is your excellent taste in books and games. Maddy, you're the best. Badger, you're all right (kidding! I love you, thank you for always being there). Henry, your imagination constantly inspires me. And to Faustus, for being perfection per-catified. I know that there are many others who deserve appreciation and thanks: please believe me when I say that you have it, with all my heart.

NOTES

INTRODUCTION

1   John Strype, *A Survey of the Cities of London and Westminster* (London, 1720), pp. 76, 277–8.

2   For more on Frances Devereux and the so-called Overbury affair, see Alastair Bellany, *The Politics of Court Scandal in Early Modern England: News Culture and the Overbury Affair, 1603–1660* (New York: Cambridge University Press, 2002).

3   I am not the first person—and I certainly won't be the last—to write about cunning folk. For a seminal work on cunning folk in England, see Owen Davies, *Popular Magic: Cunning-folk in English History* (London and New York: Hambledon Continuum, 2007).

4   Marion Gibson has written extensively on the St Osyth witch trials, including the portrayal, experiences and background of Ursula Kemp. See especially Marion Gibson, *The Witches of St Osyth: Persecution, Betrayal and Murder in Elizabethan England* (Cambridge: Cambridge University Press, 2022) and *Early Modern Witches: Witchcraft Cases in Contemporary Writing* (London: Routledge, 2000).

CHAPTER 1: HOW TO FIND THIEVES AND LOST GOODS

1   Grieg Parker, *Probate Inventories of French Immigrants in Early Modern London* (Abingdon: Routledge, 2016).

2   'Inventory of a very poor elderly man, Germany 1544', from Merry E. Wiesner-Hanks, *Early Modern Europe, 1450–1789* (Cambridge: Cambridge University Press, 2012).

3   G. L. Kittredge, *Witchcraft in Old and New England* (Cambridge, MA: Harvard University Press, 1929), pp. 199–200.

4   Henry Thomas Riley, *Memorials of London and London Life* (London, 1868), pp. 518–19.

5   Tom Johnson, 'Soothsayers, Legal Culture, and the Politics of Truth in Late-Medieval England', *Cultural and Social History*, vol. 17/4 (2020), pp. 431–50.

6   W. H. Dawson, *A History of Skipton* (London, 1882), pp. 389–94. Skipton Public Library holds the cunning man Timothy Crowther's commonplace book in its collections, along with accompanying notes by David Ovason. The book contains a good deal of information about astrology as well as several spells for healing, finding stolen goods and lost people and some ritual magic.

7   The historians Karen Jones and Michael Zell, who first wrote about this case, have argued that Dardus probably only pretended to conjure—and, indeed, this is probably what he claimed when he was investigated for his actions. I am not entirely convinced of this; he certainly knew the method. See Karen Jones and Michael Zell, ' "The divels speciall instruments": women and witchcraft before the "great witch-hunt" ', *Social History*, vol. 30/1 (2005), pp. 45–63 (53).

CHAPTER 2: HOW TO FIND LOVE

1   The so-called 'great chain of being' model often failed to mention women in any capacity. For more on the structure of pre-modern English society, see for example Susan Dwyer Amussen, *An Ordered Society: Gender and Class in Early Modern England* (New York: Columbia University Press, 1993).

2   For more on the gendered navigation of authority, see for example Susan Broomhall (ed.), *Authority, Gender and Emotions in Late Medieval and Early Modern England* (Basingstoke: Palgrave Macmillan, 2015).

3   Catherine Rider, 'Women, Men, and Love Magic in Late Medieval English Pastoral Manuals', *Magic, Ritual and Witchcraft*, vol. 7/2 (2012), pp. 190–211.

4   For an excellent study on the spiritual and cultural significance of blood, see Bettina Bildhauer, *Medieval Blood* (Cardiff: University of Wales Press, 2006).

5   Malcolm Jones, 'Folklore Motifs in Late Medieval Art III: Erotic Animal Imagery', *Folklore*, vol. 102/2 (1991), pp. 192–219 (202–3).

6   Jessica Freeman has written about Margery Jourdemayne's life and magical career. See Jessica Freeman, 'Sorcery at Court and Manor: Margery Jourdemayne, the Witch of the Eye next Westminster', *Journal of Medieval History*, vol. 30/4 (2004), pp. 343–57.

7   *The Brut, or the Chronicles of England, Edited from MS. Rawl. B 171, Bodleian Library*, 2 vols (London: Early English Texts Society, 1906), II, p. 480.

8   For other magical cures for impotence and infertility, see Catherine Rider, *Magic and Impotence in the Middle Ages* (Oxford: Oxford University Press, 2006).

9   Translation taken from ibid., p. 124.

10   Keith Thomas, *Religion and the Decline of Magic* (Oxford: Oxford University Press, 1971), p. 243.

11   James Raine, *Depositions from the Castle of York, Relating to Offences Committed in the Northern Counties in the 17th Century* (Durham: Frances Andrews, 1861), pp. 204–5.

12   Jones and Zell, '"The divels speciall instruments"', p. 54.

13   *Calendar of State Papers Domestic: Edward VI, Mary and Elizabeth, 1547–80* (London: British History Online, 1856), secs 137, 142, www.british-history .ac.uk/cal-state-papers/domestic/edw-eliz/1547-80/pp135-138 [accessed 04/ 05/2023].

14   See especially Valerie Kivelson, *Desperate Magic: The Moral Economy of Witchcraft in Seventeenth-Century Russia* (Ithaca, NY: Cornell University Press, 2013).

CHAPTER 3: HOW TO WIN AT TRIAL

1   Daniel Jaquet, 'Six weeks to prepare for combat: Instructions and practices from the fight books at the end of the Middle Ages, a note on ritualised single combats', *Killing and Being Killed: Bodies in Battle*, ed. Jörg Rogge (Mainz: Transcript Verlag, 2018), pp. 131–64.

2   Conversion rate calculated with the National Archives' currency converter, online: www.nationalarchives.gov.uk/currency-converter   [accessed 08/05/2023].

3   Jaquet, 'Six weeks to prepare for combat', p. 143. For more on customs and regulations around judicial combat, see for example Daniel Jaquet, Karin Verelst

and Timothy Dawson (eds.), *Late Medieval and Early Modern Fight Books: Transmission and Tradition of Martial Arts in Europe (14th–17th Centuries)*, (Leiden: Brill, 2016).

4   'Gregory's Chronicle: 1451–1460', in *The Historical Collections of a Citizen of London in the Fifteenth Century*, ed. James Gairdner (London, 1876), pp. 196–210. British History Online, www.british-history.ac.uk/camden-record-soc /vol17/pp196-210 [accessed 26 July 2022].

5   Jaquet, 'Six weeks to prepare for combat', p. 145. Jaquet has also written an engaging blog about this particularly nasty battle: Daniel Jaquet, ' "Une piteuse bataille": A trial by combat between commoners in Valenciennes, 1455', *Hypotheses* (17/12/2021), martcult.hypotheses.org/1511 [accessed 08/05/2023].

6   Julia Boorman, 'Bishop Wyville's Brass', *Transactions of the Monumental Brass Society*, vol. XVIII, part 2 (2010), pp. 97–118.

7   Kittredge, *Witchcraft in Old and New England*, pp. 53–4.

8   Ibid., p. 54.

9   Kivelson, *Desperate Magic*, p. 175.

10 Trials by ordeal were only a compulsory part of English law for a short time, between 1166 and 1215. However, as seen in Chapter One, such methods were still used as part of pre-indictment investigations centuries later. See Margaret H. Kerr, Richard D. Forsyth and Michael J. Plyley, 'Cold Water and Hot Iron: Trial by Ordeal in England', *Journal of Interdisciplinary History*, vol. 22/4 (1992), pp. 573–95.

11 Conversion rate calculated with the Bank of England's inflation calculator, online: www.bankofengland.co.uk/monetary-policy/inflation/inflation-calculator [accessed 20/07/2023]; monetary conversions throughout this book use the Bank of England calculator. I have used the National Archives' currency converter to gauge the day-rate of labourers over time. Available online at: www .nationalarchives.gov.uk/currency-converter [accessed 08/05/2023].

12 Translation taken from Boorman, 'Bishop Wyville's Brass', p. 100.

13 For similar charms, see Richard Kieckhefer, *Magic in the Middle Ages*, 3rd edn (Cambridge: Cambridge University Press, 2022), pp. 85–92.

14 Kivelson, *Desperate Magic*, p. 176.

15 Michael Hicks gives an excellent summary of the enthusiasm for, and cost of, monastic endowments in Michael Hicks, 'The Rising Price of Piety in the

Later Middle Ages', in Janet Burton and Karen Stöber (eds.), *Monasteries and Society in the British Isles in the Later Middles Ages* (Woodbridge: The Boydell Press, 2008), pp. 95–110.

16   *Calendars of the Proceedings in Chancery in the Reign of Queen Elizabeth; to which are Prefixed Examples of earlier Proceedings in that Court*, vol. I (London, 1827), p. xxiv.

17   Ibid., p. xxiv.

18   Roger Lockyer, 'Lake, Sir Thomas (bap. 1561, d. 1630), administrator and politician', *Oxford Dictionary of National Biography Online* (2004), www.oxforddnb .com/view/10.1093/ref:odnb/9780198614128.001.0001/odnb-9780198614128 -e-15903 [accessed 11/05/2023].

19   For a full summary of this case, see Samuel R. Gardiner, *History of England 1603–1642*, III (London: Longmans, Green & Co., 1890), pp. 189–94.

20   See Alastair Bellany and Andrew McRae (eds.), 'The Lake–Roos Affair', in *Early Stuart Libels: an edition of poetry from manuscript sources* (online, Early Modern Literary Studies Text Series I), www.earlystuartlibels.net/htdocs/lake _roos_section/J0.html [accessed 11/05/2023].

21   *The Life and Letters of Francis Bacon*, ed. James Spedding, vol. VII (London: Longmans, Green, Reader and Dyer, 1874), pp. 77–8.

22   The original pamphlet relating the event was entitled *Newes from Scotland, Declaring the Damnable Life and Death of Doctor Fian, a Notable Sorcerer* (London, 1591). See also J. Goodare, L. Martin and L. Miller (eds.), *Witchcraft and Belief in Early Modern Scotland* (Basingstoke: Palgrave Macmillan, 2008).

23   Kivelson, *Desperate Magic*, p. 174.

CHAPTER 4: HOW TO GET REVENGE

1   *Life, Love and Death in North-East Lancashire, 1510 to 1537: A Translation of the Act Book of the Ecclesiastical Court of Whalley*, ed. Paul H. W. Booth et al., trans. Margaret Lynch (Manchester: Chetham Society, 2006), p. 95.

2   Thomas, *Religion and the Decline of Magic*, pp. 58–61.

3   Jones and Zell, ' "The divels speciall instruments" ', p. 56.

4   On this theory, see in particular Caroline Walker Bynum, *Holy Feast and Holy Fast: The Religious Significance of Food to Medieval Women* (Berkeley: University of California Press, 1988).

5   Booth and Lynch et al., *Life, Love and Death in North-East Lancashire*.

6   Marion Gibson, *Witchcraft and Society in England and America, 1550–1750* (London: Continuum, 2006), pp. 1–7.

7   Willem de Blécourt, 'Witch Doctors, Soothsayers and Priests: On Cunning Folk in European Historiography and Tradition', *Social History*, vol. 19/3 (1994), pp. 285–303.

8   For one theory on the association of women and witchcraft traits, see Stuart Clarke, 'Inversion, Misrule and the Meaning of Witchcraft', *Past and Present*, vol. 87/1 (1980), pp. 98–127.

9   Ely Assize Records, EDR E9/4/8, Cambridge University Library, Deposition taken on 20 November 1635.

10   Ibid.

11   An earlier example of cunning folk seeking justice for unfair treatment dates from the 1570s, when one Janet Milner had a can thrown at her head by a neighbour because she 'healed cattle by her charmings'. Janet sued her neighbour for defamation, and the neighbour was made to kneel before her and beg forgiveness. See P. Tyler, 'The Church Courts at York and Witchcraft Prosecutions, 1567–1640', *Northern History*, vol. 4 (1970), pp. 84–109 (100).

12   W. H. Hart, 'Observations on some Documents relating to Magic in the Reign of Queen Elizabeth', *Archaeologia* (1867), pp. 389–97 (395).

13   See Juris G. Lidaka, 'The *Book of Angels, Rings, Characters and Images of the Planets* attributed to Osbern Bokenham', in Claire Fanger (ed.), *Conjuring Spirits: Texts and Traditions of Medieval Ritual Magic* (Pennsylvania: Pennsylvania State Press, 1998), pp. 32–75.

14   Quotation taken from Rider, *Magic and Impotence*, p. 97.

15   Quotation from ibid., pp. 79–80.

16   '1290: Poppet—Curse', Museum of Witchcraft and Magic website, museumof-witchcraftandmagic.co.uk/object/poppet-curse-4/ [accessed 17/08/2022].

17   Edward Bever, *The Realities of Witchcraft and Popular Magic in Early Modern Europe: Culture, Cognition, and Everyday Life* (Basingstoke: Palgrave Macmillan, 2008), pp. 35–7; 'Signs and Symptoms of Stress', Mind (2022), www.mind.org.uk/information-support/types-of-mental-health-problems/stress/signs-and-symptoms-of-stress/ [accessed 02/10/2022].

CHAPTER 5: HOW TO SAVE LIVES

1   David Kathman, 'Stanley, Ferdinando, fifth earl of Derby (1559?–1594), literary patron', *Oxford Dictionary of National Biography* (2004), www.oxforddnb.com /view/10.1093/ref:odnb/9780198614128.001.0001/odnb-9780198614128-e -26269 [accessed 3/06/2023].

2   John Stow, *Annals of England to 1603* (London, 1603), p. 1275.

3   Ibid., p. 1277.

4   Ibid., p. 1277.

5   Ibid., p. 1275.

6   William Jackson, 'The Use of Unicorn Horn in Medicine', *Pharmaceutical Journal*, vol. 273 (2004), pp. 925–7.

7   Stow, *Annals of England*, p. 1275.

8   Judith Bonzol, 'The Death of the Fifth Earl of Derby: Cunning folk and medicine in early modern England', *Renaissance and Reformation*, vol. 33/4 (2010), pp. 73–100.

9   Stow, *Annals of England*, p. 1276.

10   Thomas, *Religion and the Decline of Magic*, p. 187.

11   Mark 5:1–20; New Catholic Version.

12   Raine, *Depositions from the Castle of York*, p. 127n.

13   Lucy Moore makes a compelling, and touching, case for the love that early modern parents had for their young children in *Lady Fanshawe's Receipt Book: An Englishwoman's Life During the Civil War* (London: Atlantic Books, 2018), pp. 229–34.

14   *Calendar of Letters and Papers, Foreign and Domestic*, Henry VIII, XIII, I, no. 1150, p. 430.

15   Alan Macfarlane, *Witchcraft in Tudor and Stuart England: A Regional and Comparative study* (London: Routledge, 1999), pp. 281–2.

16   E. Mackenzie, *An Historical, Topographical, and Descriptive View of the County of Northumberland, and of Those Parts of the County of Durham North of the River Tyne, with Berwick upon Tweed, and Brief Notices of Celebrated Places on the Scottish Border*, 2nd edn (Newcastle upon Tyne, 1825), II, pp. 35–6.

17   Quotation taken from Kate Lister, *Harlots, Whores and Hackabouts: A History of Sex for Sale* (London: Thames and Hudson, 2021), p. 50.

18   Henry Thomas Riley, *Memorials of London and London Life in the XIIIth, XIVth, and XVth Centuries* (London: Longmans, 1868), pp. 464–6.

19   Ibid., pp. 464–6.

20   D'Arcy Power, 'A Universal Panacea', *Folk-Lore Journal*, vol. 2 (1884), pp. 157–8.

21   See, for example, Mark S. R. Jenner and Patrick Wallis (eds.), *Medicine and the Market in England and Its Colonies, c.1450–c.1850* (Basingstoke: Palgrave Macmillan, 2007); Tobias B. Hug, *Impostures in Early Modern England: Representations and Perceptions of Fraudulent Identities* (Manchester: Manchester University Press, 2009).

22   Lea Olsan, 'Charms and Prayers in Medieval Medical Theory and Practice', *Social History of Medicine*, vol. 16/3 (2003), pp. 343–66.

23   Sarah Fiddyment et al., 'Girding the loins? Direct evidence of the use of a medieval English parchment birthing girdle from biomolecular analysis', *Royal Society Open Science*, vol. 8/3 (2021).

CHAPTER 6: HOW TO GET RICH QUICK

1   Quotation taken from Alec Ryrie, *The Sorcerer's Tale: Faith and Fraud in Tudor England* (Oxford: Oxford University Press, 2008), p. 8. I would strongly recommend this book for a more detailed account both of this case and of the people involved.

2   For more information on astrology and astral magic, see Kieckhefer, *Magic in the Middle Ages*, Chapters 6–7.

3   For more on this point, see Sophie Page, 'A Late Medieval Demonic Invasion of the Heavens', in David J. Collins (ed.), *The Sacred and the Sinister: Studies in Medieval Religion and Magic* (University Park, PA: Penn State University Press, 2019), pp. 233–54.

4   Catherine Rider, *Magic and Religion in Medieval England* (London: Reaktion Books, 2012), p. 111.

5   For more on the properties of angels and how to conjure them, see especially Claire Fanger, *Invoking Angels: Theurgic Ideas and Practices, Thirteenth to Sixteenth Century* (University Park, PA: Penn State University Press, 2012) and *Conjuring Spirits: Texts and Traditions of Medieval Ritual Magic* (University Park, PA: Penn State University Press, 1998).

6   Dawson Turner, 'Brief Remarks, Accompanied with Documents, Illustrative of Trial by Jury, Treasure-Trove, and Invocation of Spirits', *Norfolk Archaeology*, vol. I (1847), pp. 41–65; see also Kittredge, *Witchcraft in Old and New England*, p. 110.

7   Turner, 'Brief Remarks'.

8   Gibson, *Witchcraft and Society*, pp. 1–7.

9   Janet B. T. Christie, 'Reflections on the Legend of Wayland the Smith', *Folklore*, vol. 80/4 (1969), pp. 286–94.

10   Johannes Dillinger, *Magical Treasure Hunting in Europe and North America: A History*, Palgrave Historical Studies in Witchcraft and Magic (Basingstoke: Palgrave Macmillan, 2012), p. 62.

11   Johannes Dillinger and Petra Feld, 'Treasure-Hunting: A Magical Motif in Law, Folklore, and Mentality, Wurttemberg, 1606–1770', *German History*, vol. 20/2 (2002).

12   Turner, 'Brief Remarks', p. 58.

13   Ibid., p. 59.

14   Dillinger, *Magical Treasure Hunting*, p. 115.

15   For more on this, see Glyn Parry, *The Arch-Conjuror of England: John Dee* (New Haven, CT, and London: Yale University Press, 2012), Chapter 7.

16   W. H. Hart, *Observations on Some Documents Relating to Magic in the Reign of Queen Elizabeth* (London, 1867), pp. 5–6.

17   Giambattista della Porta, *Natural Magick: In XX books* (London, 1658), p. 175.

18   See, for example, Stephen Deng, *Coinage and State Formation in Early Modern English Literature* (New York: Palgrave Macmillan, 2011), pp. 87–102.

CHAPTER 7: HOW TO GAIN A KINGDOM

1   Jean de Waurin, *A Collection of the Chronicles and Ancient Histories of Great Britain, now called England*, vol. II, ed. and trans. William Hardy and Edward Hardy (London: Eyre and Spottiswoode, 1887), pp. 64–70.

2   A. Tuck, 'Richard II (1367–1400), king of England and lord of Ireland, and duke of Aquitaine', *Oxford Dictionary of National Biography*, www.oxforddnb.com/view/10.1093/ref:odnb/9780198614128.001.0001/odnb-9780198614128-e-23499 [accessed 15 June 2023].

3   Kittredge, *Witchcraft in Old and New England*, p. 77.

4   See Franck Collard, *The Crime of Poison in the Middle Ages*, trans. Deborah Nelson-Campbell (London: Praeger, 2008), pp. 11–27, for more on the link between poison and magic.

5   Jean de Waurin, *Collection of the Chronicles . . . of Great Britain*, p. 81. Emphasis added.

6   John Hardyng, *The Chronicle of John Hardyng, Containing an Account of Public Transactions to the Beginning of the Reign of King Edward the Fourth. Together with the Continuation by Richard Grafton, to the Thirty Fourth Year of King Henry the Eighth* (London, 1812), p. 360.

7   See H. A. Kelly, 'English Kings and the Fear of Sorcery', *Mediaeval Studies*, 39/1 (1977), pp. 206–38, for further discussion.

8   For more on this case, see J. R. Veenstra, *Magic and Divination at the Courts of Burgundy and France* (Leiden: Brill, 1997), Chapter 2.

9   Thomas Walsingham, *Chronicon Angliae, Ab Anno Domini 1328 Usque Ad Annum 1388: Auctore Monacho Quodam Sancti Albani*, ed. Edward Maunde Thompson (London, 1874); Thomas Walsingham, *The Chronica Maiora of Thomas Walsingham, 1376–1422*, ed. and trans. David G. Preest and James G. Clark (Woodbridge: The Boydell Press, 2005).

10   W. M. Ormrod, 'Who Was Alice Perrers?', *Chaucer Review*, 40/3 (2006), 219–29.

11   Walsingham, *Chronicon Angliae*, p. 97; Walsingham, *Chronica Maiora*, p. 33.

12   Kittredge, *Witchcraft in Old and New England*, p. 106.

13   Walsingham, *Chronicon Angliae*, p. 160. My thanks to Matt Bennett for his help with the translation.

14   T. J. Pettigrew, 'Original Documents No. II: A Certain Confession of the Earl of Kent. MS Cotton Julius C11', *Journal of the British Archaeological Association*, VII (1851), pp. 140–2.

15   'Henry V: October 1419', in *Parliament Rolls of Medieval England*, ed. Chris Given-Wilson, Paul Brand, Seymour Phillips, Mark Ormrod, Geoffrey Martin, Anne Curry and Rosemary Horrox (Woodbridge, 2005), British History Online, www.british-history.ac.uk/no-series/parliament-rolls-medieval/october-1419 [accessed 20 July 2023].

16   For a contemporary account of Lambe's activities, see Anon., *A briefe description of the notorious life of Iohn Lambe: otherwise called Doctor Lambe. Together with his ignominious death* (London, 1628); see also Roger Lockyer, 'Villiers,

George, First Duke of Buckingham (1592–1628), Royal Favourite', *Oxford Dictionary of National Biography* (Oxford: Oxford University Press, 2011), www.oxforddnb.com/view/10.1093/ref:odnb/9780198614128.001.0001/odnb -9780198614128-e-28293 [accessed 15 June 2023]; Anita McConnell, 'Lambe, John (1545/6–1628)', *Oxford Dictionary of National Biography* (Oxford: Oxford University Press, 2004), www.oxforddnb.com/view/article/15925 [accessed 25 September 2017].

17　*Poems and Songs Relating to George Villiers, Duke of Buckingham; and His Assassination by John Felton,* ed. Frederick W. Fairholt (London: Percy Society, 1850), p. xv and frontispiece.

18　See Roger Lockyer and Anita McConnell's articles on Villiers and Lambe in the *Oxford Dictionary of National Biography* (n. 16 above) for more on this.

19　Steven Ellis, 'Dacre, William, third Baron Dacre of Gilsland and seventh Baron Greystoke (1500–1563), magnate', *Oxford Dictionary of National Biography* (Oxford: Oxford University Press, 2008), www.oxforddnb.com /view/10.1093/ref:odnb/9780198614128.001.0001/odnb-9780198614128-e -46514 [accessed 15 June 2023].

20　'Henry VIII: December 1532, 16–31', in *Letters and Papers, Foreign and Domestic, Henry VIII, Volume 5, 1531–1532,* ed. James Gairdner (London, 1880), pp. 681–700, *British History Online,* www.british-history.ac.uk/letters -papers-hen8/vol5/pp681-700 [accessed 20 July 2022].

21　Ibid.

22　Ibid.

23　Ibid.

24　Ibid.

25　Kieckhefer, *Magic in the Middle Ages,* pp. 94–5.

CHAPTER 8: HOW TO TELL THE FUTURE

1　G. O. Sayles (ed.), *Select Cases in the Court of King's Bench under Edward III,* vol. vi (1958), pp. 162–3.

2　All quotations relating to this case are taken from ibid., pp. 162–3.

3　Ibid., p. 163.

4　For a discussion of literary exchange between Muslim, Christian and Jewish medieval cultures, see Suzanne Conklin Akbari and Karla Mallette (eds.), *A*

Sea of Languages: Rethinking the Arabic Role in Medieval Literary History (Toronto: University of Toronto Press, 2013); for an interesting recent debate about the Islamic conquest of Iberia and the ensuing cultural exchange, see the special issue 'What was the Islamic Conquest of Iberia?', *Journal of Medieval Iberian Studies*, vol. 11/3 (2019).

5   *The Poetic Edda*, ed. and trans. Carolyne Larrington (Oxford: Oxford University Press, 1996).

6   See Kieckhefer, *Magic in the Middle Ages*, Chapter 6; Rider, *Magic and Religion*, pp. 221–8.

7   A charming but silly Elizabethan comedy by Robert Greene portrays Roger Bacon's adventures with the 'brazen head', demonstrating the longevity of this belief. See Robert Greene, *The Honorable Historie of Frier Bacon, and Frier Bongay, As It Was Plaid by Her Majesties Servants* (London: Edward White, 1594), p. 12.

8   For more on where these beliefs were recorded, see Rider, *Magic and Religion*, Chapter 1.

9   Macfarlane, *Witchcraft in Tudor and Stuart England*, p. 290.

10 Thomas, *Religion and the Decline of Magic*, p. 214.

11 Jones and Zell, ' "The divels speciall instruments" ', p. 55.

12 Ibid., p. 55.

13 Heinrich Harke, 'Astronomical and Atmospheric Observations in the Anglo-Saxon Chronicle and in Bede', *Antiquarian Astronomer*, Issue 6 (2012), pp. 34–43.

14 'Explore the Bayeux Tapestry Online', *The Bayeux Tapestry Museum*, www .bayeuxmuseum.com/en/the-bayeux-tapestry/discover-the-bayeux-tapestry /explore-online/ [accessed 21/06/2023].

15 See Liana Saif, *The Arabic Influences on Early Modern Occult Philosophy* (Basingstoke: Palgrave Macmillan, 2015), Chapter 2.

16 Quotation taken from Kieckhefer, *Magic in the Middle Ages*, p. 152.

17 *Catalogue of Manuscripts in The British Museum, New Series*, 1 vol. in 2 parts (London: British Museum, 1834–40), I, part I: *The Arundel Manuscripts*, p. 14.

18 Elizabeth I was equally concerned about horoscopes cast during her reign. The Act Against Seditious Words and Rumours was introduced in 1581 and explicitly outlawed 'Casting Nativities, or prophecying, &c as to the Duration of the Queens Life, or who shall succeed to the Crown, or wishing the Queen's

Death': '1580–1: 23 Elizabeth c.2: Against seditious words and rumours', *The Statutes Project*, ed. John Levin, statutes.org.uk/site/the-statutes/sixteenth-century/1580-1-23-elizabeth-c-2-against-seditious-words-and-rumours/ [accessed 12/05/2023].

19 Parry, *The Arch-Conjuror of England*, p. 49.

20 Bernard Capp, *English Almanacs, 1500–1800: Astrology and the Popular Press* (London: Faber & Faber, 1979).

21 William Lilly, *Anglicus, Peace or No Peace, 1645* (London: John Partridge and Humphrey Blunden, 1645), p. 67.

22 Nicholas Campion, *Astrology and Popular Religion in the Modern West: Prophecy, Cosmology and the New Age Movement* (London and New York: Taylor & Francis, 2012).

23 Nicholas Campion, 'How Many People actually Believe in Astrology?', *The Conversation* (2017), theconversation.com/how-many-people-actually-believe-in-astrology-71192 [accessed 05/09/2022].

24 Fleur MacDonald, 'What, if Anything, Can Psychics Tell Us About All of This?', *New York Times*, (15/01/2021).

25 Jessica Contrera, 'For Psychics, a Year Like No Other: "Everybody wants to know what's coming"', *Washington Post* (31/12/2020); Christine Smallwood, 'Astrology in the Age of Uncertainty', *New Yorker* (28/10/2019).

26 For more on chiromancy and other forms of fortune-telling, see Matthias Heiduk, 'Prognostication in the Medieval Western Christian World', in Matthias Heiduk, Klaus Herbers and Hans-Christian Lehner (eds.), *Prognostication in the Medieval World* (Berlin: De Gruyter, 2021), pp. 109–52.

27 For more information on palmistry in France, see Michael R. Lynn, 'The Curious Science: Chiromancy in Early Modern France', *Magic, Ritual and Witchcraft*, vol. 13/3 (2018), pp. 447–80.

28 David Cressy, *Gypsies: An English History* (Oxford: Oxford University Press, 2020), pp. 5, 15.

29 Ibid., p. 41.

30 Richard Saunders, *Palmistry, the secrets thereof disclosed, or, A familiar, easy and new method whereby to judge of the most general accidents of mans life from the lines of the hand withal its dimensions and significations as also that most useful piece of astrology (long since promised) concerning elections for every particular occasion, now plainly manifested from rational principles of art,*

not published till now . . . (1663), text made available through the Text Creation Partnership and Oxford Text Archive, ota.bodleian.ox.ac.uk/repository/xmlui /bitstream/handle/20.500.12024/A62237/A62237.html?sequence=5 [accessed 21/06/2023].

CHAPTER 9: HOW TO STAGE MAGIC

1   This link is noted in Elina Gertsman, 'Illusion and Deception: Construction of a Proverb in Hieronymus Bosch's *The Conjurer*', *Athanor*, 22 (2004), pp. 31–7.

2   Reginald Scot, *The Discoverie of Witchcraft*, ed. Montague Summers (New York: Dover Publications, 1972), pp. 182–3.

3   On Chaucer's translation and the later dissemination of *Treatise on the Astrolabe*, see Christine Chism, 'Transmitting the Astrolabe: Chaucer, Islamic Astronomy, and the Astrolabic Text', in Faith Wallis and Robert Wisnovsky (eds.), *Medieval Textual Cultures: Agents of Transmission, Translation and Transformation* (Berlin: De Gruyter, 2016), pp. 85–120.

4   Can in the space of one natural day—
    This is to say, in four and twenty hours—
    Where-ever you desire, in drought or else showers,
    Bear your body into every place
    To which your heart wishes to go,
    Without harm to you, through foul or fair;
    Or, if you desire to fly as high in the air
    As does an eagle when he desires to soar,
    This same steed shall bear you ever more,
    Without harm, until you be where you wished,
    Though you sleep or rest on his back.

    Translation from *Harvard's Geoffrey Chaucer*, chaucer.fas.harvard.edu/pages /squires-introduction-and-tale [accessed 22/06/2022].

5   when you desire to ride anywhere,
    You must turn a peg, which stands in his ear,
    Which I shall you tell between us two (secretly).
    You must name him to what place also,
    Or to what country, that you want to ride.

And when you come where you desire to abide,

Bid him descend, and turn another peg,

For therein lies the essence of working the device,

And he will down descend and do your will,

And in that place he will abide still.

Though all the world the contrary had sworn,

He shall not thence be drawn nor carried away.

Or, if you wish to bid him go thence,

Turn this peg, and he will vanish at once

Out of the sight of every sort of creature,

And come again, be it by day or night,

When you wish to call him again

In such a manner as I shall to you say

Between you and me, and that very soon.

Ride when you wish; there is nothing more to do.

Ibid. [accessed 22/06/2022].

6   E. R. Truitt, *Medieval Robots: Mechanism, Magic, Nature, and Art* (Philadelphia: University of Pennsylvania Press, 2016), Chapter 5.

7   See Kieckhefer, *Magic in the Middle Ages*, Chapter 5.

8   Parry, *Arch-Conjuror of England*, pp. 11–12.

9   Geoffrey of Monmouth, *The History of the Kings of Britain: An Edition and Translation of the* Britonum [Historia Regum Britanniae], ed. Michael D. Reeve and trans. Neil Wright (Woodbridge: Boydell and Brewer, 2007), pp. 138–40; on the evolving portrayal of Merlin, see Anne Lawrence-Mathers, *The True History of Merlin the Magician* (New Haven, CT: Yale University Press, 2012).

10   Thomas Malory, *Le Morte Darthur: The Winchester Manuscript*, ed. and abridged by Helen Cooper (Oxford: Oxford University Press, 1998), see especially pp. 58–81.

11   On the moral ambiguity of magic in medieval romance texts, see Corinne Saunders, *Magic and the Supernatural in Medieval English Romance* (Woodbridge: Boydell and Brewer, 2010).

12   John Lyly, *Mother Bombie: As It Was Sundrie Times Plaied by the Children of Powles*, 2nd edn (London, 1598), p. E3v. Thomas Heywood, *The Wise Woman of Hoxton*, ed. Sonia Massai (New York: Routledge, 2003).

13 Heywood, *The Wise Woman of Hoxton*.

14 Lyly, *Mother Bombie*, p. E3r.

15 Ibid., p. D3v.

16 All quotations in this paragraph are from ibid., pp. E3r–E4r.

17 *The Merry Devil of Edmonton . . . Edited with a Preface, Notes and Glossary by H. Walker*, ed. Hugh Walker (London: J. M. Dent, 1897), pp. 26–7.

18 Robert Greene, *The Honorable Historie of Frier Bacon, and Frier Bongay, As It Was Plaid by Her Majesties Servants* (London: Edward White, 1594).

CONCLUSION

1 Terry Pratchett, *Hogfather* (London: Gollancz, 1996).

2 The sociologist Max Weber's ideas on the supposed 'disenchantment of the world' were especially influential in the first half of the twentieth century. Max Weber, *The Sociology of Religion* [1920] (London: Methuen, 1965); for a recent study demonstrating the continued enchantment of the world, see Thomas Waters, *Cursed Britain: A History of Witchcraft and Black Magic in Modern Times* (New Haven, CT, and London: Yale University Press, 2020); see also Owen Davies, *Witchcraft, Magic and Culture 1736–1951* (Manchester: Manchester University Press, 1999) and Owen Davies, *A Supernatural War: Magic, Divination, and Faith During the First World War* (Oxford: Oxford University Press, 2020).

3 Thank you to Henry M for sharing these thoughts with me. I have included the quotations with his permission.

4 Rhonda Byrne, *The Secret* (London: Simon & Schuster, 2006).

5 Oliver Wainwright, 'In Iceland, respect the elves—or else', *The Guardian* (25/03/2015), www.theguardian.com/artanddesign/2015/mar/25/iceland-construction-respect-elves-or-else [accessed 30/06/2023].

6 Will Pavia and Chris Windle, 'Fairies stop developers' bulldozers in their tracks', *The Times* (21/11/2005, www.thetimes.co.uk/article/fairies-stop-developers-bulldozers-in-their-tracks-dhk3qfz3rr7 [accessed 30/06/2023]; Mary Phelan, 'Ireland takes fairies more seriously than you might think', *Irish Central* (24/07/2021), www.irishcentral.com/roots/ireland-fairies [accessed 30/06/2023].

SELECT BIBLIOGRAPHY

PRIMARY SOURCES

Anon., *Newes from Scotland, Declaring the Damnable Life and Death of Doctor Fian, a Notable Sorcerer* (London, 1591)

Anon., *The Merry Devil of Edmonton . . . Edited with a Preface, Notes and Glossary by H. Walker*, ed. Hugh Walker (London: J. M. Dent, 1897)

Anon., *The Brut, or the Chronicles of England*, edited from MS. Rawl. B 171, Bodleian Library, 2 vols (London: Early English Texts Society, 1906)

Gairdner, James (ed.), *The Historical Collections of a Citizen of London in the Fifteenth Century* (London, 1876), accessed through British History Online, www.british-history.ac.uk/camden-record-soc/vol17/

Geoffrey of Monmouth, *The History of the Kings of Britain: An Edition and Translation of the* Britonum [Historia Regum Britanniae], ed. Michael D. Reeve and trans. Neil Wright (Woodbridge: Boydell and Brewer, 2007)

Greene, Robert, *The Honorable Historie of Frier Bacon, and Frier Bongay, As It Was Plaid by Her Majesties Servants* (London: Edward White, 1594)

Heywood, Thomas, *The Wise Woman of Hoxton*, ed. Sonia Massai (New York: Routledge, 2003)

Lyly, John, *Mother Bombie: As It Was Sundrie Times Plaied by the Children of Powles*, 2nd edn (London, 1598)

Malory, Thomas, *Le Morte Darthur: The Winchester Manuscript*, ed. and abridged by Helen Cooper (Oxford: Oxford University Press, 1998)

Raine, James, *Depositions from the Castle of York Relating to Offences Committed in the Northern Counties in the 17th Century* (Durham: Frances Andrews, 1861)

Scot, Reginald, *The Discoverie of Witchcraft*, ed. Montague Summers (New York: Dover Publications, 1972)

Stow, John, *Annals of England to 1603* (London, 1603), accessed through archive .org, archive.org/details/annalsofenglandt00stow/page/n21/mode/2up

Walsingham, Thomas, *The Chronica Maiora of Thomas Walsingham, 1376–1422*, ed. and trans. David G. Preest and James G. Clark (Woodbridge: The Boydell Press, 2005)

SECONDARY SOURCES

Amussen, Susan Dwyer, *An Ordered Society: Gender and Class in Early Modern England* (New York: Columbia University Press, 1993)

Bailey, Michael D., 'From Sorcery to Witchcraft: Clerical conceptions of magic in the Late Middle Ages', *Speculum*, 76 (2001), pp. 960–90

Bailey, Michael D., *Magic and Superstition in Europe: A Concise History from Antiquity to the Present* (Lanham, MD: Rowman & Littlefield, 2007)

Bailey, Michael D., 'The Age of Magicians: Periodization in the history of European magic', in *Magic, Ritual and Witchcraft*, 3 (2008), pp. 3–28

Bellany, Alastair, *The Politics of Court Scandal in Early Modern England: News Culture and the Overbury Affair, 1603–1660* (New York: Cambridge University Press, 2002)

Bellany, Alastair and Andrew McRae (eds.), *Early Stuart Libels: an edition of poetry from manuscript sources* (online, Early Modern Literary Studies Text Series I), www.earlystuartlibels.net

Bever, Edward, *The Realities of Witchcraft and Popular Magic in Early Modern Europe: Culture, Cognition, and Everyday Life* (Basingstoke: Palgrave Macmillan, 2008)

Bildauer, Bettina, *Medieval Blood* (Cardiff: University of Wales Press, 2006)

Bonzol, Judith, 'The Death of the Fifth Earl of Derby: Cunning folk and medicine in early modern England', *Renaissance and Reformation*, vol. 33/4 (2010)

Booth, Paul H. W. et al. (eds.), Margaret Lynch (trans.), *Life, Love and Death in North-East Lancashire, 1510 to 1537: A Translation of the Act Book of the Ecclesiastical Court of Whalley* (Manchester: Chetham Society, 2006)

Broomhall, Susan (ed.), *Authority, Gender and Emotions in Late Medieval and Early Modern England* (Basingstoke: Palgrave Macmillan, 2015)

Burton, Janet and Karen Stöber (eds.), *Monasteries and Society in the British Isles in the Later Middles Ages* (Woodbridge: The Boydell Press, 2008)

Bynum, Caroline Walker, *Holy Feast and Holy Fast: The Religious Significance of Food to Medieval Women* (Berkeley: University of California Press, 1988)

Campion, Nicholas, *Astrology and Popular Religion in the Modern West: Prophecy, Cosmology and the New Age Movement* (London and New York: Taylor & Francis, 2012)

Capp, Bernard, *English Almanacs, 1500–1800: Astrology and the Popular Press* (London: Faber & Faber, 1979)

Clark, Stuart, *Thinking with Demons: The Idea of Witchcraft in Early Modern Europe* (Oxford: Oxford University Press, 1999).

Collard, Franck, *The Crime of Poison in the Middle Ages*, trans. Deborah Nelson-Campbell (London: Praeger, 2008)

Collins, David J., *The Sacred and the Sinister: Studies in Medieval Religion and Magic* (University Park, PA: Penn State University Press, 2019)

Davies, Owen, *Witchcraft, Magic and Culture 1736–1951* (Manchester: Manchester University Press, 1999)

Davies, Owen, *Popular Magic: Cunning Folk in English History* (London and New York: Hambledon Continuum, 2007)

Davies, Owen, *A Supernatural War: Magic, Divination, and Faith During the First World War* (Oxford: Oxford University Press, 2020)

de Blécourt, Willem, 'Witch Doctors, Soothsayers and Priests: On Cunning Folk in European Historiography and Tradition', *Social History*, vol. 19/3 (1994), pp. 285–303

Dillinger, Johannes, *Magical Treasure Hunting in Europe and North America: A History*, Palgrave Historical Studies in Witchcraft and Magic (Basingstoke: Palgrave Macmillan, 2012)

Fanger, Claire, *Conjuring Spirits: Texts and Traditions of Medieval Ritual Magic* (University Park, PA: Penn State University Press, 1998)

Fanger, Claire, *Invoking Angels: Theurgic Ideas and Practices, Thirteenth to Sixteenth Century* (University Park, PA: Penn State University Press, 2012)

Freeman, Jessica, 'Sorcery at Court and Manor: Margery Jourdemayne, the Witch of the Eye next Westminster', *Journal of Medieval History*, vol. 30/4 (2004), pp. 343–57

Gibson, Marion, *Early Modern Witches: Witchcraft Cases in Contemporary Writing* (London: Routledge, 2000)

Gibson, Marion, *Witchcraft and Society in England and America, 1550–1750* (London: Continuum, 2006)

Gibson, Marion, *The Witches of St Osyth: Persecution, Betrayal and Murder in Elizabethan England* (Cambridge: Cambridge University Press, 2022)

Goodare, J., L. Martin and L. Miller (eds.), *Witchcraft and Belief in Early Modern Scotland* (Basingstoke: Palgrave Macmillan, 2008)

Heiduk, Matthias, Klaus Herbers and Hans-Christian Lehner (eds.), *Prognostication in the Medieval World* (Berlin: De Gruyter, 2021)

Hug, Tobias B., *Impostures in Early Modern England: Representations and Perceptions of Fraudulent Identities* (Manchester: Manchester University Press, 2009)

Hutton, Ronald, *The Witch: A History of Fear from Ancient Times To the Present* (New Haven, CT, and London: Yale University Press, 2017)

Jackson, William, 'The Use of Unicorn Horn in Medicine', *Pharmaceutical Journal*, vol. 273 (2004), pp. 925–7

Jaquet, Daniel, Karin Verelst and Timothy Dawson (eds.), *Late Medieval and Early Modern Fight Books: Transmission and Tradition of Martial Arts in Europe (14th–17th Centuries)*, (Leiden: Brill, 2016)

Jenner, Mark S. R. and Patrick Wallis, *Medicine and the Market in England and Its Colonies, c.1450–c.1850* (Basingstoke: Palgrave Macmillan, 2007)

Johnson, Tom, 'Soothsayers, Legal Culture, and the Politics of Truth in Late-Medieval England', *Cultural and Social History*, vol. 17/4 (2020), pp. 431–50

Jones, Karen and Michael Zell, '"The divels speciall instruments": women and witchcraft before the "great witch-hunt"', *Social History*, vol. 30/1 (2005), pp. 45–63

Jones, Timothy S. and David A. Sprunger, *Marvels, Monsters, and Miracles: Studies in the Medieval and Early Modern Imaginations* (Kalamazoo, MI: Medieval Institute Publications, 2002)

Kelly, H. A., 'English Kings and the Fear of Sorcery', *Mediaeval Studies* (1977), pp. 206–38

Kieckhefer, Richard, 'Magic and its Hazards in the Late Medieval West', in Brian P. Levack (ed.), *The Oxford Handbook of Witchcraft in Early Modern Europe and Colonial America* (Oxford: Oxford University Press, 2013), pp. 13–31

Kieckhefer, Richard, *Magic in the Middle Ages*, 3rd edn (Cambridge: Cambridge University Press, 2022)

Kittredge, G. L., *Witchcraft in Old and New England* (Cambridge, MA: Harvard University Press, 1929)

Kivelson, Valerie, *Desperate Magic: The Moral Economy of Witchcraft in Seventeenth-Century Russia* (Ithaca, NY: Cornell University Press, 2013)

Klaassen, Frank, *The Transformations of Magic: Illicit Learned Magic in the Later Middle Ages* (University Park, PA: Penn State University Press, 2013)

Klaassen, Frank and Sharon Hubbs Wright, *The Magic of Rogues: Necromancers in Early Modern England* (University Park, PA: Penn State University Press, 2021)

Lawrence-Mathers, Anne, *The True History of Merlin the Magician* (New Haven, CT, and London: Yale University Press, 2012)

Lawrence-Mathers, Anne and Carolina Escobar-Vargas, *Magic and Medieval Society* (London: Routledge, 2014)

Macfarlane, Alan, *Witchcraft in Tudor and Stuart England: A Regional and Comparative Study* (London: Routledge, 1999)

Moore, Lucy, *Lady Fanshawe's Receipt Book: An Englishwoman's Life During the Civil War* (London: Atlantic Books, 2018)

Olsan, Lea, 'Charms and Prayers in Medieval Medical Theory and Practice', *Social History of Medicine*, vol. 16/3 (2003), pp. 343–66

Parry, Glyn, *The Arch-Conjuror of England: John Dee* (New Haven, CT, and London: Yale University Press, 2012)

Rider, Catherine, *Magic and Impotence in the Middle Ages* (Oxford: Oxford University Press, 2006)

Rider, Catherine, *Magic and Religion in Medieval England* (London: Reaktion Books, 2012)

Riley, Henry Thomas, *Memorials of London and London Life in the XIIIth, XIVth, and XVth Centuries* (London: Longmans, 1868)

Ryrie, Alec, *The Sorcerer's Tale: Faith and Fraud in Tudor England* (Oxford: Oxford University Press, 2008)

Saif, Liana, *The Arabic Influences on Early Modern Occult Philosophy* (Basingstoke: Palgrave Macmillan, 2015)

Saunders, Corinne, *Magic and the Supernatural in Medieval English Romance* (Woodbridge: Boydell and Brewer, 2010)

Thomas, Keith, *Religion and the Decline of Magic* (Oxford: Oxford University Press, 1971)

Truitt, E. R., *Medieval Robots: Mechanism, Magic, Nature, and Art* (Philadelphia: University of Pennsylvania Press, 2016)

Tyler, P., 'The Church Courts at York and Witchcraft Prosecutions, 1567–1640', *Northern History*, vol. 4 (1970), pp. 84–109

Veenstra, J. R., *Magic and Divination at the Courts of Burgundy and France* (Leiden: Brill, 1997)

Wallis, Faith and Robert Wisnovsky (eds.), *Medieval Textual Cultures: Agents of Transmission, Translation and Transformation* (Berlin: De Gruyter, 2016)

Waters, Thomas, *Cursed Britain: A History of Witchcraft and Black Magic in Modern Times* (New Haven, CT, and London: Yale University Press, 2020)

Wilson, Stephen W., *The Magical Universe: Everyday Ritual and Magic in Pre-Modern Europe* (London and New York: Hambledon Continuum, 2001)

Wright, Sharon Hubbs and Frank Klaassen, *Everyday Magicians: Legal Records and Magic Manuscripts from Tudor England* (Pennsylvania: Pennsylvania State University Press, 2022)

Young, Francis, *Magic as a Political Crime in Medieval and Early Modern England: A History of Sorcery and Treason* (London: I. B. Tauris, 2018)

Young, Francis, 'The Dissolution of the Monasteries and the Democratisation of Magic in Post-Reformation England', *Religions*, 10(4)/241 (March 2019), doi.org/10.3390/rel10040241

INDEX

ABOUT THE AUTHOR

Tabitha Stanmore, PhD, is a specialist in medieval and early modern magic. She is a postdoctoral researcher at the University of Exeter, UK, the first university to offer a master's degree in occult history. She has been interviewed on BBC Radio and TV. Her monograph, *Love Spells and Lost Treasure*, was published by Cambridge University Press in 2022. *Cunning Folk* is her first book for general readers.